High Praise for
DON'T HIDE THE MADNESS

"A CONVERSATION BETWEEN two literary geniuses of the 20th century whose impact on worldwide culture is so profound that it touches the fabric of our existence on levels we may not fully comprehend. This oral trove is a compendium of trenchant, ordinary and magical gnosis . . . A tangible, tender, and totally engaging tour de force, and balm for the dystopic time we're caught in."

ANNE WALDMAN, feminist, activist, poet, *Fast Speaking Woman*

"A BEAUTIFUL BOOK where you are pleasantly sitting with two originators of Beat-ism, amazing to hear them talk with each other touching many different things. I love them so much. I will buy more copies of this book."

GUS VAN SANT, director, artist, author

"THESE CONVERSATIONS HIGHLIGHT the "seer" William Burroughs' Post War Vision of the Word Virus and Ugly Spirit multiplying in its own image. . . . His influence in Punk Rock, Underground Comix, Cut Up in Associative Resonance Literature, Abstract Blast Art, and Drugs is legendary. His histories of Shaman Headlines and a cold case or two tell us what was really going on. In this scholarly didactic book, he trained Ginsberg to handle a .357 Magnum into the kill zone of Storm Troopers. That the Shaman is always there. . . . It's all here, in this futuristic compendium. Get your copy now before the country sinks into senescence or worse. Take this book home to unwind the mummy roll by roll."

CHARLES PLYMELL, first printer of *Zap Comix*; author, *Last of the Moccasins/Apocalypse Rose*

"STEVEN TAYLOR'S TRANSCRIPTIONS of Bill and Allen's table talk are so accurate that it is just like being there with them: Bill restless, changing the subject—Allen doggedly pursuing his point. I learned much from it. If only we had them with us now."

BARRY MILES, author, *Call Me Burroughs, Hippie*

"FAR AND AWAY the best book I've read in a long time. Burroughs and Ginsberg were the closest of friends for more than fifty years and this book gave me the chance to sit in again on their insightful, absorbing, and at times witty conversations. For those who are just discovering the Beat Generation, their enthralling dinner-table talks will help put a human face on these literary giants. It's like pulling up your own chair and eavesdropping on genius at work. Editor Steven Taylor has done noble work here."

BILL MORGAN, author, *The Best Minds of My Generation*

"TWO OF THE best minds of my generation, are certainly the angel-headed hipsters, Burroughs and Ginsberg; I read them at 18, again at 40 and have fumbled through their brilliance ever since. This book, their dialogue is a 20th century headstone! Like a crab's eye at end of a stick, a penetrating riff on the starry dynamo of America."

DR. PETER WELLER, PhD/Dept. of Art History /UCLA, MANCAT PROD. INC.

"DON'T HIDE THE MADNESS, the audio-taped conversations between William Burroughs & Allen Ginsberg, makes for a marvelous and very important contribution to American Letters and to the overwhelming gathering of knowledge that could've easily been lost along the way. The mere existence of these tapes' survival is a testament to Allen Ginsberg & Bill Burroughs for their foresight early on, that what they had to say and did say to each other would be transformed into a shared experience down the line."

GERARD MALANGA, poet, photographer, archivist

"SHOUT OUT FROM the highest high: Let us deify these two men great men of letters! William and Allen intersected every critical counter-culture signpost of the late 20th century as confidantes, critics, lovers and true representatives of our radical minds. Let us bask in their beatific banter and glean their energy of intellect, eros and rapacious vision. Straight world be damned!"

THURSTON MOORE, poet and musician

"HOW LUCKY WE are to have access to these extended taped conversations between these two writers, lovers, and lifelong friends, which Steven Taylor has lovingly assembled. Allen and Bill, still talking, all the many years later, still examining life's expanse—much of which they traveled in well documented tandem—now from the far shore. We have their nimble old-age (and age-old) words to guide us still. How lucky we are!"

LEE RANALDO, writer and musician

"BEAUTIFULLY TRANSCRIBED AND lovingly edited by Steven Taylor, this book unfolds like a literary salon with the two Beat icons as genial hosts. Laid down only a few years before they would both be gone, this Madness is a prescient time machine landing squarely upon the insanity of the now. for any fan, student, or scholar of Allen Ginsberg, William Burroughs and the Beat Generation, *Don't Hide the Madness* is an absolutely essential read. A treasure trove of insight, humor, beauty and wisdom."

   S. A. griffin, *Carma Bums*

"A SURPRISING PAGE-TURNER, full of hilarity and intimate asides, transcribed into an extremely readable and satisfying fly-on-the-wall of literary history . . . will make both fanboy and scholar sit up straight at attention. Oh, and the R. Crumb cover portrait of Allen & Bill is magnifcent! Highly recommended."

   MARC OLMSTED, author, *Don't Hesitate: Knowing Allen Ginsberg*

"FOR THOSE OF us who missed our chance in meeting Burroughs, books like *Don't Hide the Madness* prove invaluable. They capture a moment in time, in this case a pivotal moment for the late Burroughs, a time of public acceptance and coming to terms with the past. . . . Essential reading for those interested in experiencing Burroughs the man."

   JED BIRMINGHAM, *RealityStudio*

AG: O ho! WSB: What am I shooting, a flower? Bug powder.
Kulchur Kansas AG: Where did you do that with Jack?
Crispo! Gregory Mailer Miller WSB: Sparks in his mouth
"for Ugly Spirit shot Joan because" Tangier Exorcism. Demons.
Bypass. WSB: It's a Buddha... AG: A Buddhist .45 entities?
AG: Don't point it at my machine. WSB: W.C. Fields, carny, carny.
WSB: thrust a snake in his face. AG: I must have been drunk.
WSB: I can't be hypnotized. AG: That's pretty normal.
(tape ends)

   EXENE CERVENKA, *poet, musician*

———∞———

Don't Hide
the Madness

———∞———

Don't Hide the Madness

—∿—

WILLIAM S. BURROUGHS
in conversation with
ALLEN GINSBERG

—∿—

edited by
STEVEN TAYLOR

photos by
ALLEN GINSBERG

THREE
ROOMS
PRESS

NEW YORK
WWW.THREEROOMSPRESS.COM

EACH BOOK BORN IN GREENWICH VILLAGE

DON'T HIDE THE MADNESS
William Burroughs in Coversation with Allen Ginsberg
edited by Steven Taylor
© 2018 by The Ginsberg Estate, The Burroughs Estate, and Steven Taylor

ISBN 978-1-941110-70-6 (hardback)
ISBN 978-1-941110-71-3 (ebook)
TRP-069

BISAC Coding:
LCO020000 Literary Collections / Interviews
BIO007000 Biography & Autobiography / Literary Figures
BIO001000 Biography & Autobiography / Artists Architects, Photographers

Library of Congress Cataloging-in-Publication Data

Names: Burroughs, William S., 1914-1997. | Taylor, Steven, 1955- editor. |
  Ginsberg, Allen, 1926-1997, photographer.
Title: Don't hide the madness / William S. Burroughs in conversation with
  Allen Ginsberg ; edited by Steven Taylor ; photos by Allen Ginsberg.
Description: New York : Three Rooms Press, October 2018. | Includes
  bibliographical references and index. |
Identifiers: LCCN 2018025841 (print) | LCCN 2018028472 (ebook) | ISBN
  9781941110713 (eBook) | ISBN 9781941110706 (hardcover : alk. paper)
Subjects: LCSH: Burroughs, William S., 1914-1997--Interviews. | Ginsberg,
  Allen, 1926-1997--Interviews. | Beat generation--Interviews. | Authors,
  American--20th century--Interviews.
Classification: LCC PS3552.U75 (ebook) | LCC PS3552.U75 Z466 2018 (print) |
  DDC 813/.54 [B] --dc23
LC record available at https://lccn.loc.gov/2018025841

COVER ILLUSTRATION:
R. Crumb

INTERIOR PHOTOS:
Allen Ginsberg (unless otherwise noted)

BOOK DESIGN:
KG Design International | www.katgeorges.com

Printed in the United States of America
1   3   5   7   9   10   8   6   4   2

PUBLISHED BY:
Three Rooms Press / New York, New York
Visit our website at www.threeroomspress.com or
write us at info@threeroomspress.com

DISTRIBUTED BY:
Publishers Group West / Ingram Content Group | www.pgw.com

To Éamonn

The method must be purest meat
and no symbolic dressing,
actual vision & actual prisons
as seen then and now.

Prisons and visions presented
with rare descriptions
corresponding exactly to those
of Alcatraz and Rose.

A naked lunch is natural to us,
we eat reality sandwiches.
But allegories are so much lettuce.
Don't hide the madness.

ALLEN GINSBERG, "ON BURROUGHS' WORK," 1954

*Allen Ginsberg and William Burroughs at Steven Lowe's house, Lawrence KS,
19 July 1992*

Contents

Don't Hide
the Madness

Allen Ginsberg and Steven Taylor, Paterson Falls, 1978

INTRODUCTION

by Steven Taylor

Allen Ginsberg and I met in May of 1976 when an English professor of my acquaintance asked me to sit in as the poet's accompanist at his reading at my college. We went on to work together for twenty years.

Allen made his living as a performer. The most famous poet of the twentieth century earned only about twelve-thousand dollars a year on book royalties. He paid his rent and ran his home office by touring. Between 1976 and the early nineties, we played hundreds of shows in Europe and America. When we weren't touring, I sometimes worked in his office.

He had a full-time secretary, Bob Rosenthal, who had started at about the time Allen and I met. There was a small office in the apartment at 437 East 12th Street. Initially it was the square front room between his bedroom and the toilet closet. A makeshift desk—a sheet of plywood atop several low filing cabinets—was set up against one wall. There was no living room in the apartment, nowhere to lounge about; one either worked or ate or slept.

One of my between-tour jobs was to compile all the footnotes from the foreign editions of Ginsberg's work and then go through his whole oeuvre to make more footnotes explaining various persons, events, etc. This was aimed at the *Collected Poems 1947–1980*, then in preparation. I asked him what should get a footnote. He said, "Anything a high school kid fifty years from now might not understand." So, for example, one of the foreign editions had a footnote

PHOTO BY BRIAN GRAHAM

Bob Rosenthal and Allen in the apartment office, June 1992

explaining "supermarket." At the time, I thought it kind of crazy that in the US edition of the *Collected*, "supermarket" would need explanation. But fifty years ahead would have been 2032, so who knows? Young readers might need that explained, just as my generation needed a footnote explaining the "automat" of the 1940s. The man thought long-term. Many of my footnotes were culled later in the editing process by less prophetic heads.

Bob was in the office five days a week. Much of the time there were other people there, usually poets in need of paying work. Allen and Bob hired them to do various chores—reorganizing the files, updating the Rolodexes,[1] filing news clippings on pet subjects, keeping up with the correspondence, and organizing the photographs. Ginsberg generated enough work for a half-dozen people. As Bob said, "Allen was a cottage industry."

---

1   The Rolodex, marketed from 1958 on, was standard office equipment, a rotary card file (or "rolling index") of addresses and telephone numbers that computers largely rendered obsolete in the 1990s.

The industry served to channel Allen's workaholism and insomnia; he often sat up until dawn scribbling instructions for tasks with which we barely kept up. The industry also did activism on various issues, supported artists in the community, and generated income-tax exemptions—to fund poets rather than the war chests of Washington. It is not widely known that Ginsberg channeled into the community as wages, grants, or gifts much of what he earned. He set up a non-profit, the Committee on Poetry (COP), to which he made donations and which collected donations from philanthropically-minded lovers of literature. COP made it easy for patrons of the arts to discreetly support writers in need. One of my first jobs was writing checks for writers whose supporters donated to COP. Allen was the industry, but Bob kept it all running.

In November of 1978, Allen introduced me to William Burroughs backstage at the Entermedia Theater on Second Avenue. It was the Nova Convention, and William was the star. According to Burroughs biographer Ted Morgan, Columbia University professor Sylvère Lotringer and poet John Giorno had approached William's assistant James Grauerholz proposing a convention to discuss and celebrate Burroughs's work. "Lotringer saw Burroughs as they did in France, where he was acclaimed as a philosopher of the future, the man who best understood postindustrial society." The idea was to have academic discussions as well as performances by various avant-garde and pop figures associated with Burroughs, a "gathering of the counterculture tribe which would enshrine Burroughs as its leader."[2] That seems a bit overstated, but it does speak to James's acuity in looking after William's interests, and to Burroughs's importance as a visionary artist.

Allen told him I was English. "Well good for you, Allen," he said in his adenoidal drone, "got yourself an *Ing*lish boy." I might have expected to be thought of as his boyfriend, but it was a new experience then and it disturbed me.

---

2   Ted Morgan, *Literary Outlaw: The Life and Times of William S. Burroughs* (New York: W. W. Norton & Company, 2012), 581.

The next time I recall seeing William was at the Naropa Institute in the summer of 1979. Allen had co-founded the writing school there with Anne Waldman, and Burroughs had become a regular visitor to the Summer Writing Program, along with a couple of hundred poets, writers, musicians, scholars, and visual artists who rotated through the summer faculty. I arrived in Boulder ahead of Allen. James Grauerholz would be arriving after William, so Allen called and asked me to help Burroughs for a couple of days in the meantime.

That summer I got to know him a little. I had the impression of great shyness hiding behind a stern exterior and formal manners. He wasn't so much stern as blank; it's familiar to me as the manner of my people. Ed Sanders calls it "Protestant armor." James was friendly enough for them both.

William and James visited Naropa several times in the 1980s. Sam Kashner, in his memoir of his time at Naropa, recalls Burroughs teaching UFO literature.[3] This is no doubt true: UFOs and all sorts of paranormal phenomena were among his interests. But Sam neglects to mention that Burroughs also taught Fitzgerald and Melville. Upon learning of William's reading list, I read Melville's *The Confidence-Man*. That was an important book for me; it brought alive a body of writing that literature classes had bludgeoned into dull irrelevance.

In December of 1981, Burroughs left New York and moved to Lawrence, Kansas. According to biographer Barry Miles, William's New York rent had doubled and he was looking for a place to buy in cheap and settle down. James had already moved back to Lawrence, where he had gone to college; the cost of living was reasonable, and they could always travel back to New York for special occasions. William had been raised in St. Louis, so moving to the Midwest was, as Miles puts it, a "return to roots."[4]

In 1984, the filmmaker David Cronenberg told William he wanted to make a movie of *Naked Lunch*. In 1989, he sent the first draft of

---

3   Sam Kashner, *When I was Cool: My Life at the Jack Kerouac School* (New York: HarperCollins, 2004), 173.

4   Barry Miles, *Call Me Burroughs: A Life (New York: Twelve/Hachette Book Group, 2014), 563.*

William with James Grauerholz, Lawrence, Kansas, 21 July 1991

a script, which Burroughs rejected, but Cronenberg persisted. His fifth draft was completed in January of 1991 and, with Burroughs's approval, the movie went into production.[5] Burroughs was involved in discussions with Cronenberg throughout the process, traveled to Tangier with the director to scout locations, and had been at the studio in Toronto while the film was in production. While visiting Toronto in June, William had bouts of chest pain, and upon returning home was told by his doctor that he was at risk for a heart attack. Angioplasty was performed, but it became clear that bypass surgery was needed.[6]

In July of 1991, William had the operation. While in recovery in the hospital, he fell getting out of bed and fractured his hip. At seventy-seven years old, recuperation was bound to come slowly.

---

5   Miles, 580; 609.

6   Miles, 617.

Naked Lunch had a limited initial release in the US on 27 December 1991. It went on to make $2,641,357 in North America. *Chicago Sun–Times* critic Roger Ebert wrote, "While I admired it in an abstract way, I felt repelled by the material on a visceral level. There is so much dryness, death and despair here, in a life spinning itself out with no joy." *New York Times* critic Janet Maslin said, "For the most part this is a coolly riveting film and even a darkly entertaining one, at least for audiences with steel nerves, a predisposition toward Mr. Burroughs and a willingness to meet Mr. Cronenberg halfway." *Entertainment Weekly* noted that actor Peter Weller "greets all of the hallucinogenic weirdness with a doleful, matter-of-fact deadpan that grows more likable as the movie goes on. . . . By the end, he has turned Burroughs' stone-cold protagonist—a man with no feelings—into a mordantly touching hero." The *Village Voice*'s J. Hoberman wrote, "Cronenberg has done a remarkable thing. He hasn't just created a mainstream Burroughs on something approximating Burroughs's terms, he's made a portrait of an American writer." And Jonathan Rosenbaum in the *Chicago Reader* said, "Cronenberg's highly transgressive and subjective film adaptation of *Naked Lunch* [is] fundamentally a film about writing—even *the* film about writing."

Interest in Cronenberg's movie and its pending UK release, scheduled for 24 April 1992, prompted the London *Observer Magazine* to request an interview. After some back and forth, it was arranged that Allen would visit William and conduct the interview. He asked me if I would transcribe the tapes, and I agreed. Allen spent March 17–22 in Lawrence and came back with eleven ninety-minute cassette tapes comprising some sixteen hours of talk. I spent a couple of weeks working on the transcription and wound up with a typescript of some three hundred pages. A short excerpt from the transcript appeared in the *Observer*.[7] The same material, somewhat amended, appeared in *The Collected Interviews of William S. Burroughs*, edited by Sylvère Lotringer,[8] but the bulk of the material remained unpublished.

---

7   Allen Ginsberg, "Exorcising Burroughs," *Observer Magazine* (26 April 1992): 26–30.

8   Sylvère Lotringer, ed., *Burroughs Live: The Collected Interviews of William S. Burroughs, 1960–1997* (Los Angeles: Semiotext(e), 2001): 803–15.

In the autumn of 2014, while going through some archive boxes in my study, I came upon the original transcript and contacted Peter Hale at the Ginsberg office about making a book of it. I'd had an electronic copy of the work on an old computer disc, but no longer had a compatible computer, so Peter kindly scanned my 1992 manuscript, and I set about correcting the original, which had been hastily transcribed on a news deadline, and began adding footnotes for context. The question then became where to add notes, of what kind, and on what subjects. Should I follow Allen's advice of 1982 and explain everything that a high school kid fifty years hence wouldn't understand? I think not. But one should not need to be a Burroughs scholar to understand the references, so I have added some notes and commentary.

On visits to Burroughs in Lawrence in 1991 and 1992, Allen took a number of photos. Some of these are included here, thanks to Peter Hale and Bob Rosenthal.

Allen Ginsberg's visit of March 1992 to the home of William S. Burroughs in Lawrence, Kansas came at a crucial time for William. Now in his late seventies, Burroughs had made a career as a writer for four decades since the event that he believed set him on his path as a writer: his fatal shooting of his common-law wife Joan Vollmer Burroughs in Mexico City on September 6, 1951. William came to believe that he was possessed by what his collaborator Brion Gysin called "the Ugly Spirit." Ginsberg's visit coincided with an exorcism of that spirit performed by Navajo shaman Melvin Betsellie. Allen's account of the ceremony, in which he participated, is included below.

A Note on the Transcript

As noted above, the original impetus for the conversations was to provide the *Observer* with material for a brief article. Allen took the opportunity to record some sixteen hours of conversation.

My job was to transcribe the tapes, so that Allen could go through and edit a brief excerpt to send to London. My mandate, I knew without having to be told, was to transcribe everything as accurately as possible, for the sake of the "literary history" that was part of Allen's overall mission. However, a couple factors led me to exclude some things from the transcript. One was the pressing deadline. Surely the seemingly endless task could be relieved somewhat by skipping over mundane table talk with friends and neighbors. I also thought to protect the privacy of William and some others then still living, who might not wish to have the details of their health or finances discussed in print.

For present purposes, I have listened through digital dubs of the tapes; restored hitherto excluded material of literary-historical interest; corrected such things as spellings of names and places; corrected for words misheard or skipped in the rush to meet the magazine's deadline; and have consulted texts that figure importantly in the conversation. As with the 1992 unpublished manuscript, I have largely concentrated on the conversation of the principals.

Transcribing the tapes in 1992 was the last editorial job I did for Ginsberg before entering Brown University as a PhD candidate in ethnomusicology. My ethnographic training has, of course, influenced my approach to the present project. This is why that conversation of a quarter-century past is included here in perhaps too much detail by conventional standards. As Allen often said, "Maximize the information!" I believe the persons involved justify a minimally edited account of their conversation.

Some explanation is in order regarding the Table of Contents and section headings of the book. My transcript of 1992 and the present work number the tapes 1–11. Allen, however, numbered his tape cassettes 1, 2, 3, 4, 5, 6, 7, 8, 8A, 9, 10. The transcript of 1992 contains material not present in the digital archive recordings, and there is a substantial and important conversation in the digital audio that I did not transcribe from tape in '92. (Since the latter conversation concerns details of William's psychoanalysis in the 1940s, it is possible that I chose not to transcribe this material in '92.) That material is restored here under the heading of "Tape 11." Some cassette labels are undated, and some are obviously misdated. Finally, there is some indication that Allen mistakenly recorded over some already-recorded audio, and there has been at least one substantial erasure.

My purpose in explaining these difficulties is to note that beginning with my "Tape 9," the tape numbers given here do not conform to the content notes Allen made at the time. Where there is uncertainty regarding the tape order, I have sequenced the conversation so as to make sense. My final section, "Tape 11 Side B," does reflect Allen's preparing to depart for New York, and so does accurately reflect the final conversation. I will leave it to some future Beat PhD candidate to make a dissertation of correcting my sequence.

A Note on the Text

What is given here is a casual conversation between friends and not a formal, written text. Grammatical errors and occasional non sequiturs are endemic to the mode. Punctuation is here meant to convey the flow of speech, not to conform strictly to a style manual. Three ellipses indicate pauses in speech, interruptions of one speaker by another, or brief excisions of stutters and stumbles; four elipses indicate longer excisions. Brackets indicate unclear words, guesses at what's being said, corrections of misspoken names and misquoted material, or brief notes for clarification. "[Tape stops]" indicates points where a recording has been paused or otherwise interrupted. The synopses given in the Table of Contents and at the top of each section are derived from Ginsberg's original notes on cassette labels (where he has made such), but are edited to reflect the present transcript.

—◆—

Don't Hide
the Madness

—◆—

The Conversation:
March 18–22, 1992

William S. Burroughs, 22 March 1992

TAPE 1 SIDE A

3/18/92. Breakfast talk. AG with Wes Pittman cooking & WSB at table. The shaman. Favorite foods. Health concerns. The Gettys. Gregory Corso. W. B. Yeats. Zines. Cats. Jane and Paul Bowles. Tangier eccentrics. Kerouac the Celt.

WSB: Is that glass of water still standing there from the shaman?

AG: Yeah, that is.

WES: Did he drink from it?

WSB: He took a sip of it, then he gave it to me. He can see the spirit in the water.

WES: Is he Navajo or Hopi?

WSB: I think he's Navajo.

WES: He looks Navajo. With a real wide . . .

WSB: Yep, wide face.

WES: Really beautiful people.

WSB: They are?

WES: Except when they eat American food.

WSB: Huh?

WES: Except when they eat American food.

WSB: They get depressed.

1

WES: Hot dogs and . . .

WSB: Oh yes, hot dogs, all that sort of stuff . . . candy bars, all that sort of stuff I deplore.

WES: They really get depressed.

WSB: Ribs and what have you.

AG: Starch.

WSB: Starch. I could easily get along without meat. I like meat but just potatoes and gravy . . .

AG: Uh hm.

WSB: Rice and gravy . . . vegetables would be all right with me.

AG: So the question . . . That is . . . have you . . . what is the cause of your, the plaque? [Arterial blockage resulting in heart disease]

WSB: Well, the doctor says he didn't know. He says it was partly smoking.

AG: Ah ha.

WSB: See I stopped smoking of course, in mid June . . . and I haven't smoked since. And I wouldn't think of it, 'cause that is one of the causes. It constricts the arteries.

AG: I'm glad I stopped.

WSB: Well, I had to. I mean, smoking on top of heart surgery is like smoking on top of cancer of the lungs. Suicide. Anthracina.[9]

AG: Brion [Gysin] continued to smoke didn't he?

WSB: Hm?

AG: Did Brion continue to smoke?

---

9   *Latin:* "coal black"; an archaic term for melanoma, a darkly colored lesion on the skin.

WSB: No . . . just, just a little time. That's all very well, to stop when the damage is already done. And also I was helped by the fact that I didn't start to smoke till I was forty-five.

AG: Right, I remember you, you were always . . . unsmoking.

WSB: Yes . . . and I know how I got *on* was mixing tobacco with hash.

AG: Ah.

WSB: And that's how I got back on when I was off for two years. So . . . but now . . . I can't and that's all. So I don't. It's so necessary that I don't even miss it.

AG: So you got a hash pipe?

WSB: Well I'd have to just smoke it pure, that's all.

AG: Are you smoking much grass now?

WSB: No. Well . . . two or three joints a day.

AG: That doesn't do much.

WSB: No.

AG: I mean to the veins.

WSB: No . . . no . . . apparently. I don't know whether they on my program even test for it. 'Cause it stays in the body a long time. See morphine and heroin are out of the body in about twenty-four hours, at most forty-eight. But pot stays for about two weeks, and also a lot of other drugs like Valium stay a long time.

AG: Say Wes, did you make me any of those potatoes? I'll have some. Thank you, looks good.

WSB: Now proceed to whack this thing. These are good farm eggs, brown eggs, you know, thick shells, good thick shells. That means plenty of calcium. The hens get out and *scratch* instead of being confined. I think it's terrible, these sort of factories, big sort of chicken factories.

3

AG: Yes.

WSB: And the eggs have thin shells and no taste. See, it doesn't seem to bother most Americans. I don't think they taste their food . . . horrible. Pretty soon they won't have a living being, living creature there at all, just sort of a container. But already the chickens raised that way, they taste like lard. Lard with a little chicken broth, chicken flavoring.

AG: Can you get organic chicken here?

WSB: Oh sure . . . yeah, you can get that old . . . farm chickens, get out and scratch daily . . .

AG: I mean do you get 'em here?

WSB: Out to the right there's a place that sells farm eggs, brown eggs, brown and speckled green ones. Have you seen green eggs?

AG: No, those I haven't seen.

WSB: They're good . . . you know, they taste like *eggs*, not some nameless *ick*.

AG: Well, but chickens themselves . . . Are you able to get organic chickens themselves for cooking, or d'you get those from the supermarket?

WSB: Well, I can get those yes, sure. I'm not too fond of chicken. I like it in chicken soup.

AG: You do.

WSB: Stew, yeah, a sort of heavy . . . What I do is I take the . . . cut all the meat off the chicken and take all the bones, carcass, and make a stock with that. And then in that stock, cook your veggies, vegetables, with the potatoes, leeks, and onion, and carrots, well whatever. That's usually what I . . .

AG: Have them make one of those today for me.

WSB: It's more or less soup. But then, finally you put all the meat back in and heat it up.

AG: But how do you get the meat off? Raw, or do you cook, boil it first?

WSB: No, the chicken is cooked. Like roasted or whatnot then you just cut the meat off and then if it's a little rare it doesn't matter because you're going to cook . . .

AG: What I do, I just put the chopped chicken . . .

WSB: You mean a raw chicken?

AG: And boil it.

WSB: A raw chicken?

AG: Yeah, and boil it for some time then when it's about ready, half hour, I put in the vegetables.

WSB: Sure, then it's about the same.

AG: So then you get the bones in there but they come off very easily.

WSB: I know.

AG: Celery, celery tops and carrots and carrot tops.

WSB: Well sure. I put celery in there too. Mainly I like leeks.

AG: Yeah, I just discovered leeks actually.

WSB: Like a more delicate onion.

AG: You know what's also good is leeks and potatoes. That's the classic thing.

WSB: That's also the way you make vichyssoise. Leeks, just one onion, a small onion and then potatoes. Cook those, it goes through a blender.

AG: Did you ever make it?

WSB: Oh yes. It's one of our staples. I can make it. And then, well if you want it cold . . .

AG: Put it in the ice box.

WSB: Yeah, but you put cream, or half-and-half. You make it a cream, leek, and potato soup. You can put it in the ice box . . . alright but, if you're going to eat it hot . . . put the cream in and heat it, but don't boil it. No cream soup or preparation should ever be boiled. You don't boil cream . . . or milk . . . So that's it; we have that kind of soup about once a week.

WES: Michael actually makes some really good vichyssoise.

WSB: Yeah. Makes great vichyssoise.

AG: I made a sort of interesting vichyssoise out of leeks and beans.

WSB: What kind of beans?

AG: Um . . . white beans, navy beans.

WSB: Navy beans.

AG: A mixture of navy bean and black-eyed peas.

WSB: Oh, I could see that would be good.

AG: And put it in a sort of Osterizer [blender] with leeks. You know, the same sort of thing.

WSB: Something else I like is lentils. That's like, sort of like navy beans. Navy beans or lentil soup with ham hocks.

AG: Well, that's the classic thing . . . except I can't do that no mo'.

WSB: Ham hocks or . . .

AG: Now my Chinese roommate[10] taught me this is another way of eating a grapefruit. Just peel it. Segment it, you get it all.

---

10 City University graduate student Jack Shuai lived at Allen's apartment (1989–91), cooking and doing household chores in return for lodging.

WSB: I eat it with a spoon. Spoon it out of there and then squeeze the juice out.

AG: This way it's open, a little less messy actually.

WSB: Not messy? Looks kind of messy to me. I read that article about Getty, did you? Horrible, gruesome really. See I haven't seen him since the accident. What happened apparently was . . . overdosage of barbiturates or something like that, resulting in brain damage. Which is irreversible.

AG: It said his father was a junky in that?

WSB: *Is* a junky.

AG: Father, huh?

WSB: Yeah, sure. Oh God yes. Heavy junky.

AG: Is his father still alive?

WSB: Yeah, yeah, sure he is. He lives in a hospital. He had a big house on Cheyne Walk where he never went upstairs. He had very severe bursitis or leg problems, stayed downstairs the whole time . . . attended by one of Doctor Dent's old nurses,[11] and she was married to a policeman. They were always mucking about in the kitchen fixing tea and stuff. And he had a heavy heroin habit . . . ten grains a day, something like that.

AG: How'd he get away with it legally?

WSB: It's prescribed. All quite legal, my dear. Legal as hell. Yeah. And he'd contribute . . . then he moved into his new suite in the hospital to which he contributes substantially. The doctors prescribe his heroin. He's got painful conditions. He has this bursitis thing. Without heroin, he'd be in a hell of a state.

AG: Is he able to get out and run around?

---

11 Dr. John Yerbury Dent (1888–1962) developed a treatment for alcoholics and heroin addicts, a "painless" detox using apomorphine. Burroughs traveled to London in 1956 to take the cure.

WSB: If he wants to, I guess. He doesn't seem to move very much. But he started the Getty Foundation, where he gives away money to certain people. Brion got . . . not a fortune, but he got about 4–500 dollars a month.[12]

AG: Really? How nice. Is that through the son?

WSB: Yeah, well the old man is close to dead.

AG: Was that through the grandson or the elder Getty? I mean was it Getty Jr. that liked Brion or was it the grandson?

WSB: No, it was Getty Jr., the son. And *his* son is the one that was kidnapped.

AG: His son is the one we know.

WSB: Well, I knew the father too.

AG: You did?

WSB: Yeah, sure.

AG: Where?

WSB: In London.

AG: I didn't know that.

WSB: Not too well, but I knew him.

AG: Was he very literate or something . . . I mean that he patronized Brion?

WSB: Yeah, well sure. He also had a huge house in Marrakesh, which he hardly ever used and he started to rebuild it and it was just too much. One of those great houses made of mud would fall apart . . . Can I have a spoon, Wes? So then from his suite in the hospital he set up something called the Getty Foundation and gave money to

---

12 Brion Gysin (1916–86).

people. He said he would give money away as long as he had money to give. I'm surprised that he's still alive really.

AG: I wonder how you apply to that.

WSB: It's just a matter of his . . .

AG: I know, but how do you go about reaching him? Interesting to ask for money, say for Gregory.

WSB: Well, I wouldn't be surprised if he'd give Gregory money.

AG: You wouldn't be?

WSB: I wouldn't be surprised at all.

AG: How would one communicate with him?

WSB: I don't know. I haven't seen him in years. He had all kinds of troubles too. His wife died under very suspicious circumstances. If he ever went back to Italy, he'd be arrested.

AG: Is that where his wife died?

WSB: He'd be insane to go back there. 'Cause they did an autopsy, and found that she had died from a massive dose of heroin. Massive overdose.

AG: Was she on junk too?

WSB: Oh yeah. Yeah. So it must have been a really huge whopping dose. The story is that he was with her and she became comatose and he called Dado Ruspoli.[13]

AG: Who is that?

WSB: He's an Italian playboy. And he came over and said, "Things look bad."

AG: He get out of town?

---

13 Alessandro "Dado" Ruspoli (1924–2005), Italian "playboy prince . . . rebel and eccentric" who "embodied the dolce vita" ("'Dado' Ruspoli, Italian aristocrat and playboy of the post-war dolce vita," *The Guardian*, 26 January 2005).

WSB: I think that possibly was Dado's recommendation. Said you just better get along out of Italy, and he did. Then they performed an autopsy. Massive overdose of heroin . . . It was very, very, you know . . . *suspect* [French pronunciation]. It would be insane, once you got an idea of going back to clear your name or some such nonsense. Fortunately wisdom prevailed. God's sake, out of your mind to go back there. So he went to London; he's been there ever since. And the old man was afraid to fly.

AG: The grandfather.

WSB: Grandfather, old man. Seems stupid to me, you know, if your number's up, it's up.

AG: Let's see. I've got this tripod. First time in my life, I've never used it before. Something new.

WSB: What's it for?

AG: Well, so if I take your picture, instead of hand-holding it [the camera] so things become fuzzy because of trembling of the hand. It's a long exposure. This would be say a quarter of a second, I guess.

WSB: You can get a longer exposure.

AG: Well, I can have a quarter of a second without my hand trembling, without disturbing . . .

WSB: How long was Gregory actually in the hospital [rehab]?

AG: Twenty-three days.

WSB: Which one?

AG: Hazelden. He went to the classic place, it was really amazing.

WSB: They pay . . . a sum.

AG: No, it isn't. How much do you think a hospital is per day, any normal hospital?

WSB: About five hundred, three hundred.

AG: Well, say four hundred's the mean. So that would be four hundred a day times thirty days, say thirteen thousand. Hazelden is only 7,500 for a month.

WSB: Well that's very reasonable.

AG: Yeah. Now when you go to some of the private hospitals, they're fourteen thousand. You know, the private detox. Smithers, for instance, in New York, is fourteen thousand a month. It's just for rich people. Hazelden is the mother hospital for AA; it's the best. Even Gregory liked it. It penetrated Gregory even emotionally, in that he felt the people were good people, that really cared for him, that they were out for his best interests. You know, he didn't resent them, he didn't put them down, and that's amazing from Gregory.

WSB: Did they put him [on any kind of] reduction program?

AG: No. It was pretty much cold turkey except they did give him a little . . . It turned out he was massively undernourished, or malnutrition, so no iron at all, so they fed him a lot of vitamins and it was more or less cold turkey and he said he had a very difficult time, couldn't sleep, but pulled through.

WSB: That's good.

AG: And he actually even began talking in terms of . . . you know the AA term of can't do it by myself have to rely on some higher power?

WSB: Yeah.

AG: To him it doesn't mean God, just means some destiny, fate, fortune, or something. But he felt that . . . He did begin adopting that terminology . . . to throw himself aside . . . put himself aside and depend on not poetry, not fortune, just something, some spirit.

11

WSB: Sure. Sure.

AG: And he liked his counselors and a lot of the people there. So it was actually quite a plus. So I told him, or he knows if he's in trouble and he wants to go back, he can go back. The money is there.

WSB: Did he . . . did his legs heal up?

AG: Yeah. Much. Apparently the legs were all swollen.

WSB: Well I've seen it. I remember in Amsterdam.

AG: When was that?

WSB: Quite some years ago.

AG: Well it got so bad.

WSB: Terrible state.

AG: It got so bad that apparently he couldn't sustain it anymore. And then when *you* got ill, then when Harry Smith died[14]—he took it very hard when Harry died—and when you got your bypass, and when I got heart failure, something got into him. He realized that he was mortal.

WSB: "In him nature's copy is not eterne."

AG: What is that? Sonnets?

WSB: The immortal bard.

AG: Sonnets or where?

WSB: No no no, *Macbeth* . . . not a particularly good line.

AG: Amazing what sticks in your mind.

WSB: Well, yeah. Long passages of Shakespeare . . . in my mind.

---

14 Harry Smith (1929–91) was a painter, filmmaker, and folklorist whose multi-LP *Anthology of American Folk Music* was a primary instigator in the folk music revival of the 1950s and 60s.

AG: I have endless passages of Yeats for some reason or other. It just sticks in my mind. You know what I got? You know what I began digging lately . . . remember "Sailing to Byzantium?"

WSB: Um hm.

AG: I began understanding it a little differently the other day on the way to Florida. I'd had this heart attack.[15] I finished a poem that I'd started at the end of *The Fall of America* in 1971 that's been sitting around waiting for me to correct the typescript, and for twenty years I never got to it but I finally did for an art book with Roy Lichtenstein. Then in Holland I suddenly got inspired and wrote a twenty-seven-page poem listing and characterizing everyone I'd ever been to bed with in my life, a complete sexual history, and suddenly realized that I had enough poems for another big long book, and that it was going to be really good. You know with some very amazing things in it. And then Hal Willner started putting together all my old records for this Rhino boxed set of four CDs, which will bring back the Blake and everything else. And I felt that things that I had done . . . I had laid up treasures in heaven, which were now coming into fruition. And I was feeling good. And I realized that, well I only had a few more years, twenty years, ten years [he had four]. And then I began thinking of "Once out of nature I shall never take my bodily form from any natural thing." That's the "Sailing to Byzantium"?

WSB: Yessss.

AG: I mean, once dead, once out of nature, dead and waiting to be reborn, if you get reborn at all, I shall never take my bodily form from any natural thing. I'll not come back as flesh. "But such a form as Grecian goldsmiths make, of hammered gold and gold enameling." In other words, a work of art.

WSB: Yeah, sure.

---

15 Allen never had a heart attack. He must be referring to the congestive heart condition that he had at the time, which was relieved somewhat by dietary changes—hence all the talk of diet and salt in the present conversation.

AG: "And set upon a golden bough to sing to lords and ladies of Byzantium of what is past or passing or to come." And I realized that this record collection of mine would be up there on a golden bough singing to the lords and ladies of America past present and future, and that what I had to say was . . . because . . . not eternal but . . . it was not immortal but it was eternal. Dig? Not immortal but eternal, i.e., emptiness. So that I figured I had made my golden bough actually. I'd made my golden bird. And I had set it on a golden bough and I could kick the bucket happy [laughs]. In other words, no more desire to come back.

> [. . . Once out of nature I shall never take
> My bodily form from any natural thing,
> But such a form as Grecian goldsmiths make
> Of hammered gold and gold enamelling
> To keep a drowsy Emperor awake;
> Or set upon a golden bough to sing
> To lords and ladies of Byzantium
> Of what is past, or passing, or to come.]

WSB: Yes. [Looking at a magazine.] Did you see this, it's something called *Scab*. It's the . . . attack on the . . . it's so ridiculous . . . They said my idea of a vacation is going to Tangiers and raping children.

AG: *Scab #2* from Toronto. Were these the people that Mark Ewert knew?

WSB: He knows them.

AG: Ah well, they're just punk kids having fun.

WSB: I wrote a sort of rebuttal . . . . They're getting ready to spew out another . . .

AG: Oh, that's a picture of you here.

WSB: Of *course* it is . . . I didn't realize . . .

AG: It's the same face as over here except . . . It's a false femme, false faggot. A *breeding faggot* no less . . . that's what your trouble is.

wsb: Yes, exactly, a *breeding* faggot.

ag: They got some eye mascara on you and a bullet in your brow.

wsb: Yes, I see.

ag: . . . image here. Maybe that's the Ugly Spirit in the glass?

wes: Well that's the stigmata.

ag: Yes.

wsb: [Looking at cat photos] That Ruski? Oh man, I must go over and see him today. These are pictures of my Ruski. Oh, that's good color.

wes: That's Boy, and there's Ajax.

wsb: Boy looks like a statue, doesn't he? Course you can't really see him clearly. Look Allen, these are my pictures of Ruski. I'm going over to see him later today. My Ruski. Where is the best picture? He is such a . . . what's so good about him is his disposition . . . a cat that never bites and never scratches.

ag: So why is he over there [in another house], because of the other cats?

wsb: I couldn't have him here with too many cats. He's timid.

ag: He's that young male?

wsb: No, heavens no.

wes: He's ten years old.

wsb: He's ten years old.

ag: I see, so too old for the younger guys.

wsb: Shy. Well I couldn't have him here with Fletch and [Mona?] No, he's too . . .

ag: Is he your oldest cat, the cat you've had longest?

WSB: No, no. Ginger's the same age, maybe older,

AG: How come they don't mess with Ginger?

WSB: Ginger's a female.

AG: Ah.

WSB: Ginger's female and this is a male. A female cat could be assimilated, but a male cat's much more difficult. And we had this . . .

AG: Did he come later than the others?

WSB: No, he was the first cat. One of the first cats . . . Cronenberg gave me a Korat cat.

AG: Oh yeah. Where is that?

WSB: In the apartment here, with Udo. Now he is terribly active. He rushes around, and he's a beautiful cat. It's a pedigreed one. They cost about a thousand dollars . . . He doesn't even look like a cat. When it was first brought here in a little carry bag. I looked at it and said my God, you've given me a monkey. He's six months old and he has a pedigree; here's a picture of him. Look at that.

WES: He's really small.

WSB: They're small; they don't get more than about seven pounds, seven and a half pounds. They're terrifically active and agile. A Korat.

AG: Think you find him likeable?

WSB: Oh he's cute. He's great. Oh yes.

WES: He loves people.

WSB: He loves people. He's great. Yeah, I love cats. Yeah, he's a beautiful beast. So is Fletch. Look at his coat. He has the same color, sort of silver-gray.

WES: Allen, what time would you like to go to the store? I found some more energy.

AG: You did? What do you think? What do you want, what's your . . . ?

WES: What's good for you?

AG: I'll put on my clothes. What's your plans this morning, Bill?

WSB: Nothing in particular. I have to shave I guess, and, let me see.

AG: What's on our schedule for the day? Are you gonna go downtown at all?

WSB: Well, yeah, I'd like to stop in the pawn shop. See if I can get some . . .

AG: So shall we all go together? I'll go to the bathroom, I'll be right back.

[Tape stops.]

AG: It's expansively explained in this one. Is it in the other too?

WSB: [At a distance] It revolves around Jane Bowles, and Paul.

AG: The other book revolves around Jane Bowles. Around Jane and Paul. Well this has some long chapters about them. This has a number of chapters about them. And gives an account of her last illness. Did the other one also have that? About her going to the Parade Bar naked and giving out money?

[William inaudible at a distance.]

AG: You weren't around for that time were you?

WSB: No, I wasn't there. I heard about it.

AG: Well, I'm surprised they didn't put that in the movie.

WSB: You read the Michelle Green book?

AG: The sheltering..? [Paul Bowles's *The Sheltering Sky*.]

WSB: The book by Michelle Green . . .

AG: No, I haven't seen that.

WSB: *The Dream at the End of the World.*

AG: No I haven't seen *The Dream at the End of the World.*

WSB: Well it's very good.

AG: I thought that [indicating another book] was good too. It had a lot of information and gossip I'd never known. Particularly her [Jane Bowles's] end, I hadn't *realized* that she was so far out, so ill, and had lost so much of her reason.

WSB: Oh, absolutely.

AG: But Paul must have been a saint to put up with all that, to take care of her. That must have been really excruciating for him. I didn't realize he'd gone through that ordeal.

WSB: She'd fallen in love with Lily [Wickman].

AG: Who was Lily?

WSB: The Parade Bar . . .

AG: That owned the . . .

WSB: The Parade Bar after Jay Haselwood died. She looked awful. She was a nice enough woman, but my God. She was about seventy years old and all wrinkled.

AG: And Jane fell in love with her. Then what happened to her relationship with Cherifa?

WSB: Oh, that went on.

AG: Also.

wsb: Where Cherifa is now, I just don't know.

ag: Nobody knows, huh?

wsb: I don't know how Paul ever got her off his back.

ag: Well, just, cutting off I imagine.

wsb: Well, it's not so easy. The ferocious Moroccan lesbians, they don't cut off so easy.

ag: Hold it a second, don't move [camera click]. This is good, I don't have to worry about trembling. Don't have to worry about my hand. [He's using a tripod.]

wsb: I don't know whether the book is here or someone's borrowed it.

ag: Yeah, I want to see it.

wsb: It's very good, very readable, all that stuff about . . . [that woman who] had all these animals, foxes, minks, dogs . . . went there. She gave a party and some of the guests were severely bitten.

ag: Who was that?

wsb: Daphne [(*sic*) Phyllis[16]] . . . that was the Melton set, led by Lord David Herbert.[17]

ag: Did you know him? I don't remember seeing him, but I think he came after I was there. After '61.

wsb: No, man, he was there when I got there. But he didn't have much to do with the beatnik set.

ag: Not even later? Wasn't interested in Bacon and Williams.

---

16 Countess Phyllis della Faille collected numerous animals domestic and wild. At one of her parties, "Two guests were severely bitten by the dogs . . . and a young man had the top of a finger removed by an infuriated macaw" (David Herbert qtd. in Green, 64).

17 The Honourable David Alexander Reginald Herbert (1908–95), second son of Reginald Herbert, the 15th Earl of Pembroke. British socialite and memoirist. He curated the high society scene in Tangier.

WSB: I saw him a couple of times.

AG: Did he say hello?

WSB: Of course. He wrote a book too.

AG: Yeah, apparently an interesting one. From the quotes that I heard here, in terms of gossip about the English coming in.

WSB: [inaudible] . . . methadone and doughnuts . . . He was a novelist.

AG: Um hm. Oh these are the Celts. That's what Kerouac always wanted to be. The Bretons were Celtic, weren't they?

WSB: I don't know.

AG: Kerouac was always preoccupied with being Celtic in origin. "Incapable of prolonged action, more addicted to bawdy banquets than the hard business of war and government." That sounds appropriate.

WSB: It's complex. Celts, yes, in Britain, in the southern part of England and in Wales, then of course Ireland.

TAPE 1 SIDE B

3/18/92. Table talk. Poets are lazy prose writers.
The ceremony of the previous afternoon.
How much to pay the shaman, Melvin Betsellie.

AG: I was interested in his [Kerouac's?] poetry, and I related it to you, but I didn't put you directly onto the poetry.

WSB: I've always said that . . . get away with some definite structure like rhyme or meter, there's no clear line.

AG: How'd you like what [Robert] Creeley said about that? He made that point.

WSB: It seems to me a pretty obvious point. I said once that poets are simply lazy prose writers.

AG: Well, that's what Jack said . . . . So what did you think of the Shaman, you didn't see him put the coals in his mouth?

WSB: No I did not.

AG: How did you feel about it?

WSB: Well, I thought, my God, it's great that he has [touched me] and I didn't feel any burns or anything.

AG: He actually touched you with the body of the coal?

WSB: Oh yes. And I felt nothing . . . and I said, well, I'm certainly not injured 'cause there's nothing happening to me and I was very impressed but I couldn't see, I didn't know where the coals were. They were in his mouth!

AG: Yes . . . did you have any . . . how did you feel in terms of this sort of emotionally or psychologically during that time? I was quite moved in the sense, you know I thought . . . what I was thinking is all those people, very much your, your affectionate friends really wishing you well.

WSB: Oh, that's what *I* felt too, they were really great and I just felt, you know, sort of laying myself open just completely . . . undirected thought, undirected thought. I did nothing, no sort of intellectualizing.

AG: Blank, huh?

WSB: Yeah. Yes.

AG: What occurred to me is that we were sort of like focusing on your well-being but also I was realizing at the time, you know, what almost brought me to tears was, I don't know if you realize how many people I've ever met who really love your work and felt a great deal of affection . . . but it must be hundreds of thousands or millions of people . . .

WSB: Yes. Well, yeah I feel it. I feel it very deeply. I like the shaman very much . . . the way he was crying.

AG: Later in the evening?

WSB: Yeah.

AG: When he was thinking of his mother and his grandfather. Father dying too.

WSB: Deeply sad, deeply . . .

AG: Well, we're lucky to have seen that . . . lucky to have heard that . . . . Well, I was energetic, I don't know why, this morning I got up at 6:30 and then tried to write what little fragments I could of recollecting the ceremonies last night.

WSB: That was something—he had *coals* in his mouth.

AG: Yes, but I didn't see it in his mouth, see, Steve [Lowe] did.

WSB: Well, even in his hand . . .

AG: Did you see them in his hand?

WSB: Well I don't know. He, he came and blew on me with a coal, it was very close and I was surprised [and reacted to the] burning.

AG: Did you see him holding it, or was it being held in his palm or . . . ?

WSB: I couldn't tell.

[Bill Lyon, the anthropologist who had arranged for the previous day's shamanic ceremony arrives.]

WSB: Should I write out a check? This is the eighteenth? What?

AG: Nineteenth I think. [It was the eighteenth.]

BL: So what's all the other money for?

WSB: The shaman.

BL: Then here's what we have to do. So I told you, last night was your thank you ceremony. And if you didn't have enough money and you want to give more money, then that's still part of your thank you ceremony. But you've got to give it to Mel directly. So I'll take this check downtown, cash it for you, and then I'll bring Mel later by, after your photography session, and I'll just tell Mel that you want to see him again before he leaves. Did you give Mel . . . you didn't give Mel any money last night? OK. Because there's two things that happened that I noticed because of that. And one was both of the cooks [fire-tender assistants] took the money that you gave them and gave it to Mel, and said, "Here's some money for you." Because evidently they didn't see you give him any money. So they wanted to make sure he got money, so they gave him your money. And then Mel said a funny thing to me, he said, "I wish he'd left that tag on the blanket." And I thought, what he means is, I know what an Indian

23

means when he says that. He would take that blanket down and cash it in and get his money. Because you didn't give him any money, see. He needs money for his truck or whatever. But I didn't say anything to him 'cause I thought, well I'd better talk to Bill. OK, so I'll just bring him by, and you give him the other money, over the hundred and ten [given to the assistants] and say, you know, I didn't have enough money with me last night, or however you want to say it. But take care of him so he doesn't feel bad.

wsb: We should be back here around five.

bl: So I'm going to leave by eight, so sometime between five and eight we'll just drop in . . . Make it out to me, and then I'll bring the $190 back to you. And you can give $190 to Mel. That'd be great.

ag: How much are you going to pay him?

wsb: $190.

bl: He's going to give him $190, that's what he wanted to give him . . . I always give my Shamans $500 when they run their aid ceremony and stuff. So if a guy runs a four-day ceremony, I have him paid $2000. Because I treat them like doctors, you know, that's what I do.

wsb: Now listen . . .

bl: It's what *you* want to do . . . I'll tell you what he did physically. He started at two o'clock out there, worked in the rain all afternoon, chopping the wood, getting the fire pit . . . he had to bail it out three times, the water out of that thing. And then he ran the ceremony from six to nine. So he worked seven hours. So that'll give you some cost of just the physical part that he put in.

wsb: I see [additional three hundred?].

bl: Then make it so. You just, that's between you and him and that's good. That's a fair thing.

wsb: Five hundred?

BL: I mean, five hundred's what *I* do . . . You know I have a very high esteem of these fellows and I want them . . . Here's what I do, William. When I do these ceremonies, I make sure they get paid enough so that they'll have a high self-esteem. It's really hard for them in this culture to have any damn self-esteem. And one of the ways you can give people in this culture self esteem is by saying, "OK here's this, this means about a hundred dollars an hour." That puts them on the level of a lawyer. You know, give them that same self-esteem is what I do. And that's why I do it; it's not because I think they need so much money.

WSB: Let's give him five hundred.

BL: You guys do it together and bring it over and you both should present it. If you kick in a hundred, Allen, you give him the hundred, to Mel. You should say, "I really appreciate having the opportunity to meet you."

WSB: So that's five hundred plus . . .

BL: The 110 [(*sic*) 190].

AG: 690.

BL: I'll go down the bank. Nineteenth tomorrow, March 19th.

William with Melvin Betsellie, 18 March 1992

TAPE 2 SIDE A

3/19/92. You can't argue with a demon. Tabloid news.
The shaman's follow-up visit. Mel describes his methods.

AG: I've talked my way in and out and around in circles and I know that it isn't efficacious.[18]

WSB: Father Connor said never let him get you into an argument, never argue, he'll beat you every time.[19]

AG: Is that the voice of the good man or Satan saying that [laughs]?

WSB: It's the voice of the exorcist, trying to get the bad spirit Satan out of somebody, that's all. The voice of the therapist. It certainly is not the voice of Satan, who will argue and argue and argue and argue and argue, round and round and round and round and round in circles. You never get anywhere in so far as moving anything, or changing anything. The point of an argument is to keep something in place. Never to move it or to change it.

[William is looking at supermarket tabloid news.]

WSB: Now that's a ridiculous picture. Where are their ears? Both of their ears are crunched right together.

AG: Is that a trick photograph? Of a two-headed guard dog bred by cops.

WSB: Oh my God look at that.

AG: It's in the paper you bought at the supermarket?

---

18   Allen is probably referring to his relationship with Peter Orlovsky.

19   William is referring here to Malachi Martin's book on exorcism, which is discussed in detail later in the visit.

WSB: Well sure, these are . . . "Alien steals space buggy and flag off surface of moon" . . . "Jimmy Hoffa found alive."

AG: What's that one called, the News or something?

WSB: *The News.* "Runner up in beauty contest dies of jealousy . . . Eskimos killing walruses to get money for *drugs!,* say US wildlife officials."

AG: Eskimos.

WSB: "Ninety-year-old twin sisters launch recording career."

AG: Hundred-year-old twin sister nuns?

WSB: "Eskimos have been running around slaughtering rare Alaskan wildlife and selling the spoils for money to feed their nasty habits, US officials say."

AG: Oh, that's part of the war against drugs.

WSB: "Undercover agents worked for the past two years to bust a massive ring of poachers who've skinned and beheaded walruses, polar bears, and seals for their valuable fur and ivory. An ivory tusk could sell for as much as $5000, officials said."

AG: That's a walrus tusk, huh?

WSB: Walrus tusk. "Agents filmed poachers opening fire after herds of walruses, then approaching the dead ones and hacking off their heads. The money made from selling skins and ivory bought drugs that Eskimos took into their villages to use and sell, officials said."

AG: Uh hm.

WSB: "They nabbed twenty-nine of these culprits and are hunting down another eighty." Good God, what nonsense!

AG: You read those regularly?

WSB: Oh yeah, there's always some funny stuff, they're so funny, see.

AG: Have you gotten very much stuff for your books from those?

WSB: I told you about my hairy beast.

AG: What was that, a woman had a rare disease . . . ?

WSB: I conceived of this disease in *Ghost of a Chance*.[20] The hairs, the hairs just grow all over people and then there were spores . . . choke to death. So then I pick up this thing and it says "rare disease turns woman into hairy beast!"

AG: Uh huh. Well, your writing prophesied the . . . But I mean did you ever take anything out of there and exaggerate it? Do you remember any?

WSB: Well, yes I think of some. "Doomed cancer patient's suicide miracle, man shoots brain tumor out of his head and saves his life."

AG: I see, he had a brain tumor and he committed suicide and shot the tumor out . . . auto-operation.

WSB: Really. "Freezing to death don't drink booze." . . . . "Nincompoop animal lovers want to outlaw the term 'pets' . . . You ought to call them 'companion animals.'"

AG: How many . . . you got around the house, Bill?

WSB: How many what?

AG: Companion animals?

WSB: There are six. Six companions.

AG: And all cats.

WSB: Yes.

---

20 *Ghost of Chance* (Whitney Museum, 1991; High Risk Books, 1995) is a novella that begins in a pirate colony in Madagascar then moves to the present day where deadly viruses cause such things as belief that one is Jesus Christ and uncontrollable hair growth. The back cover of the 1995 edition calls it "an important story about environmental devastation."

AG: And none of them pets, but companions. Your equals, peers!

WSB: Well, I suppose. "Babysitter bites off girl's toes" . . . "Sperm banks use street bums as donors, as a result the babies are ugly and stupid." Oh man. "Space aliens are kidnapping the homeless and the government couldn't be happier, expert says." . . . "I had my baby by a four-thousand-year-old man." . . . Oh, here they are, here they are, here they are. Come in! Come in!

[Guests Jim and Susan arrive. Talk of the ceremony with Michael Emerton.]

WSB: Fletch! Get away from the dip. Get a way from the dip! Mother of God . . .

MICHAEL: Susan, have you tried it?

SUSAN: The sweat? No, I've just taken saunas, but not that.

WSB: Well this is not supposed to be a bath; this is a ceremony, a healing ceremony.

SUSAN: How long do you stay in?

WSB: About a half an hour.

MICHAEL: Allen, how long would you say we were in there?

AG: I thought we were about an hour and a half.

MICHAEL: Really, 'cause when William said a half an hour I thought no way. It was at least an hour . . . Actually Bill [Lyon] could tell us.

WSB: He would know.

MICHAEL: I'm gonna ask him.

WSB: We will, he'll be here shortly. [William describes the layout to Susan.] It was a hoop sort of house like that with places to sit. And then he had one of those horse troughs. They come in various sizes.

But this was about six or seven feet long and two feet deep. You fill it with water, cold water. So you come out of the sauna and douse yourself with water.

[Melvin Betsellie and Bill Lyon arrive.]

WSB: Sit down, sit down!

MB: Feel like I'm . . . [inaudible; everyone talking at once; laughter.]

AG: So, what were your thoughts after last night? It was quite an ordeal for you.

MB: Yeah. Feel OK.

BL: I'm gonna go run some errands.

MB: OK.

BL: And you can talk . . . I'm gonna go. I'm gonna be back after a while. I'm gonna leave him to talk to you guys for a little bit. [I will] Get out of the way. I still have stuff to get ready to get going. And you get to see me all the time anyway, so you don't need to see me.

WSB: Always good to see you, Bill.

BL: And good to see you too. You going to be OK, Michael?

MICHAEL: Yes. Thanks.

BL: OK. Hello goodbye.

SUSAN: See you.

JIM: Well, hello goodbye as well. We're gonna go to Topeka.

[Udo Breger arrives. Introductions.]

MB: Melvin Betsellie, Diné, Diné, Navajo.[21]

---

21 On 4 April 2016, friends of Melvin posted the following death notice on Facebook. "Chief Melvin Betsellie, who is of the Diné Nation, an Elder, a Medicine Man, a Sun Dance Chief, and Water Pourer, crossed over this morning."

UDO: Navajo.

MB: Yeah. I'm just going to prepare myself for sun dance. At Big Mountain, Hopi place. Then I'm going up the following month, in August, to sun dance with Leonard Crow Dog.

[Guest are saying goodbye. Lots of noise and crosstalk. James Grauerholz arrives. Allen discusses recording machine and microphone with JG.]

AG: Well, ideas, words and ideas, as Bill said all along, are a little bit like a virus . . . An idea is a virus. Somebody catches an idea and passes it on to others. They call it M-E-M-E-S.

JG: Memes?

AG: Heard anything about that?

JG: Yeah. Like morphemes, phonemes. There's also this interesting thing called morphological simultaneity or something.

AG: The hundredth monkey or something like that.

JG: Yeah. It means that once something has happened, it's more likely to happen somewhere else, although there's no direct causal link. That's interesting, and they prove it again and again.

[Tape stops.]

MB: He's my chief. Leonard Crow Dog.

AG: Your main teacher?

MB: Yeah, my main chief teacher. And then there's Archie, Archie Lame Deer Fire.

WSB: Is he the one that went to Denmark?

MB: Yeah. He was in Europe until January. January he came back. The last place he stopped was in Germany.

WSB: Didn't he bring some buffalo? I heard he brought some buffalo to Denmark.

MB: Yeah. He goes looking for them. He always likes to get those fresh buffalo skulls, still with the brains in it. We use that during ceremony. There's maybe eleven or thirteen or twelve. What we do is we tie them all together and then we pierce the back and we drag them. All the way around this arena four times.

AG: Thirteen buffalo?

MB: Skulls.

AG: Fresh?

MB: Fresh, with the brains still in it.

AG: What's the symbolism of that?

MB: The symbolism of strength. Enduring. And vision quests. Plus you do that and then you got the piercing of the horse too. I honored Crazy Horse, years ago, during the time of his birth also with the tree, hoisting me up and keeping me there for a while. Then there's different ways. The last step I took was one of the oldest ways that was ever done in the Lakota way, and that was getting two trees and standing in between it and pierced from front and back, staying there four days. That was one of the toughest . . .

AG: Drinking at all . . . water?

MB: No water for four days, no food for four days.

AG: So what happens to your awareness then, become . . . ?

MB: It stays, just that prayer. That prayer. That main little prayer and that sun. You start to work with elements and then your instruments that you have, your bone whistle, your eagle bone whistles, your feathers, and just your prayer. And your relatives. You think of all your relatives from way back and they come to you, and you call the bird, you call the four-legged animals, certain type of four-legged animals, certain type of animals, they'll help you.

AG: Crawling animals?

MB: Crawling animals, all life. Everything that was created on this earth was for a purpose. The smallest of insects are the most powerful insects. The largest animal is the most powerful, different ways. Everything has its meaning. That's the way we are taught. So I have respect for all things that were created to us, even the two-leggeds [laughing].

WSB: Those are the hardest to respect.

MB: [Laughing] I try every day.

WSB: So much possibility and they do so little with them.

MB: Five hundred years ago we used to be 25 million native people. At this time there's only two million. And within this continent from the north to the south, there's only 221 bands left. And the population is not very high, fifty or twenty. In the southwest . . . Diné . . . when I say Diné, it means Navajo . . . We used to be the largest tribe, but now I heard they took census two years ago and now the Cherokees are supposed to be . . . I don't know.

AG: That lady last night, she was what?

MB: She was Winnebago.

AG: Winnebago Creek, did you say?

MB: No, Winnebego Sioux.

WSB: Alright.

MB: Well, this year, William my friend, I'll be sun dancing in the month of July after Independence Day in Arizona, called Big

Mountain. That's within the Hopi and Navajo area. Which they have a JUA problem at this time.[22]

wsb: Is that in New Mexico?

mb: Arizona. They're having all them relocation problems. Causing a lot of difference between two tribes, Hopis and Navajos. And religion has almost come to a . . .

---

22 JUA refers to Joint Use Area. In response to shifting demographics (including a century of expansion of the Navajo people), the US government has designated for joint use land that the Hopi consider to be theirs. The government has redrawn boundaries fifteen times, exacerbating confusion and conflict.

TAPE 2 SIDE B

3/19/92. Mel's methods continued. The politics of peyote.
Changing the future by seeing. Tornados.
Michael's fears during the ceremony. Calling the animals.
Heart trouble: you shouldn't have salt. Allen says Grace.

MB: [I use the] night, I use the day, I use the morning, I use the sunset. Or, somehow I all focus into it like with a star, what I do. I use a sweat lodge for certain things, I use the fire for certain things, I use the hot coal for certain things and I use a sacred herb, which is called peyote. The peyote is being classified at this time as a drug. The reason why it's being classified that way is because white people misused it. The other . . . misinterpretation of the other walks of life. We never did that. We use it religiously. We show people. But again, it's not the peyote, it's us . . . that misinterpret that . . . In April, next month, April 17th or 21st, there will be a lot of leaders in Washington DC to defend this rightful use of it.

AG: What's the occasion there? For peyote . . .

MB: For peyote and all religion, in all bands, tribes.[23]

AG: About two years ago there was a court decision reversing judge Yale McFate's 1940 [*sic*][24] decision saying that it was legal, and then the courts reversed it in where, Seattle or Portland?

---

23 In March of 1992, the month of the present conversation, Bill SB 1100 was introduced by State Senator James Henderson, a Navajo, in the Arizona Senate to limit the use of peyote to Native American members of the Native American Church. The Arizona Senate Judiciary Committee found SB 1100 to be unconstitutional.

24 In 1960, Arizona Superior Court Judge Yale McFate dismissed a drug possession charge against a Navajo woman who had been arrested for using peyote during religious ceremonies. McFate ruled that banning the use of the drug was a violation of the woman's constitutional right to freedom of religion. The decision was upheld by the US Supreme Court.

MB: You know why? It was those two counselors, they announced they were using peyote. They were a member of the Native American Church, but they were not native.

AG: So they couldn't claim privilege.

MB: They couldn't claim it, so that made everything real rough.

AG: Did that decision affect Native American use?

MB: Very, very badly. Now the government has gone to Mexico, where it comes from.

AG: They try to get rid of peyote!?

MB: Yeah.

AG: In the desert [laughs]?

MB: This is where they're having the long walk or run. They're starting from . . . all bands are getting together, within a period of two to three months. Some tribes are going to start coming from Alaska, all the way to Mexico. Then the others are going to come from all the way from Argentina, and they're going to meet in Mexico. And they're going to set this sacred tree up. And they're going to put all these medicines that everybody believes, and put it with the tree and tie it with colors.

AG: Bill was down in South America and worked with some medicines and some medicine men. Ayahuasca.

MB: Ayahuasca, oh.

AG: You know that?

MB: Yeah.

AG: Many many years ago, and so did I. As well as peyote.

MB: They were in Illinois . . .

WSB: Very strong . . .

MB: . . . a month ago. They were in Illinois a month ago. Yeah, they were up there.

AG: From South America?

MB: From South America, Argentina. They were spiritual people.

AG: Do you have a copy of that here? *In Search of Yage.* Somewhere?

WSB: Well I've got *The Yage Letters.*

MB: What's real bad about the peyote right now for peyote members . . . you can have a sacred meeting within a teepee or hogan which we call highest divine . . . and within this practice, federal marshals can come in during your services and check to see if you all have membership cards. If you don't, they'll charge you for possession.

AG: But if you do on the reservation they won't bother you? What about off the reservation? What if you have a hogan off the reservation?

MB: Well, you have to have paper, you have to carry papers.

AG: But it's still allowed for Native Americans?

MB: Definitely.

AG: It's just us that can't do it.

MB: Well that's where the disagreement's coming from. Some say "we practice that way of life too." Like the two fellas in Oregon.

AG: I remember, then Little Joe . . . remember him?[25]

MB: Yeah, I remember.

AG: I knew him, briefly.

MB: So that's kinda getting a little difficult, but I don't know. We'll just have to pray a little harder, sun dance a little harder, work a little harder.

---

25   Little Joe Gomez, peyote guide.

WSB: Yeah, well . . .

AG: Have you been to many peyote meetings?

MB: I've been to a lot of them.

AG: Hundreds?

MB: Almost.

AG: I had maybe a dozen.

MB: I met a lot of leaders.

AG: Some center in Huerfano Valley in Colorado.

MB: Huerfano? Uh huh.

AG: Near the . . .

MB: Huerfano's in New Mexico.

AG: Also down toward lower Colorado, there's that long valley.

MB: Right, right.

AG: A guy there that raises horses and has a sort of pathway . . . a road . . .

MB: Well, when some spiritual man, elderly man wants to conduct services and he asks me to help him, I pull security for him. I get some security people for him. And I always tell him, you conduct your services and nobody will come in until you're done, and then I'll let them in. No matter if it's the National Guard or what.

AG: Have you had peyote, Bill, ever? He's had peyote. How many times?

WSB: The only time . . . it made me so sick . . . and then I had mescaline and that made me sick.

[MB laughs.]

AG: I wrote some very interesting poetry on peyote.

MB: You know I get mind visions, my friend, I'll call you my friend, I get mind visions, I put five hundred buttons of peyote in front of me. I put the lodge up, fire, and I stay there four days four nights and I eat all this peyote. No water no food.

WSB: Good God.

MB: I take my walk with life. All my sacred items. I call the eagle, he'll come, he'll dance for me. I'll call the bear, the bear will come to me. I tell him to sit with me. I call the white wolf, I call all types of animal, cougar, call the rain, tell the rain go away and let the sun shine. It's part of the way of life. That's the kind of life I like.

AG: So you have that four days of vision. Then how does that affect you when you're not on peyote? Does it give some permanent insight that you use every day?

MB: See the future.

AG: When you're high you see the future and then when you come down . . .

MB: I'm not high.

AG: Well when you're with peyote god . . .

MB: Spiritual.

AG: Then your use of it is to see the future or to change your own. . . .

MB: To see the teacher? To see the future . . .

WSB: To see the future is to change the future.

MB: Yeah.

WSB: If you see the future, you've changed it by seeing.

MB: The last time I did a quest, something about tornado. I wanted to learn about the tornado. Very powerful. One day I might ask you to help me.

WSB: By all means.

MB: [Laughing] Excuse me, my friend. The one I would like to have is that tornado that went through this area. You know what it did? It laid in the sky and it was going like a funnel. Then all of a sudden there was a whack! And it came . . .

JG: Yeah. I saw Wichita two days after. It was wiped out worse than any bomb.

WSB: I keep records of all tornados.

UDO: Does a tornado always turn in one direction or does it . . . ?

William with translator and scholar Udo Breger, 19 March 1992

JG: One direction in this hemisphere; opposite direction below the equator.

WSB: That's right.

AG: In the southern hemisphere it turns counter-clockwise?

WSB: The '81 tornado here hit the Gaslight trailer court and the KMart . . . between the two parts of the trailer court. The only casualty.

MB: I've seen it, William, where it throws a piece of straw through a tree.

WSB: It can send a straw so fast that it'll go through a door . . . comes at such a tremendous velocity it goes right through a door.

MB: [Introducing himself to Udo] Did I shake your hand, I'm sorry.

AG: Udo.

WSB: Udo Breger. He's from Germany.

MB: I know I know I heard. I see that.

MICHAEL: Would you like some milk with your coffee?

MB: No. Yeah. Little bit of milk and sugar please, Mike. How you feeling!?

MICHAEL: Very good.

MB: You know sometimes I take that into the lodge. I take those rocks until they're yellow. And I take in there fifty rocks.

MICHAEL: I think, you know, I think part of my problem was that I didn't quite know what to expect. And the smoke and the heat were rising.

MB: Smoke? Steam, steam.

MICHAEL: But there was also smoke in the air.

MB: Spirits [laughing].

MICHAEL: And my breath was going away and I didn't know if it would stop and so I panicked.

MB: That's why I'm there. I seen you but, be alright, be alright [laughs].

MICHAEL: By the end I felt very there, and I wouldn't say comfortable, that's not the right word for it.

MB: Intense . . . Next month I want to sing a song with the government conference, William.

WSB: What's that?

MB: I'm going to sing a native traditional song at the governor's conference here.

AG: Where's that going to be?

MB: Somewhere in Kansas. Then in May, I'm going to bless twenty-five college students, and I'm going to run a lodge for them. Quite a few other things are going to happen.

WSB: You said calling the animals. I can call cats. If there's a cat around, he will come to me. And I can also call toads. When I was a child we had an old Irish woman and she taught me how to call the toads. I can go out, and if there are any toads around . . .

AG: What's the sound you make?

WSB: I can't describe it. It's just I know it and I can do it, when I know there's a toad there. Sort of a [low melodic humming]. Last time I did it was . . . last time I saw Ian Sommerville, in Bath, a place he had in Bath.

JG: I saw you call a toad in your childhood backyard in 1980 in St. Louis, where you grew up.

WSB: That's right.

JG: Howard [Brookner] filmed you.

WSB: He said, "Oh, it's nonsense." I said, "Come out in the back yard. There's a little pool there. I don't know if I can . . . "

JG: It's spring now, the toads are moving, we should call some later.

[Mel laughs.]

WSB: Course, I like snakes too.

JG: But don't call any more cats, we have enough. [General laughter.]

WSB: Quite right, we have seven, no six.

MB: That's why it was raining yesterday, 'cause you called those toads [laughter]. Then today was sunny.

WSB: You saw my rain stick.

MB: Yeah.

UDO: So you went to see Ian Sommerville in Bath?[26]

WSB: That's the last time I saw him. I went down there. He was staying in Michel's place. Really weird stuff. Composing a metric system . . . and Ian Sommerville had his house. And that was the last time I ever saw him. On my birthday in 1976 or '75 . . . he died on my birthday.

AG: Who was that?

WSB: Ian Sommerville. Also Spencer Smith died on my birthday.

[Overlapping conversations. Dinner preparations.]

WSB: The final bottom line is spiritual power wins, but it has to be strong.

MB: Right.

---

26 Ian Sommerville (1940–1976) was an electronics technician and computer programmer. In 1961 Sommerville and Gysin developed "the Dreamachine," a stroboscope intended to affect alpha wave activity in the viewer's brain. Ian died in a single-car accident.

WSB: It must be strong enough to break through the dead weight of material power.

MB: I bring the wind. I can go out there and think "yo" clearly and then I bring the wind. Can see it coming. Good wind. I also do healing with the first full moon and with the river, water, river. And I do healing. The purpose of that is for migraine headaches. Very bad migraine headaches I can do with the moon and water. Man from Oklahoma taught me that . . . I work with water . . . I liked that fire [yesterday].

WSB: Yes . . . I knew . . . I just relaxed . . . the pipe, the pipe . . . Never for one minute was I worried.

MB: You seemed so relaxed. Some people they panic.

WSB: Oh yes. If they panic, they could get burned.

MB: I dropped that coal last night, dropped in here and it come back out. I blowed it, and I look up here and I could see your life. Remember I was showing you? I could see your life when you were a child. I wanted you to see that.

WSB: I was never afraid.

MB: People always wonder if I get burned. I don't get burned. I use big hot coals. I haven't done that in a long time, use big ones.

JG: William said the coal tried to get away one time.

MB: Yeah. Took off.

[Conversation drowned out by Michael and Allen discussing seating arrangements.]

MB: Mike, sometimes I go in the lodge, to the sacred ground, we take in fifty rocks, big rocks like this, like light bulbs, and all these spiritual medicine people sit there and keep that rock going. Get a bucket of water about this high, pour it all in there. We sing. That's the most beautiful thing I ever experienced with a lot of spiritual men all around. And everybody sings together. Sing sing sing sing. That's good. All that, one mind. When you're done the ground's real hard and it's baking.

AG: Want some soup?

MB: One mind, one thought. One goes off, everybody hurts. Like having an infantry of men. One makes a mistake, it hurts everybody.

JG: I'm glad to hear that you'll be here for some time.

MB: I'm lined up already with all kinds of people. It's amazing. Just like when I went to Santa Fe. I went to the park to relax. All of a sudden, people coming, "Can you help me out?" What kind of help do you want, you know? "Well I don't know if I'm right about this, but are you a spiritual man?" Yeah. I'm just a tool. He does all the work. "Can you help us?" Sure. I'll help you, but help yourself too . . . .

JG: The cat is warming your . . .

MB: He wants to give me some of them lives, the cat. [Laughter.] *Mósí*, we call it in my native language [Navajo for domestic cat].

[Tape stops.]

AG: You've had heart trouble, so you shouldn't have salt.

WSB: *I* shouldn't? *You* shouldn't.

AG: You know on the back porch I saw a salt-free diet scheme that your doctor gave you, low sodium. I saw the secret prescription relegated to the back porch, though I may be wrong.

WSB: By what doctor?

AG: I may be wrong! Try it without first.

WSB: By what doctor?

AG: From your hospital. I'll produce the evidence.

WSB: I'm sorry I need salt!

AG: I don't quite rightly know whether this was specifically sent to you, but I saw it on the back porch when I was putting the . . .

JG: They gave it to William when he got out of the hospital.

WSB: Sodium control diet. "In addition to the salt we knowingly sprinkle on our food, many foods contain sodium as a part of their normal chemical composition. Eating a nutritionally balanced diet . . . " Thing is, my big problem is my appetite, getting enough to eat. And I can't eat something that doesn't have salt on it. It will not benefit me, I won't eat it, I can't even eat it.

AG: You can put all the salt you want in.

WSB: Well, thank you, my dear.

AG: As long as you have one spoonful without it . . . then you can tell the difference.

WSB: Yes, I've heard this talk that once you get used to it, it will have enough salt taste. Think so?

AG: Naturally, it's a purely subjective matter. Though it's widely reported.

WSB: But you do not have problems of a poor appetite.

AG: Not at all, I'm a glutton.

WSB: Well, that's good. I admire gluttons. I can't, you know . . .

AG: So my problem has been to curb my gluttony.

WSB: And my problem is to have an appetite for my food.

AG: *Bon appétit*, Monsieur Burroughs.

WSB: Thank you, it's very good. It's beef. What is this, pot roast, or what?

AG: I would guess. I tried to write about what we saw last night. I called it pot roast. When it came around to trying to find a name for that.

WSB: It is pot roast, some shredded beef . . .

AG: Exactly.

WSB: Yes, of course . . .

AG: I forgot. I dug in without saying my Grace. What I said last night was alright.

We give thanks for this food which is the product of the labor of other people and the suffering of other forms of life and which we vow to transform into enlightened medicine, poetry, cooking, healing, in all ten directions of space. And in cat fancying.

It's acknowledging where the food's coming from and hoping you can turn it to some good use. Doesn't mean you can, but at least you can think about it . . . On the other hand you wouldn't want to say which energy I vow to devote to eating more and more people that are weaker than me or things that are weaker than me.

WSB: No . . . Well, did you know that chimpanzees and baboons are carnivorous as well?

AG: Didn't know that.

WSB: Yes, they are. They will eat anything.

AG: Do they choose to eat meat if they have a choice?

WSB: I threw a dead rabbit into one . . . recently dead, just killed. They ate it.

AG: They'll eat anything and that's their beauty. . . .

WSB: There's a story by Erskine Caldwell, called "Kneel to the Rising Sun" about this old man . . .

[Noise of eating drowns out conversation.]

AG: This kind of soup is called Jewish penicillin. Ever hear of that?

MB: No [laughs].

AG: We went today to meet some Japanese photographers who wanted to take Bill's picture for a magazine.

MB: Where?

AG: The house around the corner.

WSB: The house where my cat [Ruski] is. Steven owns that house. [Drowned out by food noise and conversation.]

AG: Any more meat left?

William and Allen with Ruski, 18 March 1992

TAPE 3 SIDE A

3/19/92. Supper with Melvin Betsellie. Cats. All word is healing.
WSB and AG dream narratives. Tennyson. Nanao Sakaki.
The bear cult. I could never kill an animal.
Thus the Ugly Spirit comes in. Ways to keep the spirit out.
Could you give that love to a human?
Salman Rushdie.

UDO: You saw Ruski today?

WSB: Oh yes. [To Mel] I hope you will bless him, cause he's the special cat. I like animals more than people. Very . . .

UDO: William, whenever you have time and you're in town, you should visit Boy.

WSB: I want to see him.

UDO: James saw him yesterday.

WSB: I'd love to see him. Yeah. And Negrito too. He's the black . . .

UDO: Mm hm, the black one.

WSB: I like animals.

MB: Yeah, they're very . . . I don't know how you would put it in words . . . compassion.

WSB: Yes. Yes, it's such a beautiful animal. Well, Ruski is so . . . he's just so sweet.

AG: Is that the one you want blessed?

51

WSB: Ruski. Yes. He needs . . . I mean protected. Yes. Incredible cat.

[Skipping Udo's account of napping with "Boy" the cat.]

WSB: He [Boy] was a present from David Cronenberg the film director.

AG: O ho! [Allen's typical greeting. Bill Lyon has returned.]

WSB: It costs about a thousand dollars. It's a pedigree.

JG: Korat.

UDO: I'd like to see that pedigree one day.

WSB: Boy is born of . . . a showing cat. . .[all it would do is to] pick up some disease or something to take it to the cat show.

UDO: And it says in your book that the Korat would be very nervous in shows.

WSB: Any cat. All this noise going on? No. No. I would not show any cat.

UDO: William, yesterday, for the first time, I had to slap him on the hind part as he was very successful in chewing the electric cord from the typewriter to the socket.

WSB: Well, it's *dangerous.*

UDO: Yes. And so now when going out I'm pulling the plug. And so I really was angry and I . . .

WSB: You know what Auden said, this is a very good rule, "Never hit a child or an animal, *except* in anger." None of this stuff, "Oh it's for your own good" or anything. *Only* in anger, a reflex.

AG: The idea was never with cold deliberation, like a Nazi in a concentration camp.

WSB: James once lightly slapped Ruski for pissing or spraying on his typewriter and Ruski . . . in terror, ran up to me in my room, groaning. I had to hold him and calm him down.

UDO: Well, what I did was a few minutes later, I had arranged the cords otherwise and took him up and apologized and told him, look, this can kill you.

WSB: They understand.

[Bill Lyon comes to table.]

AG: Want some soup?

BL: No, I'm fine thank you, I'm doing great. This soup you made up? Maybe I'll take a cup.

MB: Bill, I'll see William Tuesday [24 March].

BL: Oh. OK. When we come back.

MB: Cedar his home.[27]

BL: Oh, that's right, you want to do that cedar thing.

WSB: By all means. I look forward . . .

MB: Looks like he got all ready. I'm ready too.

JG: I have to go.

MB: Where you goin'?

JG: I have to meet a friend and we're going to a kind of a spiritual meeting that we do . . . .

MB: That's good. . . . All word is healing. Always remember that. Because you have that spiritual . . . within you. So pure, each time you speak, it's healing. Like when we go into a lodge and we pour that little bit of water on them hot rocks. When the steam comes, we say it's the grandfatherness breathing on us and healing us from within.

JG: I hope to see you again.

---

27   Cedar is used as an incense. It is associated with prayer, healing, dreams, and protection.

MB: Oh, you will.

WSB: He's going to be around for some time. They're coming by . . .

MB: I'm going to see William Tuesday.

JG: OK.

MB: I'm going to help him out a little more.

WSB: Purification here in the house.

MB: Purification within his home.

JG: Good, there's definitely a few things around here . . .

[Mel laughs.]

WSB: I look forward to seeing you. You watch yourself, be careful, have a safe trip. 'Cause you have made a bad enemy.

MB: Yes, I know that.

WSB: Take it slow now.

MB: Very true . . . c'mon, Bill.

WSB: I dreamed last night about a very muddy river, no lake . . . very dangerous . . . but I'm walking along . . . Thought it was going to be alright, but it's dangerous. Somebody *rose up* from the river with a gun. Shotgun. Nothing much. Not very dangerous. Not a real nightmare.

BL: You're not too much in danger when you're carrying a gun.

WSB: No . . . In the dream it was someone else had a shotgun, but it was not so dangerous to me at all. Not at all.

AG: I had a dream last night.

WSB: What'd you dream?

AG: About a friend who had AIDS and is dying, who's a composer.

WSB: You mean an actual friend.

AG: Arthur Russell.

WSB: Oh, I don't know him.

AG: And he came and asked me if I had seen the recording engineer who's making his album. Arthur meanwhile is in the hospital in real life, and can't work. He can't direct anybody to which tapes he made that should be put together and mixed. So Arthur asked me had I seen the tape engineer. And I said, "No he's not here, maybe later, I'll give him a message." So Arthur went looking for him and then I walked down the corridor and there was this fellow Kurt, the engineer. I said, "Oh, Arthur was just here looking for you." So I wonder if Arthur is alright, in real life.

BL: So he's quite bad off now?

AG: He's in the hospital, his mind is wandering. And I was concerned . . .

WSB: I showed you in that book, so many of my dreams have no relationship to anything in waking life at all. Like that strange bit where I was in this hotel and I was levitating over the hotel and came back and I met in the lobby of this hotel [dream scene] . . . then I realized the whole place was dark except for a little light in this hotel. In other words, it's sort of like, you know, in a country where they don't allow alcohol, only in a hotel. Here they allowed light in a hotel!

BL: For the tourists! For the tourists.

[General laughter.]

WSB: In the lobby I met a weathercock. He controls the weather. I get up to my room which was extraordinary, distant . . . . and I floated up to the ceiling . . . and then some people came with the hotel clerk. And there was a show going on, I was thinking of floating out the window and attending this show, but the interesting thing was that I was afraid that I would wake up and find it was only a dream because I was enjoying it very much. But that I would wake up not here in Lawrence, but in that hotel. Afraid I'd wake up in a strange hotel in this place where there was no light, but you could see. That I'd wake up in that hotel and find it was only a dream. Not that I would wake up in Lawrence and find it was only a dream. So completely unrelated to anything in my waking life, but very interesting. I loved it.

Let's see, and I look forward to many exploration of many areas, different spiritual areas. I like . . . going all sorts of places, journeys.

MB: Yeah. I like those journeys myself. I love the journey.

WSB: Me too.

MB: Spirit . . . spiritual . . . I love to travel.

WSB: "Ulysses." That part in "Ulysses" by Tennyson.

AG: Tennyson.

WSB: Yes. "How dull it is to pause and make a rest. To rust unburnished, not to *shine* in use!" You have to *shine* in use. Doing something, functioning. You're apt to stagnate . . .

> [I am a part of all that I have met;
> Yet all experience is an arch wherethro'
> Gleams that untravell'd world, whose margin fades
> For ever and for ever when I move.
> How dull it is to pause, to make an end,
> To rust unburnish'd, not to shine in use!]

AG: But it had something about old age, "that which we are we are?"

WSB: What we are we are . . . old age . . . still . . . um . . .

AG: Remember the lines?

WSB: I don't remember . . .

AG: You used it. I remember you saying "We are not what we were, but that which we are, we are. . . . Then what's the end? Forward to the gates or something? It may be that we'll . . . "

> [We are not now that strength which in old days
> Moved earth and heaven, that which we are, we are;
> One equal temper of heroic hearts,
> Made weak by time and fate, but strong in will
> To strive, to seek, to find, and not to yield.]

WSB: Yeah, we'll be washed away, here and there.

AG: Arrive at the gates, pass through the gates of Hercules. Maybe we'll return home to Penelope . . . mayhap . . . something like that. Nineteenth-century poems that he was very fond of when he was a student, seventy years ago [laughs].

BL: I see.

WSB: I still am very fond of that, "Ulysses."

AG: Where did you read that first?

WSB: Don't remember. It's Tennyson.

AG: Yes.

WSB: It's not typical of Tennyson.

AG: How did you like those little Japanese poems by [Nanao] Sakaki?

WSB: Very much.

AG: Very good. He's spent a lot of time with American Indians, that guy, the Japanese guy that I was reading.

MB: Oh yeah. What's his name again?

AG: Nanao. You ask around in maybe . . .

MB: I bet you I ran across him and didn't even know.

AG: He's got a beard . . . he's not here now, he's in Japan with the Ainu . . . He's trying to save various indigenous native places in Japan. And also to save the last blue coral reef.

WSB: There even are bears on that island . . . there was a bear cult.

AG: Bear myth and bear cult, circum-polar Bear Cult . . .

WSB: Yes. They weren't bears, they were . . .

BL: What does that mean?

AG: All around the area of the Arctic Circle, there is the cult of the bear. In Siberia, in Alaska, in Northern Canada.

BL: Right.

AG: In Northern Europe. Circum-polar bear . . . very interesting term.

BL: Yeah. I never heard it.

AG: Friend poet Gary Snyder used it . . . common phrase among archaeological . . . mythological, mythology/archaeology/anthropology . . . Another phrase they use is for the cultures of the Pacific Rim . . . China, Japan, that is the rim itself, the shoreline, there are apparently many common cultural characteristics there.

BL: Hm.

WSB: I could never kill a bear or a deer. I can't kill any animal.

BL: What should I do with a cat when I'm allergic to cats?

WSB: I like to shoot, but I could never kill an animal . . . and a deer, good heavens, never.

AG: Have you ever shot an animal? Once you shot a porcupine or something? Was that Lucien?

WSB: No, I did once in South America shoot a beautiful animal like a monkey, but it wasn't hurt bad and it ran away and I've always hoped that it was alright, survived. I've regretted that all my life. It was fifty years ago and I still . . . sometimes I wake up at night, you know, oh my God, why did I do that? The things that . . . the bad things that I have seen . . . most are very small, you say "oh well."

MB: Right. Right.

WSB: Thus the Ugly Spirit comes in. I realized that I was taken *over* by something to do these things and that's where the Ugly Spirit comes in. And it gives me a terrible feeling. It gave me a terrible feeling, to think that I am not in control, that I have gone and shot this animal . . . terrible. Terrible. Just don't want anything like that to ever happen again. I want to be rid of that emphasis forever. It's so much tuned into the . . . oh, sort of the whole western, I don't know, European WASP tradition. I remember when I was at Los Alamos and . . . with Boy Scouts . . . and suddenly there was a badger came running in, and the counselor . . . he [the badger] just wanted to play . . . the counselor rushes over and gets this .45 automatic and it's so inaccurate, he can't hit it from here to there, and finally he puts the gun right against it and kills it, shoots it. Good God! These people, all they can think of when they see an animal is to kill it. The badger was just playing around.

BL: What's that?

AG: That's a rather ripe pear with some lemon.

WSB: Help yourself. I'll have some.

BL: They told me in this channeling thing I told you about last night that the owl was going to come and help me.

WSB: And did it?

BL: Not yet. I mean, over the next twenty-one months.

WSB: Great . . . grab some [of the pear dessert] before it's all gone. It's very good. It's been ripening for a long time.

AG: You gentlemen want some coffee or tea?

BL: No. We're going to get on our way.

WSB: Drive straight through?

BL: Yeah, I like to do that. I like to drive at night too 'cause it's like, not so much traffic . . . .

MB: My friend, my friend. Take care of yourself till I see you Tuesday.

WSB: See you Tuesday.

AG: See you.

MB: Take care, take care.

[BL and MB leave.]

AG: What'd he have to say, anything interesting? [Earlier in the evening William and Melvin had gone to another room to meet privately.]

WSB: Yeah. Well, he . . . ways to keep the spirit out. And he would come back and bless the rooms of the house.

AG: Here.

WSB: Yes. He wants me to bury that skull.

AG: What did he say about it?

WSB: He said it's a way bad spirits could come in.

[Off-mic chatter about cleaning up the dinner remains.]

AG: I was wondering, what if you gave all that palpable affection and devotion, but *external* devotion, to a human? What would that be like?

WSB: It couldn't happen. Couldn't happen. It's not the same. It's not the same . . .

AG: Give me some of that . . .

WSB: No, no . . .

AG: Not that I was worthy . . .

WSB: It's something that I have created, a being that I have created . . . *my* creation. And I couldn't do that with a person. It's a different kind of love, a different kind . . .

AG: Created in the sense that you had Ruski as a child [as a kitten].

WSB: Yes. I would have liked to have had Ruski as a kitten . . . imagine . . .

AG: In what sense did you create it? By taking it in, and favoring it . . .

WSB: More than that, more than that. More than that, he was my creation. Mine . . .

AG: That's kind of mysterious.

WSB: Of course it's mysterious . . . very profound. Why is it that the mewling of a lost kitten in the alley means more to me than hundreds of thousands of human bellies distended by famine? I don't say that's right, but it's true. Just means more.

AG: 'Course you don't . . . the bellies distended are photographs or video, where the alley crying kitten is actually present to you, because it's actually there with an organic presence rather than an image or a simulacrum. I mean, if you were present with a human baby crying, you might be just as affected.

WSB: Mm hm, yeah.

AG: A baby crying lost in an alley right where you were living.

WSB: Well, I would do what I could, naturally.

AG: You might become sort of careful about the baby.

WSB: No, man, no, people don't mean as much to me.

AG: They're more work than a cat.

WSB: No, it isn't that . . .

AG: They're more uncontrollable. People are more uncontrollable than a cat. And they grow bigger and they can hit you.

WSB: Those considerations don't enter in. No, it just is a cat is more my creation, it's my creation . . . Here he is now, here he is.

AG: Do you have any photographs of yourself with the cat?

WSB: No.

AG: Well, tomorrow maybe or next time we go. . . .

WSB: Maybe.

AG: I'll try and get a photo of the two of you.

WSB: I've resisted any pictures of the human to do of Ruski in my lap. Somehow it's not right. It's so trite, very, you know, Colette. Colette with her cat alone.

[Tape stops.]

AG: I brought that for you, it's an up-to-date report on Salman Rushdie's situation.[28]

WSB: Where the hell is he now, it's not America is it?

AG: You know, I saw him.

WSB: Yeah?

---

28 On 14 February 1989, a BBC reporter told Salman Rushdie that he had been sentenced to death by the Ayatollah Khomeini for defaming Islam in his novel *The Satanic Verses*. For nine years Rushdie and his family lived in hiding.

AG: He apparently had been reading my poetry and he was in New York and asked to see me. So [Andrew] Wylie told me, so I went to a hotel, a secret hotel and had to pass the guards downstairs, and about ten big burly guys upstairs in the corridor and in the inner room.

WSB: Who from? What police force?

AG: Well, New York City police force at the moment. Then there was Andrew and Rushdie. Andrew showed me the curtains. The curtains were made of bullet-proof lead or some bullet-proof thing. So they were closed . . . and he was in this big flowery hotel room. He said he'd been reading my poetry, that he found it lively and he had two copies of my collected poems. We have the same agents [Wylie], so . . . and he'd sent me a message before that he liked it, he said it was live, you know, of the moment, lively.

WSB: Such nonsense. [William is referring to the fatwa calling for Rushdie's assassination.]

AG: Then I asked him did he know how to meditate. He said, no actually he'd never got that. So I said would you like to learn? He said, "Yeah! Why don't we do that?" So I sat him and Andrew down for like five-minute instruction in Samatha-Vipassana[29] and one of the things I said in the whole instruction suggestions was relax the eyeballs with some sense of the periphery of the optical field, rather than staring at a point and straining the eye. So when we were all over with it . . . we'd sat for about five minutes . . . he said, "That was very interesting, the business of the periphery of the optical field." And that was just one of many elements, but he must have a relatively subtle mind to pick up on that, eyeball kicks so to speak.

WSB: So, yeah, meditation can solve a trap by just seeing it. If you see a trap . . .

---

29 *Samatha* meditation develops mental focus through concentration on an object, usually the breath. In *Vipassana* meditation the mind is directed to observe phenomena such as thoughts as impermanent. In practice, the latter technique accompanies the former.

AG: Well, like that spirit we were talking about.

WSB: You see, when you see it, it's gone.

AG: Except what he was saying is that there are these several million dollars worth of paid assassins out to get him. You know, professionals, not even having to do with Islam. Just real professionals who want the money.

WSB: I tell you, the very information . . . they probably would never collect it . . . if one of these paid assassins killed him, they would deny that they had anything to do with it and kill the assassin.

AG: That might be. Except that they've already announced publically that it's officially government policy to pay someone to kill him. The head of the state said so.

WSB: Yes yes yes.

AG: So I asked him if there was anything I could do or we could do. He said the only thing to do is publicity, noise. He can't defend himself by force. The only thing is protest, publicity, public furor, pressure on the American and British governments to make it a condition of recognition.

WSB: Why shouldn't the American government put out a contract on what's his name?

AG: Rajastani [Rafsanjani?] Well, the reason they can't is that we're trying to woo Iran against Iraq. So for political considerations, France, America and various other countries are now trying to line up some kind of friendship, at least a talking relationship with the Iranians, so he's being a sacrificial lamb in the middle. That's why the Iranians have used their efforts to get the other hostages out. So he's the last hostage, actually, or the next to the last maybe. So they thought a lot about the hostage problem because that was already a public conflict, but in his case, the Americans don't seem to care.

Slowly they're relaxing the trade embargo against Iran which was imposed, reassigning ambassadors and counselors there.

WSB: Stupid barbarous nonsense. Now, if they were literate enough to read *Naked Lunch*, I would certainly be on that list with Islam Incorporated, talking about making fun of the Muslim religion, holy shit!

AG: I know but you're an infidel, he was born as a Muslim . . . so apparently their complaint against him is that it's from within the faith . . . it's inconceivable that he could be so insulting to something he knows and is part of himself, he's a traitor. *You're* just a negligible heathen anyway, boy, and you'll never be anything better.

WSB: Fine with me, but I don't know, what a bunch of nuts, nutcases.

AG: What would you do if you were in his case? Well, you wouldn't be. . . .

WSB: I wouldn't be in his case.

AG: Unless I transcribe this conversation and publish it in Japan. You know his Japanese translator got assassinated.

WSB: What?

AG: Rushdie's Japanese translator was killed by an assassin.

WSB: Where?

AG: In Japan.

WSB: When?

AG: About a year ago.

WSB: In Tokyo?

AG: I don't know what city. And then somebody else. I think the German . . .

UDO: Italian.

AG: Was attacked . . . injured. The Italian translator was injured.

WSB: But the Japanese translator was killed. Did they catch the assassins?

AG: No.

WSB: Well, eventually I'd take to carrying a gun all the time. That's all I could do. That would be something. I'm able with a gun to defend myself.

AG: The only thing is that they're professional assassins, so it'd be pretty hard, constantly to be on guard.

WSB: Oh, absolutely. Real professionals are hard to deal with, very hard. Because they know where you are and you don't know where they are. You're a sitting duck, in other words.

TAPE 3 SIDE B

3/19/92. At home after supper.
Allen reads his journal notes recounting the ceremony of the 18th.
Gelek Rimpoche. WSB, AG, and Michael discuss their experience
of the ceremony. William Blake the shaman. Catholic exorcism.

AG: So I'll describe what happened last night.

Last night with Bill Burroughs, Michael, went over to stone house in which Bill used to live on hilltop outside of Lawrence Kansas. The house which William S. Lyon rents now for sweat lodge with Navajo Indian shaman named Melvin Betsellie, his lady friend—what did he say she was, Winnebago Sioux?

WSB: Winnebego Sioux.

AG: The woman friend of Lyon. The fireman outside the Iroquois smokehouse sweat lodge was a tall stalwart handsome blond student born in Colorado Springs, studied in Missouri, now in University of Kansas engineering or chemical engineering. We sat with towels in the dark black smoky plastic igloo bower, laced with twig skeleton covered with black plastic, a fire-pit in center. Seven of us, the boy and western woman outside to tend fire and food. Bill sat by the entrance . . . The big-bellied shaman speech went round the tent thanking each one there, Bill first, for inviting him to share the grandfathers' medicine and giving him opportunity to learn more and use healing medicine to drive the bad spirit, Bill's Ugly Spirit, out of Bill's life and body. Then prayed and . . . grandfathers' water, earth, rocks, and green, coals in all four directions. First with feather, hands, smoke wafted to each of us, water on fire, too intense smoky steam heat.

Michael almost panicked after two rounds, Bill later weakly asked for air, "Please let me out." The third and fourth round. At the last round of hot coals the shaman now prayed to the coal, blew a shrill bone whistle. Bill Lyon tapped drum, he waved coal around blowing in complete darkness. Thirteen rocks had been taken into the fire-pit. We weren't to talk till the seventh was in. Rocks were glowing red, hot like coal or red like charcoal.

WSB: Hm, yeah.

AG: With each rock a lady Indian sprinkled cedar shavings so the smoke smell was all old American incense. Mel said he was a pitiful man trying to help and asked and thanked the spirits, grandfather spirit, creator spirit, who made Bill and asked and thanked the water and wood and rocks and other elements to help Bill who's had a hard way, a long road now, a hard road, to come and help Melvin help Bill, to make his heart strong and his head clear. Bill is an old man, he hoped he would be an old man, he hoped *he* would be an old man, he must be a good man to have come so long a road, to remove and take back the bad spirit that had come into Bill so long, long ago. Did Bill once live by a big water?

After the fourth round everyone sprinkled with water several times with his feathered fan. He held coals in his hand, put them in his mouth, swallowed the bad spirit coals several times and coughed or retched it up. Michael and Steve saw the coals in his mouth, lighting up his gorge . . . coughed it out. He touched Bill with a coal. Bill later said he felt nothing, couldn't see what and where the coal was moving around in, though in the air we saw it. Sitting beside the Indian lady, the Winnebago Cree [*sic*], I only saw the red glow flying in the air above the fire and back, circling around Bill but Michael and Steve said they did see it in Melvin's mouth, quote, "It looked quite terrifying the mask of his face open-mouthed, the inside of his mouth lit up, you could see down to his throat in the red coal light, almost frightening," said Steven Lowe.

So Melvin prayed to the creator, the grandfathers, the elements, to help Bill on his way, make his way easy when it's time for him to go back to the creator, make him strong to live long long time, asked us all to think of Bill and send him our healing thoughts, get rid of the bad element that was in the coal. Send the bad spirit back to the one who'd put it in Bill, maybe an animal, maybe someone angry, maybe an angry animal.

The spirit caught, jiggled in the flute, shrill flute blown into the fire, to put the spirit into the rocky fire-pit still glowing, steaming and cedar-fragrant smoke in our eyes causing burning tears to run at first till I got used to it and remembered all the people I met who liked Bill's writing, hundreds, maybe hundreds of thousands, maybe millions of people in the world who've read his work, appreciated his adventurous spirit and his insight and lonely courage and the beauty of his stubborn realism, his intelligence, his ear and all the voices and spirits he could summon up, how he'd written so many decades, so much work, essays, poems, novels, routines, movies, sketches, paintings of the different spirits he'd seen in *his* imagination, his visualization, and paintings. So we all sent Bill our best healing friend thoughts and good will wishes and prayers for help.

Last round of pipe and tobacco were passed round, one hand under the stone head, other on the shaft pointed to the lady on my left next to Mel at the door hole. Sweet mild tobacco we puffed three or four times each from the long-stemmed stone-headed heavy pipe. Share gift of tobacco, gift of water, gift of rock, gift of cedar, gift of ancestors, gift of life. Thank ancestors, thank water, stone, sky, wood, varied elements, spirits, crawling spirits, insect spirits, all asked to help us and help this old man on his way have a strong heart and clear head and a long happy life, peaceful life from now on, the bad spirit gone back to where it came from, who it came from.

WSB: Hm hm.

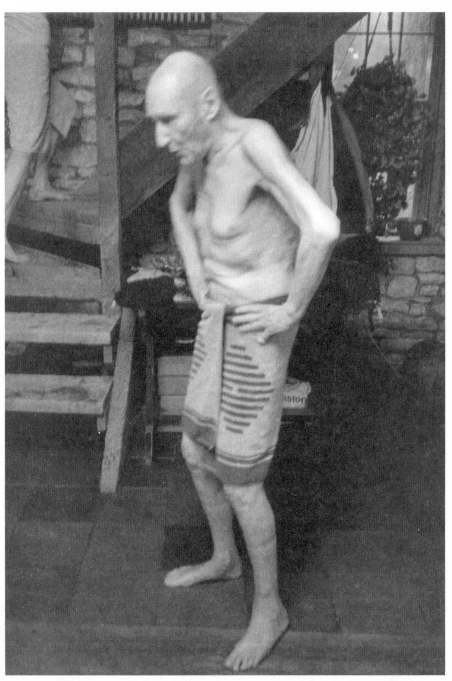

After the sweat lodge at the Stone House, Lawrence, KS, 18 March 1992

AG: The round-roofed hut was dark, everything blacked-out invisible except the fire in the center and shapes of our neighbors reflected in the smoke. We were all sweating and hot and warm and wet with sweat, my eyes and nose were running waters, my towel that I was naked in the darkness as Bill was except for his shorts, he kept saying, "Yes . . . yes . . . of course, thank you, I'm grateful" with good, subdued conscious manners, quietly responsive till at the end with the heat and suffocating smoke and occasional heart pity, "Please, please, open the door, some air." And a couple of times, "Please, let me out, I need to go out," because of the ordeal of heat and smoke sitting uncomfortably on his butt, knees folded up to his breast, till like Michael, when overcome so he couldn't breath he listened to me and Bill Lyons and lay down with his head close to cooler floor where there was more clear air, so stayed there till the course of the ceremony, till he was OK.

Before we went out, gathered undressed at the house, his chest wrinkled, the scar of bypass skin colored brown tan-like on his arms and breast, which sat wrinkled on his frame. Thin body, the back of him was stooped, soft muscled but vigorous at seventy-eight years. He said, "I always thought poets were lazy prose writers, writing paragraphs and sentences and break it up into line." So we went inside and at fireplace, Mel set up altar, bundles of feathers, medicine bundles and skins, flute, white bald eagle feather laid on . . . feather fans, laid in formation before the big fireplace in the wall of the stone house . . . his pipe, a glass globe of incense, sand from one sacred power mountain, all gifts he got from his grandfathers and teachers. And went to another hour-and-a-half elaborate ceremony on his knees asking for help to preserve old medicines, preserve old ways, stay in touch with the grandfathers, sky, wood, rock, green, "Help this old man beside me. I'm a pitiful man myself, like this man beside me, but I'm trying my best to do what's right for this old man on his way beside me, and I thank my grandfathers and my mother who passed away six years ago, and my father who went on to her a month later. I thank you all for being with us and helping me and helping this old man." He cried a little for his mother and said several times he was a pitiful man, not much good but doing his best to be the one who could be there for the creator to help others.

WSB: Um hm.

AG: Gave Bill a blanket and pillow to sit on the floor. I was sitting legs crossed, meditation posture on Bill's right. The blond tall student next on my right, who'd obeyed instructions and filled an aluminum foil covered plate with large and small hot glowing coals from the burning logs in the fireplace. Silent and thoughtful, it was his second sweat-lodge ceremony, his first as a helper. He'd met Melvin only three weeks ago. Later said he'd read some of Burroughs, happy to meet us, saw the *Naked Lunch* movie, smiled, pleased when I took his hand, still sweating in the house even.

So the shaman Mel finally asked Bill to sit in chair facing fire, gave him cedar green sprigs to smell and hold in left hand, white eagle feather in right hand. Climax of long ceremony and on his knees Mel chanted several long, long prayers. Then he repeated anaphoric word in his native Navajo tongue *con* glottal stop con word con fire con . . . that repeated phrase . . . sounded like aunt . . . and waved the smoke at all of us separately and prayed repeatedly to the bear spirit, the four-legged people, the two-legged people, the crawling people, the insects, the families, the brothers and sisters here and everywhere, the relatives and their own brothers and sisters or relatives, family all one family no matter what race we come from. All relatives together in a room.

Finally, ceremony over, we all ate, big servings of pot-roast meat, baked cheese potato slices, salad, coffee, a home-made sweet icing cake. I ate it, a little worried about the salt. I cooked up a big tureen pot of soup at Bill's, chicken, parsley, carrot-tops, parsnips, turnips, diced cut celery, waiting on the side with spinach and string beans, mushrooms later addition, onions. Got home so put it out on the porch to cool and finished the brew next day.

Bill's up talking to his cats, feeding them. I'll get up and see him on his way to Kansas City 7:30 a.m. Now was there anything that I . . . ?

WSB: I don't think so, you've got a lot of things that I missed. Um . . . I don't have as much.

AG: Well, I sat down and, you know, if you'd sat down at the time and wrote it . . .

WSB: I was a little bit under by all this. When I got into the house I felt very well and I was surprised that I could eat as much as I did. I didn't eat very much, but just a handful.

AG: I had a big appetite.

WSB: I had one drink and then I just ate a small plateful of food. And I was feeling very good. We got back here about 10:40 or 11. Back to the house, yes. And Allen stayed up writing that and I . . .

AG: No, I stayed up reading a chapter or two of Bill Lyon's book.

WSB: Oh yes.

AG: That's where I got some of the . . .

WSB: Yes, yes . . .

[Allen begins taking pictures of the company. AG directs Udo and Bill to sit together for photos. "Udo, put your chin down slightly."]

WSB: Well, very good, very good.

AG: I was surprised I remembered so much. But you know what I didn't get . . . I couldn't remember, did we go around four times?

WSB: Four times, what do you mean?

AG: Remember, he did four times around and four separate sections.

WSB: And I remember that I took four puffs of the pipe and . . .

AG: Remember what you were saying when you wanted to . . . the moments when you wanted to leave, or when the smoke was so overpowering?

WSB: Well, I don't remember except that I needed air, I needed to get out.

AG: And you finally lay down with your head near the door.

WSB: Yes, I finally lay down near the door and then I felt better . . . and . . . you know, I felt I had to stick it out and stay there, I couldn't break this . . . when he . . . putting the coals I felt better. As soon as he was using the coals, and . . . I immediately felt better . . . And I thought, I know that he knows what he's doing.

UDO: May I take a photo of the two of you?

AG: I was wondering if you felt any of the affection.

WSB: The what?

AG: The affection that was directed toward you.

WSB: Oh, yes, yes . . . His affection . . . it was very strong . . . a very good, you know, good feeling person.

AG: That's what I get from Gelek.

WSB: From what?

AG: That's what I get from Gelek Rimpoche.[27]

WSB: Oh yeah.

AG: That sense of, someone who cares for me and is really interested in my welfare. Very compassion . . . not compassionate, but giving himself to me.

---

27   Kyabje Gelek Rimpoche (1939-2017) was of the last generation of Tibetan Lamas trained in Tibet before the Chinese invasion of 1959. After the death of Allen's main Buddhist teacher, Chögyam Trungpa Rinpoche in 1987, Gelek became Allen's main teacher; he attended the poet's death in 1997.

wsb: Yes. A good person. And I felt . . . it was really tough and I could see that he was suffering . . . he was hurt by this spirit. And he says he hadn't realized the power of this entity, the full, evil power. And he was, you know, it was almost too much for him.

ag: Yes, what actually Bill Lyon was talking about, he said [reading from his notes] "scared him on a deep shamanic level. . . incautious, overconfident. He knew he'd got him, but it hit him harder than he anticipated. Something lacking in his overall sincerity in approaching it. Has to learn how to handle the public in ceremonies, the depth of sincerity needed to get into it is immense and at first there may have been some admixture of trying to impress Bill Lyon, at first." This is what Bill said.

wsb: To have to achieve complete sincerity is very difficult.

ag: Yeah. And then I said, who was he praying to? He said also the winged people, the insect people, and the crawling people. Remember the winged people? That's the phrase . . .

wsb: Yes.

ag: And the crawling people . . . . Now, Bill, were you at any point worried about having a heart attack or something?

wsb: No, I wasn't, no.

ag: What was your concern, heart?

wsb: No, I wasn't afraid of a heart attack . . .

ag: That is, if you could focus . . .

michael: The intensity. Allen . . . you were . . .

ag: In the middle.

michael: But the most far from William.

ag: No, Steve was . . . .

wsb: I thought, well, I said, he knows what he's doing. I just had to say listen, he knows what he's doing. I'm not going to get burned or anything, so I trusted his judgment. Apparently he had a hard time too.

ag: So he probably got scared himself . . . according to Bill Lyon.

wsb: Udo, are you finished with that exorcism book? I'd like for Allen to see it.

udo: I'll bring it tomorrow. I'm not finished, but I'll bring it tomorrow.

wsb: It's so pertinent, to this same thing.

michael: Did you hear . . . one of the big parts of that book is that a weak member of the family who's involved with this and you invoke these spirits can affect the weak person? Did you catch how he said to us don't let this affect our family members, and don't let this affect our friends, you know, that really helped me . . . you gave me those three books . . . I was having those fears . . . you know, play with a ouiji board and the next thing you know your furniture's flying around.

wsb: It's so similar, the exorcism, and what he was doing.

michael: William, you know, the very first time he was holding the coal in his fingers and he put it in your face and he said, "Do you see it, Bill? Do you see it?" . . . And you said, "Yes." You just kind of whispered it . . . from where I was sitting . . . that coal . . . you know that skull you have here?

wsb: Yes. No, I saw it.

michael: The little one . . . the little plastic one . . . it looked like . . . he's putting this skull in his face . . . after I recovered from my thing and my heart stopped pounding and I was right there for the coal, which was kind of the most intense part, when he was doing the whistle and the swallowing and the regurgitating.

WSB: Oh man. It was really (chuckles) . . .

MICHAEL: I guess I'm the only one who saw the thing where you were sitting here, I was here across the fire pit and it was so difficult to see. I thought that he, the shaman, had sat back down. But it looked like the coal was still doing this, flying around you, but I thought he was doing it . . .

AG: I did too.

MICHAEL: And did you hear him inside? He said, "You saw, Bill, I had to catch it."

AG: Yeah, I saw that.

MICHAEL: He . . . he . . . moved over and caught it . . .

WSB: Caught the coal, yes.

MICHAEL: It was just flying around William and that was the spirit and he was saying that it was trying to get away, it was trying to come back to you.

WSB: Absolutely.

AG: But I couldn't see in the dark whether he had it in his hand waving it around or whether it was on its own.

MICHAEL: But see the only thing is, after he had done . . . he had put it back in the pit . . . the crying, vomiting thing . . . and then he got back in his place, but . . . his body didn't move when it went back. That was . . . not the scariest, but the wildest thing.

AG: That I didn't see, actually, I couldn't follow . . .

MICHAEL: It was zipping around William.

WSB: That's true . . . that's true.

AG: See, I thought it was . . .

MICHAEL: And then I saw it go away, and then he was back over there and then inside he said, "Did you see Bill, it was trying to connect and I had to grab it?" And that's when I was sure that he was even putting it in his mouth, because I couldn't really believe . . .

AG: But then Steven said he saw it in his mouth.

MICHAEL: Oh, we both saw it. But I couldn't believe it.

AG: You saw that?

MICHAEL: Oh yeah, I mean he was going . . . he was spitting sparks on William.

WSB: Yes, he was.

AG: Spitting sparks on you?

WSB: Yes, but it didn't hurt. It didn't burn.

AG: From out of his mouth?

MICHAEL: Remember, I asked William in the car on the way back, "Did you have burns?" He was going [makes throaty, blowing noise] and then he would blow the whistle at you and the thing must have been in him while he was blowing the whistle.

WSB: Absolutely.

MICHAEL: And Steve and I both saw his cheeks light up.

WSB: He had the sparks in his mouth, there's no doubt about it.

MICHAEL: And he was spilling them on you! . . . You weren't flinching, you weren't . . .

WSB: No I wasn't . . . I didn't flinch at all . . . because I thought, well he knows what he is doing and I'm not afraid of the sparks.

MICHAEL: What a scene.

WSB: Oh, wow. He should be back here on Tuesday. . . .

AG: I have a lot of stuff on here [Sony pro Walkman cassette recorder] . . . conversation with the shaman. Though the best moment I think I missed, when you were saying . . . you said . . . that moment when you were agreeing about in order to get a spirit, to do away with a spirit, you have to see it.

WSB: Oh, yes. Have to see it.

AG: What was his word about it? He agreed you have to see it?

WSB: If you see it you gain control of it.

AG: You know Blake has a similar idea, that . . .

WSB: In order to stay in possession . . . by not seeing. It can't confront you directly. It's just a matter of . . . well if you see it *outside*, it's no longer inside.

AG: Right.

WSB: It just has to leave.

AG: Blake's idea was insistent on outlines and forms in painting. Definite form, definite outline.[28]

AG: What's the name of the anthropologist?

MICHAEL: Bill Lyon.

AG: Blake's idea was . . . Blake was insistent on outlines and forms in painting and in definite form, definite outline, because his idea was you cannot know Satan or conquer Satan or deal with Satan unless you know his system, unless you see Satan, you can't know his system, unless you identify him, give him definite outline. So he says the reason for error is that error will carry itself to extremes till you see the chaos and the form it has created.

---

28 William Blake argued that in art, in order to see the spirit world (his real world), all spirits, objects, and figures require outline. He disparaged painters who tend toward abstraction, who render form via color and light ("fog") as unable to draw.

WSB: Um hm.

AG: So that you begin to see it. In other words, unless error were allowed enough play so that it manifested itself visibly . . .

WSB: You would never see it.

AG: You would never see it. You wouldn't know it was there. It would only be there subtly, doing some damage but unless . . . it's almost as if . . . unless we saw the ozone layer . . . hole in the ozone layer, we wouldn't know that fluorocarbons were a menace.

WSB: I want you to see this book on exorcisms . . . very pertinent . . . sophisticated . . . He was a Jesuit, name's Malachi Martin. And he knew all the. . .

AG: Well, you know the political implications are interesting like with the Iraq war. Unless you can see the system or know the reasoning of the government, you won't be able to critique it. Unless . . . or the entire population doesn't see the manipulation . . .

WSB: In exorcism . . . you can never . . . a verbal argument can never do anything.

AG: A what kind?

WSB: A *verbal* argument. You can not just . . . as Father Connor said, you can't ever beat him in a verbal argument because that's what he wants.

AG: Yeah.

WSB: 'Cause that's . . . it's nothing but a *confront* . . . a non-verbal confront . . . that anything happens . . . it has to be non-verbal.

AG: Well, does that mean visual also?

WSB: Well, yes, visual. It has to be . . . it cannot be verbal, because that's the way of evading a confront. You will never beat him if you argue with him. So never let him draw you into an argument.

AG: So how would that work with Senator Helms and Joe McCarthy?

WSB: Same way. If you argue with them, they go on and on. You never argue. You never argue, never a verbal argument.

AG: So how would you then confront the Satan in Senator Jesse Helms? Make another work of art?

WSB: No. He has to come out and try to confront *you.* You have to draw them into confront. Not verbal confront, but silent confront. Otherwise, they'd argue and argue going around and around and around for a hundred thousand years. But the arguing has nothing whatever to do with what they're really doing.

AG: So now how would you confront the Satan in the Ayatollah and his followers thereafter, after he died, about this price on Salman Rushdie's head and having killed his Japanese translator?

WSB: That is not a question. You think in political terms or justifications, never get anywhere.

AG: Well, the method of confrontation is now many of the publishers have gotten together to put out his book [*Satanic Verses*] in paperback. That's not an argument, that's a deed.

WSB: Yes, it might be something but never, never a verbal argument it will never, never go anywhere except in circles.

AG: Or into anger.

WSB: Because you're not talking about the issue at all; you're talking about words.

Burroughs with painting and Mugwump from Cronenberg's Naked Lunch,
Lawrence, KS, 22 March 1992

TAPE 4 SIDE A

3/20/92. Breakfast. Malachi Martin's Hostage to the Devil.
The Don Juan books by Carlos Castaneda. Remembering Mel's prayers.
Exorcism v. psychotherapy. R. D. Laing. William's psychiatrists.
What are these entities? Word as virus. Narcissism and possession.
Trungpa Rinpoche. The demons in William's paintings. The Libertarian Party.

AG: I never read all the Don Juan books, not one of them, actually.[32]

WSB: Well, they're very interesting, particularly the cross [the cross-ing?] . . . You reach something called the place of no pity. That's very interesting and here [in Martin's book] it is repeated almost word for word. "Something subtly merciless had lodged there." That's the priest, the exorcism priest, compare [it to] Don Juan's place of no pity. It really comes down [to cat:] get away from my tea, beast, get down, to the place of no *self* pity. It isn't pity, it's self pity.

AG: What did you think of the shaman last night saying "I'm a piti-able creature, and this pitiful man beside me"?

WSB: He meant that sort of thing.

AG: Suffering.

wsb: No, not that so much as . . .

AG: Humble.

WSB: Limited. It's sort of like humility . . . humility, that he recog-nized the limits of his power, that's all. You don't want to get uppity.

---

32 This refers to the controversial anthropological writings of Carlos Castaneda, which fea-tured the Yaqui shaman Don Juan Matus.

AG: What book is that? Hostage to evil?

WSB: Now this is *Hostage to the Devil*, this case of five exorcisms.[33] And also I remember Doctor Rioch saying that there comes a point in therapy, if the therapy is deep enough, there may come a point where the therapist encourages the patient, the subject, to express his aggression. In some cases he will immediately attack the therapist. And he says that requires expert handling (chuckles).[34]

AG: R. D. Laing did that . . . with Peter.[35] He provoked Peter, but Laing was drunk and Peter was drunk and Peter attacked Laing; we had to call the police (laughs). Laing kept saying, "Well in a normal situation in England, I would have had several burly . . . "

WSB: Well exactly, there was always in any exorcism, they had two strong men there to restrain the subject if he or she becomes violent, and they have great strength. So it takes two. They often are ex-policemen or, you know, policemen. They're just there in case the . . . So I like all these intercessions where in a way they're doing the same thing.

AG: What's the guy who wrote that?

WSB: His name is Malachi Martin, he was a Jesuit.

AG: Intercession with Don Juan, you mean.

WSB: Yes, with Don Juan and with shamanism. They're trying to get an evil spirit out.

AG: So this is a formal exposition of Catholic procedure, a practicing Catholic view of exorcism?

---

33 Malachi Martin, *Hostage to the Devil: The Possession and Exorcism of Five Living Americans* (Reader's Digest, 1975; Harper One, 1992).

34 David McKenzie Rioch (1900-85), the neurologist who arranged for Burroughs to get a disability discharge from the Army in 1942.

35 R. D. Laing (1927-89), Scottish psychiatrist. Ginsberg invited Laing to the Naropa Institute in Boulder, Colorado in 1987. There Laing attempted to treat Peter Orlovsky. Laing's method involved mirroring or imitating the psychotic behavior of the subject. A violent scuffle ensued resulting in Ginsberg breaking a finger and needing knee surgery.

wsb: No. It's five cases of exorcism.

ag: But done under Christian, Catholic . . .

wsb: Done by a priest and then he has to have his helpers to restrain the person and it's very interesting because it corresponds very directly to the shaman's . . . Now he has to take, you see the priest must be able to take the . . . control the spirit. And he's attacked by the spirit, very violently. And if he doesn't watch what he's doing, he can be fucked completely or even literally. There's a case here where the spirit leaped on the priest and fucked him up the ass.

ag: [laughing] How did they put that?

wsb: Just exactly, there's no sort of prissiness here.

ag: Who is the guy who wrote it, an ex-priest or an assistant or somebody who's done research?

wsb: No. He was a Jesuit, Dr. Martin "pioneered . . . cases of spiritual affliction. It is extremely doubtful if scientists would have begun to examine such a dangerous but important subject for another hundred years." And always, the psychiatrist, if there is one present, fucks everything up. 'Cause they don't know what they're doing, or what they're up against. They think it's just some goddamned complex.

ag: What are these entities?

wsb: We don't know. That's just it. They say that they are . . . evil spirits. It would seem that they are spirits that came into existence with Christ.

ag: Spirits of what?

wsb: With Christ, they're Christian spirits, evil Christian spirits.

ag: Christ did exorcism, didn't he?

wsb: Of course he did.

AG: He drove the money-changers out of the temple but he also went down to hell and cast . . .

WSB: He sent the spirits into the swine, remember? They said well where can we go? And he put them into the swine.

AG: And then the swine ran off a cliff, into the ocean.

WSB: What the poor spirits did then I don't know. So it's very, very interesting. Now listen to this. In this he speaks of the evil spirit "multiplying its own shape in *end*less succession, soul-killing succession, baneless graves in a row." In other words a virus.

AG: Baneless graves in a row, that's good prose.

WSB: It's a virus, multiplying its own image.

AG: Um hm. What is a virus, actually?

WSB: It's . . . well in the first place it's an obligate cellular parasite.

AG: Obligate meaning what?

WSB: Well, meaning that's the only way it exists, or functions. Unless it's in a state of . . .

AG: Obligatory parasite or obligate . . .

WSB: Obligate *cellular* parasite.

AG: So a parasite onto cells.

WSB: Yeah. Now that's not true of bacteria, it's not true of parasitic entities like malaria or spirochetes. They can exist apart from cells.

AG: They can exist in solution, in vitro . . . in mucous . . .

WSB: In all sorts of things. Not a virus, and that was the trouble they had in cultivating a virus, 'cause it only grows in living tissue. But you can't cultivate it in a petri dish.

AG: So then in what sense could you call *word* a virus?

WSB: It repeats itself but only in the sense of repeating itself word for word. What a virus does is repeat its own image, word for word.

AG: However, would that be . . . in this image of word as a virus or ideas as viruses, you catch a virus, you catch a word, that wouldn't be down to the cell level, that would be another kind of paradigm, another kind of . . .

WSB: Say here is the obligate cellular parasite. You have an idea of that and an idea of that, a serial relationship. So it's sort of rough metaphor to say it . . .

AG: Yeah. It's not literally in the cell.

WSB: No.

AG: You ever think of it as literally in the cell?

WSB: Well, sure . . . originally yes, the concept of word, in the cell.

AG: Where did that come from, the idea of word as . . . that wasn't Korzybski? [Alfred Korzybski developed general semantics.]

WSB: No.

AG: No. It was what? Yours or partly Brion's?

WSB: Partly mine . . . but it's no concept at all.

AG: Where'd you first hear of it?

WSB: Well, I said it acts like a virus.

AG: Yeah.

WSB: That's all. And a virus is an obligate parasite, an obligate cellular parasite. And a word could . . . a language could hardly . . . cannot exist without . . .

AG: The speaker.

WSB: The speaker, without speakers.

AG: Without a host, yeah.

WSB: More than one.

AG: Uh hm. Well you could talk to yourself I guess.

WSB: But how? You can talk to yourself, but the concept, unless the concept of another person were there, you wouldn't . . . The concept of a language, communication . . . you couldn't talk to yourself. Unless you had a concept.

AG: Uh hm. I like the idea of . . . the idea as a virus in the sense of . . . 'cause it's obviously . . . in marketing research that's exactly what they do . . . like for political purposes, to make a little slogan.

WSB: Why sure. Now I know you've heard about the computer viruses.

AG: Yeah, now what do they do? They just sort of . . . it spreads through the telephone modems.

WSB: It can get in the program. And then it's hard to get rid of. They have to kind of call in a priest [laughter] to exorcize the computer of its virus. I don't know how the computer would attack the priest.

AG: The virus could go back to the FBI files and get everything on the priest and then spit it out on the printer and . . .

WSB: The evil spirit knows all about the priest. He knows all his early sexual experiences. That is, one of the priests went down on a woman when he was sixteen, and the evil spirit says, "Ha ha, Peter the eater." And just goes through all his sexual history. Very obscene. It's full of very overt obscenity . . . when they get going . . . you know . . . what a wretched person . . .

AG: The exorcist is . . .

WSB: Coming out between a woman's smelly legs. Yeah. Now then, if the priest tries to challenge the spirit on its own grounds, he can really get into trouble with it. He can go mad.

AG: Like what, you mean get into a metaphysical argument with a . . . ?

WSB: Well, no, that isn't dangerous that's just not productive. No. But now look, unless the person in question wants to get rid of the . . .

AG: Oh yeah.

WSB: If you have someone like . . . there's one person here, the evil spirit says, "He is ours completely." Well the priest, being experienced, knows better than to try to get in there and challenge that because the person in question is completely possessed. The only thing the priest has to work with, the desire of the . . . what's left of the person's will, desire to be cured or freed.

AG: That's a little bit like Alcoholics Anonymous. Only until you realize you have a disease and that you can't do it by yourself and that you need help . . .

WSB: That's right.

AG: And then turn to others for help.

WSB: That's right.

AG: Otherwise pride or secrecy will prevent . . . make a barrier for anybody to reach a hand in.

WSB: He spoke of all the barriers here now. As a young priest he made that mistake once, of trying to exorcize . . . someone who was completely possessed, nearly . . . just barely escaped with his life.

AG: That book was written by an ex-Jesuit who did it, who was a specialist in this?

WSB: Yes, sure.

AG: Has that got the imprimatur of the pope?

WSB: Suppose so . . .

AG: They're allowed to . . .

WSB: Oh yes . . . the priest . . . has been on television . . . an exorcism on television. I saw little bits and pieces of it. You saw doors opened up and drawers in a bureau opening and closing. All these physical manifestations. Doors slamming, things like that. And the priest there, you know saying Jesus stuff, but they finally got the spirit out.

[William reads:] Malachi Martin, a former Jesuit professor at the Pontifical Biblical Institute in Rome, was trained in theology at Louvain . . . specializing in the Dead Sea Scrolls and intertestamentary studies. Received his doctorate in Semitic languages, archaeology, and oriental history. He subsequently studied at Oxford and at the Hebrew University, concentrating on the knowledge of Jesus as transmitted in Jewish and Islamic sources. One of the many exorcists of his personal acquaintance . . . . The redoubtable Father Connor, who figures importantly in the first case in the book. Dr. Martin is the author of *The New Castle, Jesus Now, Three Popes and the Cardinal* . . . .

AG: Apparently this guy Malachi Martin is the religious editor of William Buckley's *National Review* also. You'd think he'd exorcize Buckley.

WSB: Yeah. I found it very worth reading. He wrote a book called *Vatican.*

AG: You know what Jonathan Robbins's study is for his PhD?

WSB: No.

AG: Pre-Christian ideas of the mother and how under the Christians it slowly became transformed into the witch.

WSB: The mother.

AG: How the feminine earth figure became the witch figure under Christian domination. And so he's going into something similar to what this guy was studying. That is the, non-biblical sources of Jesus from Jewish and Arabic tale or scholarship. Or Aramaic.

WSB: Very interesting. This is sort of tracing the similarities of various approaches like the shaman approach . . .

AG: There's a book by Mircea Eliade on shamanism, have you seen it? [*Shamanism: Archaic Techniques of Ecstasy*, published in French in 1951 and in English in 1964.]

WSB: No. Is this a recent work, or . . . ?

AG: Oh, about twenty, thirty years ago.

WSB: There's the classic work, another classic work, [Weldemar] Bogoras's *Chukchee Mythology*, that is the reindeer people and their shaminism [1910]. They're still practicing and it's described in *The Shaman's Drum*. And the spirits that the shamans use to evoke the helpers.

WSB: Now the Catholics tend to think that any spirit is evil . . . . One of the great sources of error of course is narcissism . . . fixed . . . try to hang on to an image.

AG: Yeah.

WSB: A fixed image . . . .

AG: Taking that external image for real.

WSB: You see [reading], "a malevolent intelligence is scanning the innards of his very self," this is the priest, "the attack finally wells up and pours over him. Father Hearty is filled with disgust and loathing he cannot control; he starts to retch, he is whipped with a ferocity he could never have imagined. . . . The keynote of that clash is an either/ or, it is conveyed to Hearty subtly that he submits, if he renounces his opposition to the evil spirit, all will be well. The attack will cease. If not he will be destroyed. . . . Now in one hurting glare of exposure he sees his weaknesses laid bare: the tawdry logic he received in his philosophy training, the self-confident, ignorantly treated facts of theology, the self indulgence and one time hypocrisies as of his piety.

The useless pride in his priesthood, all is so much drivel and dross, a dump of human trash that withers under the fire of that gaze, looking in at him and probing every darkest cranny of his weakness."

AG: Probing . . .

WSB: "Cranny of his weakness . . . "

AG: Ho ho!

WSB: "Well, father, what did you expect? A gold watch?" I wrote [laughs] Christ's sake. "For as long as it lasted it was a brutal partial possession of me. The searching gaze continues like a filthy and malicious hand, pawing each of his faculties contemptuously. Even his will is fingered and stripped of the motives he had always relied upon. His will is the last bastion. It holds. But now he sees all his apparent strength torn from him like so much cardboard, coverings from an inner treasure: his sensuous enthusiasm for beautiful ceremony, his esteem of good people; his compassion for the sick and the helpless; his pride in being a priest and a man; his satisfaction in his Welsh culture; his reliance on the approval of parents, teachers, supervisors, his bishop, the pope; the consolation of prayer and submission to law, all are torn brutally aside, and only his willing self holds at last."

AG: Hm.

WSB: "His soul, as a willing being, stands naked of all the supports and reasons of a lifetime, scrutinized by the unwavering gaze of high, unlovely, and unloving intelligence." So that's what the priest has to put up with, you see. *Everything* goes.

AG: That's pretty, completely . . . You've been in that situation, haven't you?

WSB: Sure, man. But anybody is.

AG: I guess when you, um . . .

WSB: If you go far enough . . .

AG: I remember when you were talking about falling on the hospital floor breaking your leg and your scream could be heard through the . . .

WSB: Break my hip . . .

AG: Yeah . . .

WSB: Well, yeah, well that's just pain, plain ol' pain. And there's no use to deny that it . . . you lost control.

AG: But did you ever find yourself in a situation like that?

WSB: Good God yes! Anybody does . . . if they . . .

AG: It's very familiar.

WSB: Take a look! Just take a look at yourself. What are you? Of course you do. Unless you . . . See everything that he *relied* on, had relied on, has no . . . it's vanities . . . it's all vanity. It's nothing. All that . . . *everything* goes. The only thing he can hang on to is his will. The will to resist. But that will go too if he steps into the territory of the . . .

AG: So how did he resolve that? Just withdrew from the territory?

WSB: He just hung on, he hung on. It's a question of hanging on. Until the spirit leaves, spirit goes. Maybe that was a success, but not all of them are successful.

AG: How much is that like a bum trip on acid? Or psilocybin?

WSB: It's sort of . . .

AG: It's very similar.

WSB: Similar. Similar.

AG: In a vague . . . in a lighter touch, I had . . . you know, early encounter with Lucien and Jack I had that. 'Cause I was talking about being a labor lawyer.

WSB: Uh hm.

AG: And Jack looked at me . . . gave me this withering look and said—when I was seventeen . . .

WSB: Yeah.

AG: "You've never worked a day in your life in a factory, you know [laughing] nothing about labor, what are you talking about? Being a labor lawyer . . . "

[William laughs.]

AG: Saving the laboring man and the labor union. I suddenly realized that everything I'd relied on, from my family, from my reading, my education, my temperament, was all like cardboard.

WSB: Well, exactly, he said like cardboard.

AG: That was like a crucial moment of insight. I had another one . . . well, lot of them like that. But I had another one with Trungpa once in '74. I'd built this house with Peter [adjoining Gary Snyder's land in California] and I'd done some carpentry.

WSB: Mm hm.

AG: So I came back to Boulder and happily said to Trungpa, "I've been building this house with my own hands." You know, learn . . . doing some actual labor." So he said, "Let me see your hands." And I turned out these very soft hands. "What? You've been building it with your own hands? You haven't got a . . . not one callous on them . . . that's not real labor," he said.

WSB: Yeah. Yeah.

AG: Then I suddenly thought . . . I realized how much pride I'd been taking just sort of in the *idea* of it rather than the actual action.

WSB: Here's another very interesting insight into the . . . "Every exorcist learns during pretense," that is one of the stages, "that he is dealing with some force or power that is at times intensely cunning, sometimes supremely intelligent, and other times capable of crass stupidity . . . and it is both highly dangerous and terribly vulnerable."

AG: Hm hm.

WSB: "Oddly enough, while the spirit or power knows some of the most secret, intimate details of the lives of everyone in the room, at the same time it also displays gaps in knowledge of things that may be happening at any given moment in the present."

AG: Hm hm.

WSB: So it's . . . complete and dreadful confusion. "His ears seem to *smell* foul words, his eyes seem to *hear* offensive sounds, and obscene screams, his nose seems to *taste* a high decibel cacophony."

AG: This is the priest or the spirit?

WSB: No no, the . . .

AG: Exorcist or . . . ?

WSB: The exorcist or the subject. The one who is being exorcised . . . He's talking here from the point of view of the subject. And I write "typical of LSD in flicker . . . hearing smells, smelling sounds, and so on, the overflowing of the senses."

AG: Cryptesthesia [*(sic)* synesthesia].

WSB: Huh? Yes.

AG: Cryptesthesia.

WSB: Yes . . . Barry Walters speaks of it as typical of flicker, and also of . . .

AG: Of liquor?

WSB: Of *flicker*.

AG: Flicker. Dream machine flicker.

WSB: Yes, of course, of LSD or mescaline or any of that.

AG: What do you think the shaman, Melvin, was seeing in you? What do you think he was getting?

WSB: The spirit.

AG: Something like this?

WSB: What?

AG: Something like that?

WSB: Well, not exactly, no. But he described it as a spirit with like a white, skull face . . .

AG: Hm hm.

WSB: But no eyes, and sort of . . . wings, like that . . .

AG: Aha!

WSB: Only occupies this part of the . . . but where there's one spirit, there . . .

AG: That's what Melvin saw?

WSB: Yes.

AG: And did you get any glimpse of such a thing?

WSB: Well, I have many times.

AG: Yeah, and you've painted it in a way . . . those are like . . . a little like . . .

WSB: Yes I brought out some paintings and he would say, "Well there it is, there it is, and there it is," in the painting. For example . . . let's see . . . come in here and I'll show you some of the paintings that I showed him.

AG: One thing I wanted to do is call Stephen Bornstein and find out about this phrase *m-e-m-e-s*, the idea as virus that he had. He said it was a formal phrase for that . . . [36]

WSB: Really?

AG: Yeah.

WSB: Do you know about the Libertarian Party?

AG: Well a little, that they're extreme . . . extreme . . . against the drug laws I know that, some of them.

WSB: I sent them a letter asking for more information and it's here somewhere.

AG: What roused your interest? You know somebody that's in . . . ?

WSB: No I just noticed they were the only political party that came out against drug laws.

AG: Yeah.

WSB: Now that's here somewhere.

AG: In here, in this . . . ?

WSB: Well, in my new . . . um . . . you see it's in a big envelope.

AG: Yeah.

WSB: Well, you might have a look at it, I've gotta shave.

---

36 The term "meme" derives from the Greek mimeme, "imitated thing." Meme was coined by biologist Richard Dawkins in his book *The Selfish Gene* (1976). It designates "an idea, behavior, or style that spreads from person to person within a culture." The meme is a kind of cultural gene—it self-replicates, mutates, and responds to environmental pressures.

TAPE 4 SIDE B

3/20/92. Hostage to the Devil. *U2 cutups. Word as virus redux.*
Allah is everywhere. The Libertarian test. Gun control.

AG: The book being discussed before was Malachi Martin, the book *Hostage to the Devil,* subtitled *The Possession and Exorcism of Five Living Americans.* And . . . it's Perennial Library, Harper & Row. And Bill had made a few annotations here: "The light at the end of the tunnel" was one thing he wrote at the bottom. "There are no accidents in a magical universe." And in this description of the exorcist being "whipped with a ferocity he could never have imagined," Bill has an annotation: "Well, Father, what did you expect, a gold watch?"

Continued on March 20th. The AP dispatch from Los Angeles . . . the headline in the *Lawrence Journal-World* March 19th from Los Angeles Associated Press, "The Irish rock band U2 is trying to quell a flap arising from the newspaper report that the words 'bomb Japan now' flashed on TV screens during a concert. The words actually occurred separately in a stream of words that flashed by rapidly according to a text issued through the group's Los Angeles public relations firm," . . . "a portion of the stream," . . . means quote, "everyone is racist except you, bomb . . . "

[William enters.]

WSB: I can fish, you can't.

AG: What you mean I can't fish?

WSB: Because you're out of state, you don't have a license.

AG: Oh, yes, yes, you have to have a license to fish there?

WSB: You have a special lake license, but there's also . . . the out-of-state . . . the regular fishing license, which I don't need because I'm over sixty-five. But you would need because you're from out of state.

AG: I'm over sixty-five, my dear.

WSB: I know, but you're not a resident, Allen.

AG: I see, if you're a Kansas resident and you're over sixty-five, you don't need a . . . kinda nice . . . they figure you're too doddering to go . . .

WSB: You can throw out a line, and if anything comes near I'll grab it. *I* am fishing.

AG: They figure you're too doddering after sixty-five to have to go down and sit in an office to get a license?

WSB: Well, no it's just . . . you know senior citizens . . . considerations. [William leaves the room.]

AG: Well, to continue . . . "The words actually occurred separately in a stream of words that flashed by rapidly according to the text issued through the group's Los Angeles public relations firm. A portion of the stream reads, quote, everyone is a racist except you bomb where ultimately Japan chaos I want everything I want it now gun, dot dot dot, unquote. So a concert review in March 6th of the *Atlanta Journal-Constitution* said the phrase "bomb Japan now" fed up in "a spree of buzz-words flashed by at near-subliminal speed."

> The music critic Steve Dollar said that he'd written . . . that
> he had . . . that he wrote down what he had gleaned from
> the presentation, but that the pace is so fast that there's only
> time to pick up certain words.

So I asked Bill what he thought of that and he said well, 'cause it was in the style of his cutup, obviously U2 had been influenced by his word-juxtaposition style and stream of words flashing by. The subliminal suggestions implicit in the rearrangement of the words when they were cut up. And he said, well, you can make *anything* out of that, you could have other words, like "everyone ultimately Japan" or "I want Japan" or "I want Japan now" or "everyone except you . . . I want everyone except you." "I want you now Japan," could also get that out of it.

When we first talked this morning I read him . . . some notes I had from conversation with Stephen Bornstein, he had the memes m-e-m-e-s. The idea as virus. We were talking about viruses before. A virus can't live outside the [host]. A virus is not a living creature and can't reproduce on its own outside the host, required the host in a specifically human cell or a cell and Stephen was comparing virus to . . . you catch a virus is like a . . . you catch an idea. And an idea . . . and he's saying an idea seems to be like a virus, in that someone gets an idea or catches it and passes it on to the next person who spreads it through gossip and pretty soon everybody's got the same idea. Particularly the ideas in the form of an unbreakable link of two or three or four words that make a . . . formulate the idea . . . he was comparing that to the marketing tool called quote a "positioning statement" unquote. As it's the viral idea material for a company.

He described how the company or person views itself in three words. Like a viral idea material phrase intact going from person to person. Or like a sound bite. Bornstein's idea was ideas have an existence of their own like a virus, like the "idea whose time has come." An idea is like an opportunistic virus whose time had come.

He is defining, for instance, the Egyptian religion virus was monotheism, by Akhenaten, prior to Jewish monotheism and then the positioning statement of Jewish monotheism or viral statement was the sanctity of human life as exemplified by the story of Abraham being ordered to sacrifice his beloved son, but God loved Abraham, so an angel's hands came out and stopped the knife that was going to sacrifice Abraham *(sic)* [Abraham was going to sacrifice his son

Isaac]. God didn't require a human sacrifice. So the position statement was the sacrifice of . . . that God didn't require sacrifice. God
was . . . God loved Abraham or . . . sanctity of human life. Actually
a ram came out of the thicket and so was sacrificed instead of Isaac.
The Hebrew God didn't require human sacrifice.

So you could say the Hebrew virus, instead of God is one . . . Egyptians
. . . was the sanctity of human life. Um . . . Christian would be compassion, or forgiveness of sin. That is in the sacrifice of Christ . . .
died for your sins, so Christ died for your sins . . . Jewish sanctity of
the human, Christian, additional compassion or forgiveness of sin.
So then . . . I asked Bill what the Islamic positioning statement or
virus idea of Islam was . . . we were guessing around that . . . it was . . .
Allah Akbar, God is great, God is everything. Positioning statement
of Buddhism, would be, I guess the . . . three marks of existence, or
the three jewels of the *Buddha, dharma,* and *sangha.* Or three marks
of existence as suffering, transitoriness, and *anatma,* no permanent
self. Maybe the four noble truths, then you'd have to expound those:
existence contains suffering, so forth.

I just asked Bill what was the positioning statement for Islam. He
said, " Well, Allah is everything. Allah is everything and everywhere."

[Allen reads the questions of a "Libertarian test: personal issues
and economic issues," which William got in the mail. William
answers.]

AG: "Military service should be voluntary, no draft." Yes or no.

WSB: Yes.

AG: "The government should not control radio TV or the press."

WSB: I agree. Yes.

AG: "Repeal regulations of sex by consenting adults."

WSB: No, that is yes, there shouldn't be any.

AG: "Drug laws do more harm than good, repeal them."

WSB: Yes.

AG: "Let people immigrate and emigrate in and out freely."

WSB: Yes.

AG: Now on economic issues. "Farmers should farm without quotas or subsidies."

WSB: Well, I . . . that's a pretty elaborate question.

AG: So that's yes, maybe, or no?

WSB: I would say maybe, 'cause I'm not sure, I don't know enough about that.

AG: OK. "People are better off with free trade than with tariffs."

WSB: Probably.

AG: OK so we have yes. "Minimum wage laws eliminate jobs, repeal minimum wage laws."

WSB: I wonder about that.

AG: OK, maybe.

WSB: I'd say maybe, that is, with these economic things I don't know enough.

AG: "End taxes. Pay for services voluntarily."

WSB: What you say?

[Allen repeats.]

WSB: Mmmmaybe.

AG: Medical . . .

WSB: Yes, I understand, right . . .

AG: "Europeans and Japanese should pay for their own defense."

WSB: Well, well, yes, I have to say they should. Now . . .

AG: You want the Japanese to rearm?

WSB: No, I don't want them to rearm.

AG: But pay for their own defense.

WSB: Pay for their own defense, yes, more or less, yes. Or 'maybe' for that one.

AG: Well you pass as a 100 percent Libertarian on personal issues. You pass as a 20 percent Libertarian on economic issues. And an 80 percent maybe.

WSB: Well, their position is that a lot of . . .

AG: They would classify you then . . .

WSB: Their position is that a lot of people are not voting because after all the Democratic and Republican party, there's no difference between them.

AG: Yes. They would classify you as a left-liberal.

WSB: Yeah.

AG: Not an authoritarian, not a Libertarian, not a centrist, not a right-conservative but a left-liberal.

WSB: I suppose so.

AG: This is a self-government compass. Take the scores and you make them here.

WSB: I get you.

AG: But they don't . . . it's not very clear 'cause it has only for "no" but not for "maybe."

WSB: Yeah well . . .

AG: Here's your score card.

WSB: OK. I don't want to carry that around with me, I'll put it away.

AG: Should we re-legalize drugs?

WSB: What?

AG: Here's the Libertarian Party on drugs. "Drug laws don't help but make things worse."

WSB: That's true.

AG: "Professional politicians scramble to make names for themselves as tough antidrug warriors. Experts agree that the war on drugs is lost and never could be won. Time to consider re-legalization. Alcohol prohibition in the twenties: result, organized crime."

WSB: Exactly. Well, what I've always said.

AG: "Streets became battle grounds, criminals bought-off law enforcement, adulterated booze blinded and killed people. Civil rights were trampled."

WSB: Of course, yes.

AG: So repeal. "[If] liquor was legalized, criminal gangs out of the liquor business. Today's war on drugs is a rerun of prohibition. Forty million Americans are occasional peaceful users of some illegal drug, no threat to anyone. Organized crime profits. Black market always appears to supply demand."

WSB: Of course it does, all very true.

AG: "Criminal gangs love the situation, making millions, kill other drug dealers, innocent people caught in the crossfire. Corrupt police and courts. Adulterated dope, experimental dope, injury and death. Crime increases. Half the cost of law enforcement and prisons is squandered on drug-related crime."

wsb: Exactly.

ag: "Of all drug users a relative few are addicts who commit crimes daily to supply artificially expensive habits. They're the robbers, car thieves, and burglars. American police state. Civil liberties suffer. We are all suspects subject to random urine tests, highway check-points, spying on our personal finances. Property can be seized without trial, if the police merely claim you got it with drug profits."

wsb: That's true.

ag: "America is becoming a police state because of the war on drugs." Well that's *very clear!*

wsb: Quite clear and that's what I've always said. I said all that in my article in *Spin* . . . Say no to drug hysteria.

ag: I had an article in *High Times* saying the same thing, this year. Did you see that? Big interview in *High Times* that I had?

wsb: I think I did, yes.

ag: Now they're continuing: "America can handle legal drugs. Today's illegal drugs were legal before 1914."

wsb: That's right.

ag: "Cocaine was in the original Coca-Cola recipe. Americans had few problems with cocaine, opium, heroin, or marijuana. Drugs were inexpensive, crime was low. Most users handled their drug of choice and lived normal productive lives. Addicts out of control were a tiny minority. The first laws prohibiting drugs were racist in origin, to prevent Chinese laborers from using opium and to prevent blacks and Hispanics from using marijuana and cocaine."

wsb: Why?

AG: "Some Americans will always use alcohol, tobacco, marijuana, or other drugs. Most are not addicts, they're social drinkers or users. Legal drugs would be inexpensive. Addicts could support their habits with honest work. Organized crime would be deprived of profits. Police could return to protecting us from real criminals."

WSB: Yes. There are crimes against person and crimes against property. That's it. When the police get outside those areas they become . . . disliked and so on. No good results.

AG: "Criminal laws only drive the problem underground, put money in the pockets of the criminal class. With drugs legal, compassionate people could do more to educate and rehabilitate drug users who seek help. Drugs should be legal. Individuals have the right to decide for themselves what to put in their bodies." So they are pointing out that Mayor of Baltimore, Kurt Schmoke and conservative writer William Buckley are calling for "repeal of America's repressive, ineffective drug laws." So that's pretty good. They're very succinct, very clear, and correct.

WSB: Very clear.

AG: Then they have one on responsible gun ownership. That's up your alley. "Equal rights for America's gun owners. Gun ownership by itself harms no other person and cannot morally justify criminal penalties. Most of the American Revolutionaries of 1776 used their own guns in that war. The Bill of Rights was to prevent our government from depriving them of such liberties. Gun control advocates would declare all gun owners guilty without trial simply for owning guns. Gun control advocates are like the prohibitionists of early twentieth century." That is, they're using the same parallel to prohibition, by making things illegal it didn't stop drug use, it didn't stop gun use.

WSB: People don't realize what a simple contrivance a gun is. Anyone can go down in his basement and make a gun, a single shot gun, will kill. Like my flintlocks, pistols—I may take them out today and try them. Well, they work. They shoot a great big hunk of lead. And at moderate range they're deadly indeed. So it's very easy to make a gun. Just like bathtub gin, you see. Again, supply and demand.

AG: So their proposition is, "if a person commits a crime with a gun, then impose severe penalties for injuries on the victim, hold negligent gun user fully liable for all harm his negligence does. Politicians should encourage gun ownership for a responsible, well-trained, and armed citizenry." But, you know, that the Libertarian Party view and I . . . agree on general principles. But then, there are now apparently 200 million or more guns—more guns than people in America, so you couldn't get rid of them. But also they're being used almost indiscriminately by preadolescents in New York grammar schools . . . who don't have any sense of responsibility, at that age are so full of enmity . . .

WSB: You see, alright . . . in my adolescence, it was a gun culture. There was about as many guns around then as there are now.

AG: In your class and in your group.

WSB: Yes, but nobody shot any . . . kids didn't shoot each other.

AG: Yeah, but different education and different economic conditions. You were upper-middle-class, here all these kids are living in a drug culture where there's a tremendous amount of violence so that the guns are both a form of self-defense and also a form of aggression.

WSB: No doubt about it. In other words they have let a situation get worse and worse and worse and then scream that they've got to do something about it. And what they do is going to aggravate the problem still further. Sure they could . . . New York where they have the most trouble has the most . . . the strictest gun laws of any place.

AG: New York does?

WSB: Yes! New York City has special laws that don't apply outside New York City. It's very difficult to get a permit even to own a *rifle*

. . . a rifle or a shotgun. Although you get outside of New York and you can buy a rifle or a shot gun in a hardware store. Now a rifle or a shotgun can easily be made into a pistol. All you got to do is cut off the stock and cut off the barrel and you've got an awkward perhaps but very deadly weapon.

AG: Not a big rifle, a .22 maybe but a great big one would be pretty hard to handle as a pistol.

WSB: Well, yeah, sure, but you don't need a big one. Just a rifle or a shotgun, a .410 shotgun could easily be handled as a pistol.

AG: Well nowadays there are news stories in New York saying that kids are afraid to go to school *without* pistols, because there's so much violence. So the whole level of violence escalates.

WSB: Escalates, sure, but the answer is not to pass stricter gun laws.

AG: So what is the answer?

WSB: You pass stricter gun laws, what's going to happen?

AG: The law-abiding people will throw in their guns and then the wild kids'll keep them.

WSB: Anyone can make a gun . . . zip guns . . .

AG: What they do now is they have metal detectors in high school. You can't bring your gun into school. You know that?

WSB: Yeah.

AG: Apparently that's going to be more universal than the city. Would you approve of that? No guns in school?

WSB: Well yes, no guns in bars and . . .

William Burroughs and Alene Lee, rooftop near Thompkins Park
and Paradise Alley. Bill and I assembled Yage and Queer letters,
Alene typed up the collaged manuscripts, Fall 1953. Allen Ginsberg

TAPE 5 SIDE A

3/20/92. Noon. Drunks with guns. What this interview is all about.
Japanese question list: When did you first meet?
Lucien Carr. David Kammerer. Alene Lee. Kerouac. Gregory Corso.
Junky. Queer. Naked Lunch.
Literary censorship: the case of James Joyce's Ulysses.
Tangier. Brion Gysin. Cut-ups and the facts of perception.
Naked Lunch, *the movie. Jane Bowles.*

WSB: A lot of the sheriffs would say, "alright, you come into town, you leave your guns here, in the sheriff's office, or we'll come out and get 'em." And then, when they ride out of town, they get their guns back. Simple as that. No I wouldn't support drunks in a bar with guns. It's very dangerous, not only for anyone that they might dislike or become annoyed with, but for everyone in the place. Bullets would be flying everywhere.

AG: So you were asking me what this is all about.

WSB: Yes. Sounds good.

AG: Jeremy . . . the film producer . . .

WSB: Jeremy Thomas.

AG: . . . wanted an interview for the European and Japanese opening of the [*Naked Lunch*] film.

WSB: Yeah. OK.

AG: And Jim [Grauerholz] was unwilling to have another invasion of interviewers and reporters, so they came up with the idea of sending me here and paying me well . . .

WSB: Good.

AG: . . . to do an interview. And I was too busy, but I wanted to come and visit. But doing an interview was too much, so what I'm going to do is do these tapes and then Steven Taylor will transcribe them, and edit for me and then I'll do the final edit.

WSB: OK. Fine.

AG: And I'll peel off the money for him to do that.

WSB: Mm hm.

AG: So now the main people that put up the money were the Japanese, apparently. And they left a bunch a questions which we might . . .

WSB: Alright, bring 'em out.

AG: . . . run through fast if I can find them. . . . yes . . . I got 'em. They're very awkwardly phrased questions, so I'll try and rephrase them.

WSB: OK, go ahead.

AG: "When and where did we meet each other last time?" Well, I came visiting here before the summer, after your angioplasty I believe.

WSB: Yes. That's right.

AG: And then again after your bypass.

WSB: Yeah, I guess so.

AG: So this just last summer and actually, today there should be some photographs from that time arriving here by Federal Express.

WSB: Yes.

AG: "What was their first encounter and where? Were any other persons together there?"

WSB: Well the first encounter was in Joan's apartment, that apartment in Morningside Heights. [421 West 118th St.]

AG: No. You know where?

WSB: Where?

AG: Lucien brought me downtown, Christmas 1943 or '44 [December 1943] to 44 Morton Street, where you were sitting on a kind of a long bench facing the garden door, the back door.

WSB: That was where Dave Kammerer lived, not where I lived.

AG: Yeah, where Dave Kammerer lived. And Louise Lutz lived upstairs. Remember?

WSB: Yes.

AG: I'd never been to Greenwich Village before. And Lucien . . . [I] literally never had been . . . although my father and mother had been there . . . and Lucien took me downtown from Columbia, the Union Theological Seminary where we had rooms across the hall, to meet you. And I think he was wearing a red bandana around his neck or something like that, Bohemian costume. And apparently he and Kammerer had been to a dyke bar on the corner of Bleecker and Thompson or something like that. He had gotten drunk and in a fight with somebody and bitten her ear.

WSB: Who had?

AG: Lucien.

WSB: Lucien.

AG: . . . had bitten her ear and there was blood all over, and you said, "In the words of the immortal bard, 'tis too starved an argument for my sword." That was the first time I'd heard Shakespeare quoted so . . . justly. And then you said of Louise that you liked her, because she was straightforward, manly, and reliable. Remember that?

WSB: Yes. I did.

AG: Remember that meeting at all?

WSB: I don't remember it, no.

AG: Yeah, I have a very clear visual impression of it, amazingly, and even of some sort of back door into a garden, or back door . . .

WSB: There was a back door.

AG: Was it to a garden?

WSB: It was a back door. There was a garden. Yeah, sure, it was a garden. Courtyard.

AG: Yeah.

WSB: And you could . . . Dave's apartment was on the second floor, first floor up, and you could easily climb down from his window, this door that opened up, one could easily climb down from there into the garden.

AG: Oh, his was on the second floor.

WSB: Second floor.

AG: I had an idea it was on the first.

WSB: Oh no.

AG: You know who wound up living at 44 Horatio later.

WSB: 44 Horatio?

AG: Yeah, that was the address.

WSB: It was Morton Street.

AG: Morton Street, I mean. 44 Morton Street . . . was the Nobel Prize-winning poet Joseph Brodsky.

WSB: Who?

AG: Joseph Brodsky. You know, the Russian poet who came here, writes for the *New York Review of Books*.

WSB: Yes, I heard something about that yes.

AG: So his apartment was I think at 44 Morton Street. "Any stories where they . . . stayed in New York in 1953?" How long were you in New York, do you remember?

WSB: How long was I what?

AG: How long were you on East 7th Street with me in New York in my apartment?

WSB: Oh, about a couple of months, two, three . . .

AG: I think it was the fall, because you left around Christmas . . .

WSB: I left around Christmas and I went to Rome.

AG: Yeah.

WSB: And then I didn't come back.

AG: Yeah. So let's see, they're saying "any stories" when we stayed . . .

WSB: What stories, where?

AG: About that apartment.

WSB: Well . . .

AG: What I remember is, among other things, beside the fact that we put together *The Yage Letters* and the *Queer* manuscript . . .

WSB: Yeah.

AG: . . . and that Alene was there.[37]

WSB: Who?

AG: That Alene was there, Alene Lee, typing . . .

WSB: Yes.

---

37   Alene Lee (1931–1991) was represented as Kerouac's lover Mardou Fox in *The Subterraneans*.

AG: Kerouac . . . stole a pushcart. Kerouac and Gregory stole a push-cart and left it at the front of the apartment. You remember that?

WSB: No, I don't.

AG: And I got really mad.

WSB: I would too, I think . . .

AG: We had some grass in the apartment.

WSB: That's it, you can get into all sorts of trouble. To steal some-thing that people need is not funny at all. I know some people in Paris who thought it was smart to steal a policeman's cape and boy the gendarmes were really pissed off and right, this costs money, man, they don't get paid very much. There's nothing funny about that sort of thing. I think it's bad because it's not a prank.

AG: Well, that's what I thought, but also would bring in the heat [the police] to the apartment . . .

WSB: Well, that's it.

AG: And there's grass around.

WSB: Exactly.

AG: So I got upset, course it never did bring in the heat, but I. . . .

WSB: Well, that cape certainly brought heat around.

AG: One thing I remember actually, at some point or other you and Lucien and Kerouac got me on a couch and took down my pants.

WSB: I don't remember that.

AG: [laughing] 'Cause I . . . it was thrilling and I got a hard on I remember, I was ashamed. Because it was Lucien there.

WSB: Should be.

AG: On the couch in front of the window.

WSB: Yes. I know where the couch was. Typical railroad apartment, where they usually had the bath tub in the kitchen.

AG: Yeah, I had one there.

WSB: Typical slum.

AG: Actually I ran into a girl who's living there now who keeps inviting me to come back and see it.

WSB: That'd be interesting.

AG: A friend of the rock group Sonic Youth that plays with you . . .

WSB: Who?

AG: Sonic Youth is a rock group . . .

WSB: Yes.

AG: She's one of the singer friends of theirs.

WSB: Yes.

AG: And she's now living in my old apartment. But one thing I remember very clearly is the origin of "The Market" or "Interzone" and market . . .

WSB: Yes.

AG: . . . fantasy with you and . . . looking out the window and you saw a neighbor lady lean out with a very intense expression and pull in the laundry and the laundry line. You remember that?

WSB: No. But I know how about those laundry lines.

AG: And you saw the laundry lines and then . . . all the fire escapes, and from that rose a routine about balconies criss-crossing in the void and . . .

WSB: Um hm yeah yeah um hm . . .

AG: And lines of ropes connecting buildings . . .

WSB: Exactly . . .

AG: I remember you looked out of the window and then were impressed by the expression of the woman's face, 'cause . . . if you could look up a minute . . . she leaned out like that only, you know, with a great intensity of expression and extending her body out pulling . . . with her hand out grasping . . .

WSB: Grasping . . . I remember.

AG: You were imitating her avaricious gesture, grasping and pulling the laundry line and from that was the seed of "The Market" [scene in *Naked Lunch* novel].

WSB: Yeah.

AG: Now, do you have any visual memory of that outside of the window at all, the laundry lines?

WSB: No, but I know I can see . . . the laundry lines are a feature of those apartments and their laundry's on the balcony. You'll find that in . . . balcony . . . in sort of, slums all over the world.

AG: Yeah, Naples.

WSB: Naples, I was thinking of that. Naples and Marseilles and all kinds of places.

AG: Actually that photograph of Kerouac that I have . . .

WSB: Yeah.

AG: You can actually see the laundry line . . . those specific laundry lines. Did you ever notice that in that photo?

WSB: I think so, yeah.

AG: It takes a very good printer to get them because it was very faint . . . sky. So let's see . . . that's where . . . you first met Gregory there.

WSB: I first met Gregory there. Yes.

AG: I think that day he came around with a little attaché case full of liqueurs.

WSB: Little bottles, those little bottles of liqueurs and . . .

AG: Wanting to sell them. He was living by his wits.

WSB: Yes. That he was indeed. He wanted to sell those and he burned the toast.

AG: That I don't remember, what happened?

WSB: Nothing. He was making some toast. You asked him to make some toast and the toast was burnt to a crisp and I complained and he said well . . . he got real annoyed, said well, he was a poet [laughter]. And he wasn't expected to be able to make toast properly . . . which he didn't, he burned the toast.

AG: Remember anything about Jack's visits?

WSB: Well, Jack was there a number of times.

AG: Yeah, well he was in and out a lot.

WSB: But I can't . . . I don't remember anything very specific . . . um . . . that was when he was . . . this was before he'd published anything.

AG: Well, he had *The Town and the City* out, years before [1950, Harcourt Brace]. But he'd already written *On the Road, Doctor Sax, Visions of Gerard, Maggie Cassidy.*

WSB: Yes, but it was a long time before those were published.

AG: Yeah . . . but he was having an affair with Alene . . .

wsb: Yes.

ag: . . . at that time and so sometimes staying over at her place on 11th Street in Paradise Alley.[38]

wsb: Yes. Yes.

ag: Then what did he do when he visited us?

wsb: Nothing special.

ag: Well there are those photographs of you two doing routines, remember? Fighting with the knife.

wsb: Yes.

ag: Then camping [acting campy] on the couch with him making believe he was the innocent American bumpkin and you the Hungarian countess, warning him against his mother.

wsb: And then . . . oh, he'd do routines of cops.

ag: Oh really, I don't remember that.

wsb: Yes, don't you remember that?

ag: No. What was this?

wsb: Oh, the tough cop and the con cop. He'd act it out.

ag: Both of them?

wsb: Yes. You know, "He doesn't want to talk to you I like his face, he's alright. . . . Now listen here, tell him we're not Boy Scouts. . . . lock him up . . . " This sort of tough . . .

ag: Where did he get that I wonder? Is that from you? 'Cause you knew that one.

---

38 Paradise Alley was the locals' name for a courtyard at 501 East 11th street. In *The Subterraneans*, Kerouac changes the alley's location to San Francisco. Ginsberg pointed the place out to me in the late seventies. It had been walled up. After a fire in 1985, the tenements adjoining the yard were demolished and replaced.

WSB: It's the oldest in the industry, the tough cop and the con cop. Any interrogation, well it goes back . . . all interrogations are based on the tough interrogator and the nice one. They beat the guy up, then he's all broken down, then somebody comes in that's going to be his friend, see? And of course they're both. . . .

AG: How much does that extend politically I wonder . . .

WSB: Huh?

AG: I wonder how that extends politically. The Republicans are the tough cops in America and the Democrats are the soft cops or something?

WSB: No, it doesn't extend that far, it's an interrogation technique . . . entirely . . . a very old one and a very effective one, even if you know it. Even if you know it, it's effective. The tough cop and the con cop.

AG: "Why did it take so long to be published their books?" Why'd it take so long for their books to be published?

WSB: Why?

AG: "We heard *Junky* took nine years especially. Why *Junky* was co-published with Maurice Helbrant?" That's the story of the Ace Books, the reverse story. [The original edition of *Junky* was published back-to-back with another novella, *Narcotic Agent*, by Maurice Helbrant.] But that's not true [about taking nine years to publish]. *Junky* was published within two years probably of its writing.

WSB: It was.

AG: '53.

WSB: 1953.

AG: And was written '50–'51 probably.

WSB: Yes, exactly, so it didn't take so long. They're thinking of, possibly of *Queer.*

AG: And also *Naked Lunch* actually.

WSB: Yeah, well . . .

AG: *Naked Lunch* came together about the time that it was published. *Queer*, of the same time 1953 wasn't published until 1983.

WSB: Yeah. Well it was in an archive.

AG: I think I had a copy somewhere. And I think somebody found it. Bill Morgan found it, or a version of it.[39]

WSB: They're asking why. Well, there were lots of reasons. I didn't publish *Naked Lunch* until 1959. It was published in Paris. And then, when it came to the question of publishing *Queer*, I didn't have the manuscript. Alan Ansen had the manuscript. And I wasn't too in a hurry to publish it because I felt it was a sort of amateuristic, you know.

AG: Well, you'd gone much further by then.

WSB: I'd gone much further.

AG: You already had material for *Soft Machine*.

WSB: Yes. The trilogy. *Naked Lunch*, *The Soft Machine*, and *The Ticket That Exploded*. I didn't feel very . . .

AG: No. *Naked Lunch* was one thing. Then *Soft Machine*, *The Ticket That Exploded*, and *Nova Express*.

WSB: Yes.

AG: They're all extensions of *Naked Lunch* though.

WSB: Yes. They are. You see, *Naked Lunch* was from about a thousand pages of material. A lot of it overflowed then into *Nova Express*, then *The Soft Machine*, and *The Ticket That Exploded*.

---

39 Miles found the *Queer* ms in London in 1972, as he was cataloguing WSB's archive. He assembled it from numbered pages scattered throughout a larger cache. "Allen never had a copy of *Queer*, he was probably thinking of *And the Hippos* . . . which he did have" (personal communication, 2 June 2018).

AG: And then a big huge thing, *Interzone* of that time that Kerouac had helped type.

WSB: Yes, but it wasn't . . . that wasn't published until later.

AG: Yeah, that came out a couple of years ago but that was also part of the big word-hoard.

WSB: Partly, yes.

AG: But there was another reason, as I remember, which was that *Howl* was not published till 1957.

WSB: Hm hm.

AG: And in 1954 there was the Roth case, I believe, or some time around then, the Roth decision in the courts, saying that literary merit might be considered an argument against obscenity, or against prohibition for obscene purposes. But up to that point *Queer* would have been too colorful to pass censorship.

WSB: And now . . .

AG: And then, in the *Howl* case . . . it was apparently significant, in San Francisco, because the judge said that literary merit was a criteri[on]. And then in the subsequent case a year later, '58, in a sequence of cases beginning with D. H. Lawrence and Henry Miller and culminating in '62 with the *Naked Lunch* victory, it was affirmed over and over again that literary merit was a defense against censorship for obscenity.

WSB: Yep.

AG: And that had never been established. Like in Britain during the persecutions of [Henry] Vizetelly [1888] for publishing Zola, he was ruined because literary merit was not allowed as a statement. And then in the twenties in England even, Radclyffe Hall's lesbian novel *Well of Loneliness* was condemned and the entire Bloomsbury circle went to court, including Virginia Woolf and Leonard Woolf and E.

M. Forster, and they were not allowed to speak for the literary merit of the book—which they didn't think had that much literary merit—but they went to bat for it because it was controversial.

WSB: Yes, and the Sitwells too.

AG: Yes. But the court at that time said that literary merit would not be admissible as any sort of evidence that the book . . . The question in British law was whether or not the book was obscene, not whether it had merit.

WSB: Yes.

AG: And in America the *Ulysses* decision of the twenties [1933] was not based on literary merit either, it was based on the fact that the judge who judged the *Ulysses* trial said that if the definition of pornography or obscenity is that it tends to excite or arouse lust, this book is more of an emetic and did not arouse lust.

WSB: Exactly, it might be considered emetic. I think it was Judge Learned Hand. Well, he was a cultured, intelligent man.[40]

AG: And it's true that most of the things that are called pornographic don't arouse lust actually . . .

WSB: Yes, of course . . .

AG: But then . . . so the sequence of trials that we had in the fifties, or Grove Press, culminating in yours, actually broke the back of literary censorship because at that point is wasn't a question of whether or not it aroused erotic interest, or gave you a hard-on, or got you

---

40 Learned Hand was not the sole judge; he was one of a panel of three. Lead Judge John W. Woolsey wrote: "[I]n respect of the recurrent emergence of the theme of sex in the minds of [Joyce's] characters, it must always be remembered that his locale was Celtic and his season Spring" and "To have failed to honestly tell fully what his characters thought would have been artistically inexcusable." Woolsey said the criterion of pornography is that a work "lead to sexually impure and lustful thoughts. . . . Whilst in many places the effect of *Ulysses* on the reader undoubtedly is somewhat emetic, nowhere does it tend to be an aphrodisiac." The court found that the literary worth of a book should be taken into consideration, and a book should not be banned on the basis of isolated offensive passages. The case opened the door for literary works with explicit content.

sexually aroused. It was a question of whether this arousal was on the basis of something that had artistic or literary merit. So that's why *Queer* couldn't be published until that wave of censorship had been overcome . . . or the wave of libertarian trials.

WSB: Then it became too mild.

AG: Yeah? What became too mild?

WSB: *Queer.* By then it was sort of passé. And I was not . . . in order to approach it . . . that was when I wrote that introduction, that's as long as the text. In that form it was, I felt, workable and worth publishing. When I started looking at it, at first, I said, oh my God this is amateuristic writing . . . and I had to write the introduction, and then when I started writing the introduction, I was seeing it as sort of historical, in an historical perspective, because it dated back to, oh Jesus, how many years?

AG: Twelve? '49 '50 '51, the material of the letters.

WSB: '49 '50 and *Naked Lunch* was published in 1959 first in Paris and '62 in America and when was *Queer* finally published?

AG: It was codified from letters that were years earlier; it was codified in '53 and published in '83–'84 [1985], thirty years later. [Returning to the list of questions]: "Why did it take so long to be published their books?" Yes. "Why was it [*Junky*] co-published with Maurice Helbrant . . . *The Autobiography of a Narcotics Agent*?" You remember?

WSB: Well sure. Ace Books was putting out a series of sort of contrasting books in one book, one going this way and one going that way.[41] It was a series.

AG: Well, there was another reason, which was, at that time your treatment of the subject was very realistic and accurate and not full

---

41 Two novellas were printed in one volume, back-to-back. What would ordinarily have been a front cover and back cover were, in effect, two front covers.

police-state version. So that the editors interposed a lot of footnotes.

WSB: Yes.

AG: Contradicting your statements.

WSB: Yes: "This is not the opinion of . . . established medical authorities."

AG: And they also wanted to cover their asses . . .

WSB: Um hm, yes.

AG: . . . from criticism, by publishing it with a pro-police account of the drug problem.

WSB: Exactly.

AG: OK [reading:] "How come *Naked Lunch* was started in Tangier?" Well that was [laughter] . . .

WSB: Well well (laughs).

AG: Though actually *Naked Lunch* was started. . . . before, in the sense that "The Market" . . . when was that written? "Interzone" and "The Market" were part of *The Yage Letters* actually.

WSB: Yes, that's right.

AG: So the seed of *Naked Lunch* is that Interzone market meat cafe.

WSB: Absolutely. Yes.

AG: And that's from a *yage* experience . . . your description of the *yage* experience actually 1950 or '51 or something . . . I always thought that was the seed of *Naked Lunch*.

WSB: I think it was.

AG: And actually I thought *Star Wars* stole that seed when they had that meat cafe, the interplanetary bar.

WSB: Oh yes. Well I wouldn't say that they stole it.

AG: Well, it certainly was keyed-off. "We understand that in '57, Orlovsky, Kerouac and Ginsberg visited Burroughs in Tangier. Did Burroughs receive any influences from that event to write *Naked Lunch*?"

WSB: No.

AG: No, what you received . . . we came bringing manuscripts, and Kerouac bringing his typing and editing skills.

WSB: That's right.

AG: To type up . . . did he type "Interzone" or what?

WSB: He typed some, but . . . yes, quite a lot of it. He was a very fast typer.

AG: Yeah, a hundred twenty words a minute.

WSB: Yes, go on.

AG: "Why he move, Burroughs, to Paris in 1958?" Well, let's see . . . me and Gregory and Peter were there.

WSB: Yes.

AG: We had a hotel, it was convenient. And what was going on in Tangier now?

WSB: Not much.

AG: Was Kiki still alive?

WSB: No, he was dead.

AG: Already?

WSB: Yes.

AG: In between . . . no . . . it was a little earlier.

WSB: He was dead and, well, I don't know. I felt that I'd had enough of Tangiers and I wanted to move to Paris.

AG: Also there was a community there already, of friends.

WSB: Yes.

AG: "Did Sinclair Beiles or Gysin help or contribute to write *Naked Lunch*?"

WSB: Who?

AG: Sinclair Beiles.

WSB: They helped in the typing.

AG: And editing.

WSB: And editing, yes, very definitely.

AG: "Please tell us about Brion Gysin. How was the cutups technique created? What was Mr. Burroughs's intention to create this technique? How did they collaborate?"

WSB: I did not create it. It was created by Brion Gysin. It's really a painter's technique. And it is an extension of the collage technique, which was pretty old hat in painting at that time. It is closer really to the practice of human perception. You see, just . . . should I stand in front of a landscape and paint it, I'm completely ignoring the factor of time. While I am painting it, it's changing, clouds are changing, all sorts of things are changing. So there's the myth there of someone creating in a timeless vacuum. Now, so say, take a walk around the block, come back, and put what you have seen on canvas. What have you seen? You have seen fragments. You've seen a man cut in half by a car, you've seen reflections in the shop windows. So that was the . . .

AG: Um hm, and you've seen your own thoughts . . .

WSB: Well, yes . . .

AG: . . . if you daydreamed also.

WSB: Yes, of course and how they intersect with reality. And I found that if you notice where, just where . . . what you were thinking when you saw something, you'll see that what you're thinking is reflected in what you see. I was thinking about New Mexico and I round the corner in New York and there was a New Mexico license plate: "New Mexico, land of enchantment." But I was thinking about it before I saw the license plate.

AG: Now Gysin's suggestion was that writing was fifty years behind painting, from the point of view of cutup and collage.

WSB: Yes.

AG: From the Dadaist and early collage artists.

WSB: And also . . . this is closer to the facts of perception. Every time you look out the window or walk down the street, your consciousness is cut by random, seemingly random . . .

AG: OK, this idea of the collage or cutup being closer to perception, was that Brion's idea or your evolution and rationale for it?

WSB: Oh . . . both, both, both.

AG: I mean, you've extended the thought of it, elaborated the . . .

WSB: It is closer to the facts of one's perception. Life *is* a cutup. And to pretend that you write or paint in a timeless vacuum is just simply . . . not . . . true, not in accord with the facts of human perception.

AG: And also there's the fact that arranging the portions of *Naked Lunch*, they were sent to [Maurice] Girodias in the order of their typing.

WSB: That's right.

AG: And so the arrangement of those chapters was in a sense random or cutup.

WSB: Well yeah. And then when we looked at it and the idea was that we would decide the order when we got the proofs. I remember Sinclair Beiles and Brion saying, "Well why change it? It's perfect the way it is, the way it came from the printer." We made one major change, that is, the first chapter became the last chapter. 'Cause the first chapter that came from the printers, which would be the beginning, we moved to the end.

AG: And that was . . . that's where you rise up and annihilate the detectives that had come to . . .

WSB: Yeah, that's right.

AG: So . . . actually the book exists within the parenthesis of the detectives coming to you like Kafka, and your exorcising them by shooting them, in which the entire hallucination and previous adventure disappears and is swept into oblivion.

WSB: That, in the original, was the first chapter and we made that the last.

AG: Now that always seemed to be a very model way of handling all that disparate cutup material, because then it could be placed . . .

WSB: There's no actual cutups in *Naked Lunch*.

AG: No I know, but it seemed that was the jump-cut . . .

WSB: Yes, exactly.

AG: . . . between one scene and another in *Naked Lunch*. And one routine can be handled well as dream material or hallucination material if you put them within the parenthesis of the hallucination of being arrested and waking from that hallucination by shooting the detectives, waking from the dream. But now, why didn't they use that in the movie? That's what I don't understand, 'cause it would make the movie very very model-structured.

WSB: Well he . . .

AG: Did they understand that part? That structure in the book?

WSB: They understood that structure in the book but they imposed a different structure.

AG: But their structure left it very open-ended 'cause at the end you're just entering into, what, Interzone? ["Annexia" in the film.]

WSB: Freeland. Well no, I think theirs . . . was perfectly logical and very good. When he said . . . *write* something, that means make something happen.

AG: Yeah. That was very smart. That wasn't your idea was it? You had the border guards any number of times in the Lower Slobbovia or wherever . . .

WSB: Yes.

AG: And never interrupted . . . never stopped you to say prove . . . I'm a writer . . . prove it, write something. Very funny actually.

WSB: That was very good. And . . . that was all . . . you see I had nothing to do with writing the script.

AG: Yeah, no I understand that, so that was an interesting invention. But then what do you think of . . . your response was to turn around and put a bullet through the head of the lady passenger who was supposed to be some simulacra of the wife of the Tangier resident, right?

WSB: In other words, I made something happen.

AG: Yeah.

WSB: Thereby proving that I was a writer.

AG: Yeah. 'Cause you can say then that anybody who drops an atom bomb is a writer, that they made something happen, from their premise.

WSB: Well no, not unless he *wrote* it.

AG: Yeah. Um hm. What did you think, in the movie, of the use of that autobiographical section?

WSB: I thought it was quite . . . quite all right.

AG: I thought it was sort of treading on . . . to do it twice I thought was treading on territory . . . though by doing it twice it sort of made it more imaginative and less close to . . .

WSB: Well that's what I meant . . . the whole thing was so bizarre that, the use of all the biographical material, which became part of such a bizarre surrealist structure . . . That was the reason that he didn't want me to take any part in the film. That would destroy the whole illusory structure, by putting somebody in there that the audience would know just who it was . . . it would have been a bad note.

AG: So the film is basically a hallucination on the *basis* of some autobiographical material already fictionally hallucinated in the book.

WSB: Yes. Exactly.

AG: But then what was really interesting was shifting . . . Jane . . . the simulacrum of Jane Bowles . . . or whoever the imaginary personage was . . . who was the resident writer in Tangier and his wife . . . to shift that . . . there's always the myth of blaming Paul for Jane's illness, if not blaming Cherifa, which I think is unjust, shifting the blame onto William Lee. So [laughs] an amazing piece of hallucination there. I wonder what Paul Bowles thinks about that. Have you had any response from him about the picture?

WSB: No.

AG: I like the idea of generalizing the narcotic thing by making it black meat addiction.

WSB: Yes, so you can't say it's a film about drugs, all the drugs are made up. Nor can you say it's a film about sex, because, well there are all sorts of sexual references as there are in these other films . . . it was not explicit, human sex. It's kept totally inhuman, people turning into centipedes. It is not . . .

AG: So it's not specifically homoerotic either.

WSB: No, no.

AG: Except in the one scene where you're in bed with Kiki.

WSB: Yeah. But by and large . . .

AG: How did you like the figure of Kiki there?

WSB: He's fine.

AG: Was that too effeminate?

WSB: No I don't think so, well that's just a . . .

AG: Too campy.

WSB: Too campy for the real life, but after all, they're similar.

AG: I thought it was a little bit a stereotyped idea of an effeminate but masculine Moroccan. Too much like a cat actually, rubbing up against you. There's one other thing I was wondering about, let's see . . . Actually the picture in the cage was kind of interesting, the idea of shlupping him up that way.

WSB: Yes, it was.

AG: The big giant insect, that was the most realized thing. The type-writers were amazing . . . 'cause that combined the talking asshole and the typewriters.

WSB: Yes, but I never would have thought of that. That is, the impor-tance, the symbolic importance of the actual *instrument* with which you write, the typewriter. Never occurred to me.

AG: Well, it's already . . . however it's an extension of the idea that you had that the writer writes the future or writes reality or writes what is going to happen.

WSB: Yes.

AG: And in that sense, the typewriter 'tells the fortune' so to speak. The typewriter tells . . . or the imagination tells the writer what to write.

WSB: Exactly. Yes.

AG: So the typewriter is both the machine and the imagination itself. But it also combines it with what looks to be an anus.

WSB: Yes, very much so.

AG: Which talks out of turn, which is in the talking asshole routine, and it also combines it with an anus addicted to bug powder [laughs] pleasures. So he actually made a composite image and that's the most interesting thing in the movie. That was an invention worthy of your prose I thought. So that was a contribution.

WSB: Um hm.

AG: I think the film will always be a cult film because it's so far out. But I had one strong objection to the acting, which is that the figure of Martin, which is based presumably on me, is a wimp, and I don't mind that because I did feel somewhat wimpy [laughs], still do, but reading the "Market" section at the beginning when the straight guy is screwing your supposed wife . . . when the straight guy, Kerouac, what's his name in the film the guy who plays Kerouac? . . . Anyway remember they're screwing on the floor and I'm sitting there making believe I'm ignoring it and reading or encouraging it by reading the "Market" section, or this character Martin is doing it. And it's read in such a flat, toneless, uninteresting voice! That it doesn't bring out the vigor and humor and color of the soliloquy.

WSB: Yes, well that's another interpretation.

AG: Yeah . . . but I thought it was lame because I had . . . before I saw the film, before I knew it was in the film, I had read that to my class three days earlier, four days earlier. I had a class in the literary history of the Beat Generation at CUNY [City University of New York] grad school, and I picked that to read to them. And it was a knockout, because it was entertaining. And here it's used as a kind of . . . well it's toneless. And I also thought, in the car, the recitation of the talking asshole was done in such a flat monotone, that it lost a lot of the raucous humor and color and vaudeville. 'Cause it's a vaudeville story to begin with.

WSB: Sure.

AG: And it lost that whole vaudeville thing and becomes more heavy, a little heavy that way. It's not outrageous enough. It's as if they were afraid to be outrageous by pronouncing it very subtly and intelligently and acting it out. And I thought maybe because Peter Weller the actor came and visited you and you were too much on your dignities or something like that, so he thought you were always monotone . . . Did you get . . . when you met him, did you at all get a little far out at all or were you just sort of very straight with him?

WSB: Well, I was there in Toronto.

AG: Oh, he didn't come out here to see you?

WSB: Yeah, he did, he was here once to see me I think, with David. Then I went to Toronto, I was in Toronto for a week and . . .

AG: You met him there?

WSB: Yes.

AG: Was that after he did that scene I wonder.

WSB: Well, I'm not sure because this was the . . . the shooting was by no means finished. And I saw some rushes and did a lot of press conferences and stuff like that. But I was having these chest pains and then I got back, I called the doctor and he said, "Come at nine o'clock tomorrow." And I didn't even go back to the . . .

AG: They put you right in the hospital.

WSB: Right in the hospital for the angioplasty, angiogram. And that only lasted about a month or two. Let's see, this was in . . . it was mid-June, because I went back to the hospital for the by-pass surgery . . . the angioplasty . . . They usually . . . it's sort of a bad . . .

AG: Five or six years sometimes . . .

WSB: What?

AG: Few years sometimes.

WSB: Sometimes, that's rare.

AG: Well, the thing that builds up the plaque is diet . . . Exercise, and stuff like that . . . but you have exercise, the rowing, quite more than me, actually.

WSB: But it didn't work. So about mid-June I had a recurrence, this time the doctor says, "you have to have surgery, there's no point . . . "

AG: What did you feel when he said that?

WSB: Well I said OK . . .

AG: 'Cause you'd never had . . . you've hardly been in the hospital in your whole life except for a little early . . . I remember for years and years you were . . .

WSB: So the doctor came to see me, the surgeon came to see me and said, "Well, you understand the risks? It may cause a heart attack, it may become infected, there may be complications and there's a possibility of dying on the operating table." Well, I said let's go ahead. There was no choice. Those pains are terrible, those chest pains. Really awful.

AG: Had you ever had any other pain like that? How's it compare with kidney? [AG had periodic kidney stone pain.]

WSB: It's a different . . . different . . . Kidney pain can be immediately relieved by morphine. This cannot. Morphine just doesn't seem to do a thing.

AG: Kidney pain is a spasm.

WSB: Yeah.

AG: A muscle spasm caused by the irritation of the grain phosphored crystals going down through the urethra. So the morphine relaxes the muscles.

WSB: That's right. But this is . . . I had some of my worst pain when morphine didn't relieve it at all.

AG: Would heroin have relieved it?

WSB: I don't think so.

TAPE 5 SIDE B

3/20/92. 1:30 p.m. to 2:30 p.m. WSB's and AG's heart issues. Getting back to the film. W. B. Yeats. Queer. Exterminator! *Japanese questions continued.* Towers Open Fire. *New video tech.* The Western Lands. The Place of Dead Roads. Cities of the Red Night. *Norman Mailer. Don Juan. Trungpa Rinpoche. Bill Lyon and Black Elk. Nuclear proliferation. Science is a lie. Tennyson. Blake. Rimbaud. J. D. Salinger. Hemingway. Desire dissolves. Going shooting tomorrow. L. F. Celine. My greatest influence is Denton Welch.*

WSB: [It is] only relieved by something that affects the cause of the pain, mainly nitroglycerine which expands the arteries. And that's the only thing.

AG: Did you ever have to wear a nitroglycerine patch?

WSB: I did.

AG: Yeah, I did for a month. You don't have it now?

WSB: Oh no no no no no no. I have not had any need of nitroglycerine since the surgery.

AG: I wore a nitroglycerine patch to Europe after I got out.[41]

WSB: I had those when I was in Toronto.

AG: Oh, already?

WSB: Yes.

---

41 Allen spent a period of days around Christmas of '91 in hospital with water on the heart and a slight weakness of a valve resulting in a spiral of fatigue and slow failure which was remedied by rest, medication, and strict diet.

AG: Oh, I see, you saw the doctor before you went up there and he advised against it?

WSB: No, he didn't advise against it strong enough. He felt . . . he told me later that he felt very bad about that, that he should have said flatly, "You should not go, this is too dangerous."

AG: All I had was shortness of breath, so it wasn't so bad. It turned out I had a gallon of water surrounding the heart and the heart was not getting enough oxygen to pump, so I took Lasix, which is a water pill, and that drained it. But they put it in my arm and I spent a week in the hospital and got drained of the water and felt . . . and the heart comes back to normal. Then what I found was . . . then I did an angiogram and they said my veins were completely clear, and unblocked.

So what was the problem? So my cardiologist said that probably what happened was that in the last five, six, seven years you've had a virus of some sort which you thought was a cold. It might have put you down in bed and it was some virus around the heart that did some damage, thickened the wall a bit, so it's not fully performing. But it's not a big deal if you just take it easy physically, don't over-exercise, walk a little, watch your salt, absolutely no salt, that's very important. Because that gathers water . . .

WSB: Oh yeah.

AG: Four times as much water to the amount of salt. So you didn't have a water problem?

WSB: I had no water problem.

AG: So that's why I'm so hung on the salt thing. I really have to worry about that.

WSB: I never had any accumulation of fluid. Since mid-June, when I had the surgery, I stopped absolutely smoking. I was in the hospital for two weeks . . .

AG: Was stopping smoking hard?

WSB: In a hospital you can't smoke anyway. No, it wasn't hard, no.

AG: Actually I find that true. If you stop for some reason or other, after two days it's gone, it isn't like a long habit . . .

WSB: No, I didn't find it difficult but I just . . . I just loathe the hospital. The food is so . . . why they serve such execrable food.

AG: I was in a good hospital, good food. Bassett Hospital in Cooperstown is notorious for its cuisine. Good kitchen.

WSB: This was just vile.

[Tape stops. Talk of Nichol's Diner. William is in and out of the room. Inaudible. Tape stops.]

AG: Getting back to the film.

WSB: Yes.

AG: One other touch I thought was quite good was the scene with the rather pudgy version of Paul Bowles, the other writer in Tangier beside Lee. I forgot the name of the guy in the film . . . where he's talking to you in this . . . his words were . . . he's saying he's telepathizing with you because his words are saying something desynchronized with what the sound track is. Remember, when he's moving his lips . . . that's an interesting touch.

WSB: Yes, yes. That was very good. Did you notice the bit where suddenly outside the window was Central Park?

AG: Um hm. How'd they do that anyway? I guess it's a picture.

WSB: Very easy.

AG: Actually I didn't notice that, where is it?

WSB: I forget where it is in the film, but it was there. Suddenly, just for a few minutes, less than that, say, just a flash. There was Central

Park outside the window. Those touches and the special effects of course are what Cronenberg is known for.

AG: I liked the character who was the sort of slimy German . . . the one has the voice sort of like Alan Ansen imitating a German. The louche queen, or whatever, double agent or whatever he was. I thought Benway was a little too serious. They made him into sort of a secret villain rather than . . . Benway as much more playing both sides of the fence.

WSB: Yes, but always remember there's no point trying to be faithful to the book because film and writing are just two completely different mediums.

AG: Yeah. I like your . . .

WSB: Any film stands on its own apart from whether it's based on a novel.

AG: Does this film stand on its own as logically as the book? In other words, the book has that logical frame. The film I couldn't tell, it was sort of like . . . Yeats has the phrase *hodos cameliontos*, chameleon-like, in that you don't know where the beginning or the middle or the end is.[42] So it's an unrelieved hallucination, because you don't know where you're coming in and you don't know where you're going out or where it ends. You're going into the hallucination, or maybe coming out of it I don't know. Freeland might be waking up from having committed killing or waking from a dream of having committed a killing or maybe a continuation of the hallucination. But we don't . . . it's kind of an indecisive moral, so to speak, or morale, or conclusion or an indecisive resolution of the condition of hallucination. In the book you touch on the reality. Here reality is touched on when Martin . . . the two writers come in occasionally.

---

42 "Yeats worried that his poetry might be destroyed if he wandered too far down what he called the *hodos chameliontos*, the chameleon road, in which the imagination . . . kept producing images in such profusion that the images became unintelligible. In a number of passages deleted from his plays, we can see Yeats experimenting with these wild profusions of images. In the art historical writings he studied, Yeats found visual analogues to the *hodos chameliontos* in the world of Persian art" (Daniel Albright, "Yeats, A Vision, and Art History," *The Yeats Journal of Korea* (2011): 5-29.)

WSB: Remember that . . .

AG: What do you think of the figure of Kerouac? I've forgotten who he was.

WSB: In the film I thought he was . . .

AG: Well, he wasn't as good looking as Kerouac. In fact he had kind of pock-marked or warty-faced or something.

WSB: Now remember that there isn't any Kerouac in the book.

AG: Yeah. So that's just added in from biography.

WSB: Yes.

AG: And what other elements? So they took from *Queer* and they took from *Exterminator!* . . . the opening chapter of *Exterminator!* with the addictions to bug powder.

WSB: Bug powder, yes.

AG: Any thing else from *Exterminator!*?

WSB: It's too bad that . . .

AG: They used that up in a way.

WSB: No, there's a book called *Mummy*, and the people actually seem to have become addicted to mummy dust.

AG: Ah huh.

WSB: And mummy dust was somehow made from people who've died of the most loathsome diseases. It's too bad that Cronenberg didn't see this book, see I only saw it after the film was made. It might have been of interest to him. [William leaves the table for a moment.]

AG: But you know what I was noticing in the *Exterminator!* thing, I was looking at that first chapter. I don't know if that comes in and out very much in the rest of the book because I haven't . . . when you get back here [waiting for William to return]. I was looking at it and

141

I noticed there are a number of voices in that first chapter. The first one, "You need the service?" That's the exterminator himself; then the narrator's voice "During World War One worked for A. J. Cohen Exterminators ground-floor office dead-end street by the river. An old Jew . . . " etc. Then there is . . .

WSB: Then there's the woman.

AG: No, then there's the older brother, "You vant I should spit it right in your face, you vant, you vant you vant?!" That's used in the film isn't it?

WSB: I think so.

AG: Incidentally if you ever did another one [another edition], "The brothers would retreat, shadow-boxing presences invisible to my goyish eyes" . . . it's to my *goyishe* eyes, g-o-y-i-s-h-e not goyish. And the fourth voice is, "They eat it and run around here fat as hawgs!" That's the old southern sheriff or some . . . redneck.

WSB: No, he was a young man.

AG: Oh, OK.

WSB: Well, middle aged, "They be runnin' roun' here fat as hawgs."

AG: Then there's the lady, "Well, come in young man and have a cup of tea, that wind has a bite to it."

WSB: Yes.

AG: That's the fifth voice. Then there's the sixth . . . is a German lady, "Ach so the vine is not enough." Then there's a seventh voice. The college-trained brother, "We'll slap a Board of Health summons on them if we have to. I'll go along with you on this one. Get in the car." Then the eighth voice is the Jewish matron, "Let's not talk about the company. The company makes too much money anyway. I'll get you a drink of whiskey."

WSB: Yes, that's correct.

AG: And that's eight voices, and then the ninth voice, "We serviced an old theatrical hotel. Rooms with rose wall paper, photograph". . . . "Yes that's me there on the left," the old actress. So there's eight, nine voices in that one . . .

WSB: Oh yes.

AG: And then it ends, the first voice, "Exterminator!" So what I was complaining about was the reading of "The Market," the talking asshole, one other routine that they did what was that? Remember?

WSB: Hm?

AG: There was one other routine they ran in the movie, I forgot.

WSB: Not sure.

AG: Anyway, all these voices are missing in the movie when you're . . . they're all different characters . . . but they apparently took this directly almost, this Exterminator . . . The Chinaman shoveling the foot powder [bug powder] and the guy taking arsenic, not addicted, but so used to arsenic he could take it.

WSB: There is a considerable tolerance.

AG: So let's see what other questions we had. How did they, which is to say Gysin, "did he collaborate on the other *Exterminator?* The other book *Exterminator.* That's the cutup book . . . pamphlet.

WSB: Yes, he did.

AG: What was that?

WSB: It was called *Exterminator,* but not with an exclamation.

AG: Yeah. And that was . . . there's rubbing out the word. Exterminator there means rubbing out the word.

WSB: "That petty king's in England, does the party know where I come I kill both friend and foe." Which was the Duke of Buckingham's satire on the conquest of Granada by Dryden, which is all in heroic couplets. It's ridiculous. He would rush in and kill 20 people, like the conquest of Granada.

[Allen laughs.]

WSB: An absurd play in heroic couplets.

AG: Was that Buckingham's play? It was a satire on Dryden?

WSB: Yes. But it was Buckingham's satire on Dryden's *Conquest of Granada.*

AG: But is there any special thing about collaborating on *Exterminator?* Apparently they're interested in that.

WSB: Brion Gysin and I collaborated on *Exterminator.*

AG: But what did you do? Put text out and you both cut it up together, or separate texts that you worked on?

WSB: Well, yeah. We did all sorts of things—we were certainly collaborating. It was definitely a collaborative effort as was *Minutes to Go.*

AG: *Exterminator*'s later.

WSB: Yes, but very shortly later.

AG: So an extension of the same stuff.

WSB: Yes, exactly.

AG: But I guess that [*Exterminator*] had more varieties of cutup than *Minutes to Go.* More applications of it or something, I forgot.

WSB: Well, it was an extension. Extension.

AG: That's what, done in Paris?

WSB: Yeah.

AG: So that would be around 1960-ish.

wsb: Yes.

ag: Now how was the experimental film with Gysin and Antony Balch produced? Did Gysin work on that? Was Balch a friend of his? [*Towers Open Fire* (1963) and *The Cutups* (1967)]

wsb: Yes. Very definitely. How it was produced was . . .

ag: Piecemeal, I think, when we had some money, we put it . . .

wsb: We didn't have much money but the only expenses were the film and the laboratory, but Antony had a wind-up, hand-held 35 millimeter camera. Those cameras were very rare then. They were usually used by film crews that who were going back into somewhere where they didn't have access to regular equipment. They used hand-held . . . but they didn't want a sixteen [millimeter], they wanted thirty-five.

ag: Winding it up, how long can you shoot? Just a minute or less?

wsb: You can shoot, as I remember, several minutes.

ag: That's pretty good then. You can get a several-minute scene, that's about as long a scene . . .

wsb: That camera's probably worth quite a lot of money now.

ag: Well nowadays they have battery-operated . . .

wsb: Yes.

ag: And the new videos actually are almost, or will be soon, of film quality and reducible to cassette. . . . The new Hi-8. Have you heard about those? Practically, twice the size of this little tape machine.

wsb: Oh really?

ag: And they work on a small cassette like a DAT and they're almost of film quality. In fact what Robert Frank has been doing for making films . . . or just making video with Hi 8, like one day

Gregory and I went to see him. Gregory had a poem about his ass, or ass, all the . . . so Robert filmed him with it and then . . . He did a film with Peter, one hour continuous shooting, an hour of real time and the last half hour is Peter, in a manic phase, taking him down into the subway and threatening go walking happily down the subway tracks. So Robert finally had to come out from behind the camera and say wait a minute Peter don't go down there and Peter said OK and it ends with Peter going up. Anyway, so Robert . . . then takes photographs of the video screen of the large video screen and it has a grainy but very recognizable and interesting Robert Frank still photograph. So the quality of the film is good enough for that.

WSB: This is the thing . . .

AG: So that was done where, London, Paris?

WSB: Most of it was done in London, some in Paris, and some in New York.

AG: New York too . . . with Balch?

WSB: Yes, sure.

AG: What year was that?

WSB: That would be . . . I don't remember. It was done . . . That would be in '65, when I was in New York and had that apartment on Centre Street.

AG: Was I around then? I don't think I was even around.

WSB: I don't think so. 210 Centre Street.

AG: Where was I then? '65 I was half a year in socialist countries. Did I miss you in New York then completely?

WSB: I stayed for a while in the Chelsea [Hotel]. Then I moved down to 210 Centre Street. And this loft. I had a loft there.

AG: For some reason or another I have absolutely no recollection. That's when I was in Prague, Cuba, Czechoslovakia, England, so I was about half year or longer away. So how long is that film? It's about half an hour.

WSB: More like twenty minutes.

AG: Yeah. Then the next question they have is why didn't you use the cutup method when you began, well, they say *Western Lands* . . . but in the last trilogy, you didn't use it hardly at all in *Western Lands*.

WSB: I used it to some extent. It wasn't appropriate to the . . . to the structure. Was not appropriate to the structure.

AG: So what was the structure?

WSB: It had a very definite structure. The beginning of *The Western Lands* is just after the death of Carson.

AG: Right, from *The Place of Dead Roads*.

WSB: Yes. At the hands of Joe the Dead. And then developed from there, it makes a circle and comes back.

AG: It comes back to somebody shooting him from a distance in a cemetery or something like that.

WSB: That's *The Place of Dead Roads*. This is much more a tight trilogy.

AG: Yeah.

WSB: The *Cities of the Red Night*, *The Place of Dead Roads*, and *The Western Lands* is a very tight trilogy with the same characters . . . from the beginning to the end.

AG: I don't think I've ever understood the full structure of that. I haven't read it that carefully. I read them separately over a long . . .

WSB: It has a very definite structure.

AG: That evolved during your writing.

WSB: It did indeed.

AG: Who do you read now, among American writers? You read Mailer's *Ancient Evenings.*

WSB: I read Mailer's *Ancient Evenings* with great interest because I was interested in . . . and I used a lot of that in *Western Lands* . . . that is . . .

AG: His explanation of the . . .

WSB: The seven souls structure, which was very helpful to me in *Western Lands* . . . Mailer's. And also in *Place of Dead Roads* too. So that's Mailer. But I read a lot of books for information, like doctor books, spy books . . .

AG: Like this book actually . . . exorcism.

WSB: Exorcism is a subject that interests me and books on shamanism I've read through. I've read all the Don Juan books.

AG: How do they stand up now, the Don Juan books?

WSB: Alright.

AG: Trungpa liked them, the first couple. But by the third or so he didn't take to it. He said it offered no way of connection into the teaching.

WSB: I agree with that. It's too much . . . well, there's no way that you can apply it.

AG: So, he was saying in comparison to the Tibetan system where you actually have a teacher and a method and specific exercises . . .

WSB: Well, you could never find such a teacher and it's a sort of closed system.

AG: Of course, inspired by that you might pick . . . like that young blond kid . . . you might pick up on some teacher who might know a shaman and then get into it that way once you get respect for shamanism from the books.

WSB: Yes, now the shaman . . . being a shaman takes years. They have the vision quest, and first they have to have some . . . the calling, and then they study, or not study, but they have these vision quests and then application, discipline. It goes on for many years. I don't know how long this shaman . . . he's a comparatively young man . . . Black Elk was sixty-five or seventy.

AG: I think he's been fourteen years or so or fifteen . . .

WSB: Well you see, Bill Lyon was twelve years with Black Elk, spent twelve years with him. He gave up a tenured professorship, the coveted tenure, in order to follow through with Black Elk.

AG: You know . . . you read a lot of spy novels. Did you see Mailer's new huge spy novel?

WSB: I have seen it, yes.

AG: Did they give it to you or send you one?

WSB: Yes, it was sent to me.

AG: Did you get to look at it at all?

WSB: *Harlot's Ghost*. Quite something, yes.

AG: Have you read it at all?

WSB: Not all.

AG: Looked a little like Dos Passos. You know that composite of realistic news and news headline and journalism and fiction. But apparently he's come to funny ambivalent feeling about the CIA, both admiration and loathing for some people. Sort of like life itself, complicated and . . . a big complicated organism that you shouldn't kill necessarily.

[William laughs.]

AG: Or it's a replica of a psychological situation in any individual sort of . . .

WSB: Of course the disintegration of the Soviet Union must be a terrible blow to the CIA.

AG: I think so now the atom bomb is spreading like mushroom spores . . . they need to spread like mushroom spores themselves to keep track of who's got the bomb! It complicates matters.

WSB: I suppose so. Yes.

AG: Now everybody can be a little Russia. Everybody can be a little monster. They've already got . . . what . . . you know almost immediately they had North Korea may have the bomb, Pakistan may have the bomb, India may have the bomb, Israel may have the bomb.

WSB: Israel does have the bomb.

AG: South Africa may have the bomb. You know anybody might have the bomb at this point.

WSB: That's right.

AG: Libya's building the bomb . . .

WSB: Oh my God.

AG: The Brazilians! No. The Argentinians or the Brazilians or somebody else is building the bomb.

WSB: Oh my gosh.

AG: So there's no end to it now.

WSB: There is not any end to it. Terrible. Terrible. What they're going to do about it . . .

AG: You know what Harry Smith said?

WSB: No, what?

AG: "Science leads inevitably to ecological degeneration or nuclear disaster. Science is a lie."

WSB: Well, if you say science is a lie, it's not . . .

AG: Well, he was coupling that as part of that one state . . .

WSB: It certainly doesn't lead anywhere except to disaster. I'll agree with him there.

AG: Well, that is to say, lie in the sense that the claims of science to perpetual progress, that's the lie.

WSB: That is, good God, yes. Who believes it anymore?

AG: So who was the first one to denounce that notion of progress? That was the nineteenth-century idea. Probably Elizabethan idea . . . expansion . . .

WSB: No it came in with the Industrial Revolution. Remember Tennyson saying China didn't have our glorious gains? "Better a year of Europe than a century of Cathay." Their glorious gains indeed.

AG: You know who was the first one to denounce the Industrial Revolution and that notion of progress would be Blake. "Dark satanic mills." And that's also his pun for the mills of reason, the mills of mind.

WSB: That was the very beginning of the Industrial Revolution.

AG: Then Rimbaud . . . *le progrès la science la nouveau nobilite . . . Le monde marche. Pourquoi ne tournerait-il pas?*

[La science, la nouvelle noblesse! Le progrès. Le monde marche! Pourquoi ne tournerait-il pas?—"Mauvais Sang" from A Season in Hell]

WSB: Of course. Oh yes. It seems to me that a person would have to be very naive indeed to believe in progress at this point.

AG: Now the Japanese probably do, they've made a lot of progress . . . at the top of the economic heap.

WSB: Well, not progress, they believe in work. The whole idea that science is going to lead . . . where *could* it lead? Where could it possibly lead? Suppose everybody does have enough to eat. I've got enough to eat. Most of us do, where's that get us?

AG: Well, most of us in America do.

WSB: Well, yes, so that doesn't . . . naturally it's a good thing to have enough to eat, I don't want to starve but it's just a beginning, it is no end in itself.

AG: Did you read *The Naked and the Dead*? [Norman Mailer]

WSB: Yes.

AG: How was that?

WSB: It's a good read, a solid novel. I liked *From Here to Eternity* [James Jones] better. There were two novels . . . and I don't know, I just had more sort of . . . it got more of the army.

AG: Yeah, it was more about an army. . . .

WSB: It was an army book and it's about what it means to be a peacetime soldier, a twenty-year man. Someone who's going to make a career of the army.

AG: We're talking about *From Here to Eternity*.

WSB: Whereas Mailer's was about a wartime army with all sorts of miscellaneous people who were not professional army men at all.

AG: Did you ever read *The Catcher in the Rye*?

WSB: Yes. I thought Caulfield, he was a *wretched* specimen. Talk about a wimp. God, he really turned my stomach.

AG: [laughing] Why? I don't remember, I didn't read it.

WSB: Oh, man.

AG: Somehow I'd never gotten into it.

WSB: He just, I don't know, he's just such a nowhere.

AG: Apparently he got a lot of young people who read it into Zen.

WSB: Oh man, did he ever.

AG: Introduced a lot of people to Zen in some funny way. And *The Old Man and the Sea.*

WSB: Yes, now . . .

AG: That's quite something. I thought that was very good when I read it.

WSB: It's good from a mythological point of view. All this talk about the noble fish and all that.

AG: Well the fact that the guy strives so hard and he gets his fish home but it's been eaten to a skeleton by then. So you get what you want . . . But I'm thinking of that lately, that now I have enough money to travel wherever I want but I haven't got the health.

WSB: Well exactly.

AG: I've got enough money to live where I want, but I don't want to move, it's too hard (laughs).

WSB: Exactly, exactly, exactly. I've gotten enough money so I could travel if I wanted to, but I can't.

AG: Why can't you?

WSB: Well, what am I going to do?

AG: Go out and have sexual adventures in Burma.

WSB: Yes, I am not as interested in that any more and there's the question of . . . various questions. My health and so on. It's just . . . [William exits]

AG: Hobbling into the bathroom to take another pill? What pill is that? [To tape recorder]: Now 2 p.m. on March 20th.

WSB: It's nice to be able to buy more or less things that I want. If I see a gun and I want to buy it I can buy it. If I . . . well, like the shaman.

AG: Yes, you can pay the shaman well.

WSB: I can afford to pay the shaman and live comfortably, look after my cats, things like that . . . which is good, but . . .

AG: Actually I like the image in *The Old Man and the Sea*, of striving and succeeding but finding that the success was ghost success.

WSB: Exactly.

AG: In other words, in the long run, after a certain age, the motives for success, pride or oppressing people or getting power . . .

WSB: They're gone.

AG: The desire to have power dissolves.

WSB: That's right, that's right.

AG: The desire to dominate people for love dissolves.

WSB: So many things go.

AG: Luxury dissolves when you realize you can't eat caviar anymore [laughing]. Now I can afford any kind of food I want and I can't eat salt so I get all sorts of foods that are forbidden but I used to love good Roquefort cheese and caviar and now I can buy 'em but I can't eat 'em. On the other hand, it's a relief to realize you can let go.

WSB: That's true too.

AG: It's quite a relief to know that they're not absolutely essential to your existence . . .

[Tape stops.]

AG: [overhears and relates WSB phone call to tape recorder] "Hello George. You want to go out shooting this afternoon?"

WSB: Oh, I see yes . . . We want to go tomorrow because they got a funeral tomorrow . . . OK . . . well, I'll see you soon. Thank you. Bye.

AG: They have a question here: "Does he still do the shooting sometimes?"

WSB: Oh, every week, once a week. It's one of my pastimes, go out and shoot, then go out to the lake.

AG: Are you rowing? You've gotten back to rowing?

WSB: Yes, a little bit.

AG: I have some good photos of you rowing from last time.

WSB: I take it real easy though.

AG: Yeah. Remember that time you rowed the wrong way?

WSB: Yeah. I rowed up around . . . well I rowed for about twenty . . .

AG: Rowed downstream and then we had to row back upstream and that was quite an ordeal I remember. Good thing your heart was in shape then.

WSB: Well, it wasn't, apparently wasn't.

AG: It says here: "Why did you use the pen name William Lee for *Naked Lunch*?" You didn't use it for *Naked Lunch*, that was for . . .

WSB: *Junky*. My parents were still alive.

AG: Yeah, I hadn't intended to publish "Howl" 'cause I didn't want my father to read it . . . but then it seemed to be such a hit in San Francisco that I lost my embarrassment.

WSB: I see, well . . . any other questions?

AG: Ya. "Any influence from Henry Miller?"

WSB: No, I wouldn't say so.

AG: Had you read any of Henry Miller?

WSB: Oh yeah, sure.

AG: 'Cause I didn't until 1955 or '56.

WSB: I read *The Tropic of Cancer.*

AG: When?

WSB: Oh, way back, way back.

AG: Obviously more influence from Miller's original, which was Céline.

WSB: Oh Céline of course, yes. [Louis-Ferdinand Céline.]

AG: Now what is the influence of Céline? In tone, subject matter, sort of unofficial world, but any syntactical or prose influence . . . vernacular?

WSB: The vernacular, the . . .

AG: Slang, 'cause . . . you know he's supposed to be almost untranslatable into English on account of his argot and you're supposed to be untranslatable into Bulgarian on account of your argot.

WSB: No, but just the general . . . I think he's so funny. I read this whole despair and all this . . . and it's a very very funny book. That bit on the ship where they're going to beat him up, he talks them out of it . . .

AG: Yes.

WSB: I thought that was *uproariously* funny.

AG: I always thought that the scene where they wind up . . .

WSB: The whole scene . . . in Africa. Consumed by hatred so he can't stay off the drop dead, poisoned by themselves like scorpions.

AG: [laughing] Is that his phrasing?

WSB: *Yes.* Exactly his words . . . Oh, that is such a funny book. *Death on the Installment Plan* is very funny.

AG: But *Journey to the End of the Night* has the African scene. And also his visit to America, isn't it? To Detroit.

WSB: Yeah, that wasn't as funny to me as the African scene and the scene on the boat.

AG: The scene I remember was vomiting . . . everybody vomiting on the boat till they vomited up the last raspberry.

WSB: That's *Death on the Installment Plan.*

AG: And from *Journey to the End of the Night* the thing I also remember is the sort of black humor, Kafkian entrance into the army, they get drunk and they follow a parade and all of a sudden the gate shuts behind them, and then there's a jump-cut, in the next chapter they're in the middle of a battle and he wakes up and realizes he's surrounded by . . .

WSB: Vicious men . . . yes.

AG: He'd better get out of here.

WSB: And that scene on the boat where the officers try to beat him up, he grabbed their hands and says *vive la France!* It was very difficult [laughing] for anyone to hit him while he was screaming "*vive la France.*" Very funny. "And all this time I felt my self-respect slipping away from me and finally as it were completely gone as it were officially removed [laughing] I've always felt better as a result."

AG: That's quite an imprint.

WSB: Oh man, great. Well, my greatest influence stylistically is Denton Welch.

AG: Yeah, really?

WSB: Yes. Audrey Carson is very much built on, patterned on Denton Welch.

AG: Which book of Welch, *In Youth Is Pleasure?*

WSB: All of them, there were four.

AG: Yeah, I've only read one, *In Youth Is Pleasure.* Remembered that from the forties.

WSB: *Maiden Voyage* . . . I remembered whole passages. Like . . . "His horrid little black pony galloped through the roses showing its awful yellow teeth. How I hated it." Horrid little black pony. So yeah. He's a great influence stylistically. *Maiden Voyage* and *In Youth Is Pleasure*, then some short stories called *Brave and Cruel*, and his diaries, journals.

AG: You have them all here?

WSB: Yes.

AG: Yeah, I should look at them while I'm here.

WSB: Yes. Oh man, he . . . what was the other one? *A Last Sheaf.*

AG: What did he die of?

WSB: He had an accident. He was hit by a car for no apparent reason. *A Voice Through a Cloud*, that's about his illness. He was hit from behind by a car and he never recovered. He was an invalid, he had to use a catheter. He's this invalid, and is taking morphine.

AG: Oh. So from the pleasurable youth to the sudden "old age sickness and death."

WSB: He only made it to thirty.

AG: How did he take it? What was his temperament?

WSB: He kept working but he took it very hard. He loved things, you know to just go have teas, bric-a-brac, he loved bric-a-brac, he enjoyed the details of life very much and this was taken away from him. He was a permanent invalid, and a very difficult invalid.

AG: And did he have money at all to sustain that situation?

WSB: Oh ya, he had . . . wasn't wealthy but his family . . . they lived in . . . his father lived for years in China in Shanghai and was some sort of merchant. So he got enough money to live on. That is, he had an income, that's all. And he had bought a small house, a cottage.

AG: You know it reminds me of Bruce Chatwin, you know . . . have you ever heard anything of him?

WSB: No.

AG: He wrote *The Songlines*. Apparently he was gay and was a very brilliant writer and rather nice looking.

On Star Lake, Douglas County, KS, 30 March 1991

TAPE 6 SIDE A

3/20/92. 2:30 p.m. to 5:45 p.m. Hector Munro (Saki). Cities of the
Red Night. *Get your guns together. Shooting at Fred Aldrich's place.*

WSB: Eccentric gay . . .

AG: Sitwell?

WSB: No.

AG: Oh, um . . .

WSB: I read it I know . . . it's just my name thing. I think that it's
somewhat in the line of Denton Welch but I like Denton Welch much
better. He [whose name Bill can't recall] wrote a thing called *Prancing
Nigger* [Ronald Firbank].

AG: That's a familiar title.

WSB: Yes, and typical of the English gay eccentric, what the hell was
his name? Sort of not quite turn of the century and a little later. I
also have got recently . . . the complete works of Hector Munro.

AG: I never heard of him.

WSB: Well, that was Saki!

AG: Oh, well I never read anything of his.

WSB: Why not? It's great. Saki is another great gay . . .

AG: Oh really?

WSB: Yes, of course.

AG: What were his novels about? Somehow I thought they were animal adventure or something like that.

WSB: No, my dear, he wrote . . .

AG: Or children's stories.

WSB: No no no, God no. He wrote, what is it? *The Unbearable Bassington*, from which I borrowed the concept of the door dog. It follows someone across the threshold as a harbinger of death. His work's all been published in one volume. He was killed in the First World War. It's all about the, you know the real period of St. Louis, [laughing] not St Louis, London society, Edwardian London Society. Lords and ladies. Quite a writer. Also had been known as a short story writer.

AG: When did you read him?

WSB: I read him first when I was a child . . . fifteen, sixteen. And I read *The Unbearable Bassington* when I was in college.

AG: Is that him, Saki?

WSB: Yes.

AG: I remember that title.

WSB: Hector Munro. He was known as Saki.

AG: What else they got here? [Reading question] "How do you evaluate *Cities of the Red Night* among your works?

WSB: Writers are notoriously bad judges of their own work.

AG: That's the beginning of the trilogy.

WSB: Yes.

AG: That was written in Boulder, wasn't it?

WSB: No, it was written more in New York.

AG: "What are you planning right now?" Let's see, we're expecting . . .

wsb: We're expecting Steve and Wes to come over and I have got to get my guns together.

ag: OK. Get your guns together.

wsb: I'm getting 'em together now.

ag: What are you going to bring today?

wsb: Oh, I'm going to bring . . . [He exits, enters.] Let's see . . . now [Putting things down on the table]. . . . .45 revolver . . .

ag: A .45 automatic [*sic*], what make?

wsb: Colt.

ag: .45 what's the revolver, single shot or something?

wsb: No it's not, revolver . . .

ag: Oh it revolves, yes, well I don't know.

wsb: What? Single shot . . . a single shot revolver.

ag: Any rifles?

wsb: No.

ag: Ah. How come?

wsb: Well, I . . .

ag: Have you been using rifles since you . . .

wsb: Not much.

ag: Is it too much of a shock to the body?

wsb: No . . . the body, it's just that . . . not at all . . . I mean a shot gun is much more of a shock, but no. It's just enough if you've got a .45 automatic, .45 revolver, a .38 revolver and a 9 mm. . . . four guns. Plenty to do.

AG: OK, ready. Ready for the wild-western action.

WSB: Yeah. Good. Excellent.

[Resuming at the shooting range at Fred Aldrich's place. Sounds of shooting, checking target.]

WSB: See what I did, Al?

AG: What you got there, Bill?

WSB: Yeah, take it down, might as well.

SL: It's a great group, right on the patch.

AG: Right on the heart, huh?

WSB: Right on the fucking badge.

AG: When did you make these drawings?

SL: Just now.

WSB: What?

AG: When did you make the drawing?

SL: You should do one, Allen.

WSB: Forty-five, the old Colt forty-five.

AG: When did you make the drawing itself?

WSB: Just this second.

AG: Oh, I see. I'd like to try one of those.

WSB: Try it?

AG: Yeah, I'll try it. Let me get rid of this apparatus.

WSB: Alright, here.

AG: That's a Colt .45 you got there huh? OK.

wsb: OK, Allen. Here you are, .45.

ag: Let me get my weapons straight over here. [Under his breath:] Got a .45, just don't point it at me [laughs].

wsb: Now . . . alright, Allen, wait a minute.

ag: Why don't we prepare . . . should I prepare a . . . ?

sl: Do you want to draw a target real quick?

wsb: Go ahead.

ag: OK but should I prepare a painting first, Bill?

sl: Here's the marker, just draw over here . . . .

ag: I think I'll choose vertical. Do my Buddha.

sl: You're going to shoot the Buddha? [Laughs.]

ag: Now I'll shoot my Buddha, Bill.

wsb: He deserves to be shot!

sl: This is tantric, baby.

ag: The heart is on the left side.

wsb: Well, it won't hurt him.

ag: No.

wsb: Don't feel right about shooting a baby. [Allen's Buddha looks like a chubby infant.] Here, Allen, here's you.

ag: I'm about ready, Bill. OK.

wsb: Come here. Come here and let me show you. Now Allen look, come here.

ag: OK, I got my Buddha ready and I'm gonna shoot him right through the heart.

WSB: That's the six [cartridges]. This here . . . It's gonna be a Shanghai . . . target with a . . . I'll draw a chink on there.

AG: Um hm. Maybe you could do some Japanese bashing too.

WSB: Five, six, six . . . [loading gun.] Alright, draw a chink. Somebody else . . . you go ahead and shoot, Wes, I gotta draw a chink here.

SL: (laughing) Allen, your ears.

AG: I gotta do it both sides. So what kind of gun you got there?

WSB: There's my .45 . . . six, six, and seven . . . alright . . . This is a .45 RV automatic, one of the best hand guns ever made. . . . Wes,

WES: Yeah.

WSB: Wanna try this one?

WES: Sure.

WSB: It's ready to go. Now then I can put it on safe. Try the target on my . . .

WES: To the left?

WSB: Yeah, just bring it up . . .

[Tape stops.]

WSB: [To Allen] Pretty mild recoil. But it's the army gun now.

AG: You see the creature I created there.

WSB: Yeah.

AG: What does he look like?

WSB: I think . . . [preparing gun] . . . here, go ahead. You don't cock it, you just pull the trigger.

AG: Alright.

WSB: A longer pull. Not a . . . this is a police gun, plain-clothesman's special, snubby . . . right . . .

[Five shots in rapid succession.]

SL: Draw a flower, each of you guys, and we'll shoot em . . . . First day of spring today.

[Tape stops.]

SL: Allen.

WSB: Yeah go ahead, try it double action. You better get in a little closer.

SL: Yeah.

WSB: That's a little far for that gun. What you gonna shoot?

WES: Maybe the head on the left.

WSB: Alright, go ahead . . . you got some tape?

[Five shots.]

WSB: That's it, five shots. Man that's good. [Checking targets.]

WES: It took me a long time to sight.

WSB: Yeah.

AG: The double action?

WES: Yeah.

AG: What kind is it?

WSB: That grip makes a lot of difference.

WES: Yeah. Feels really nice.

WSB: I'm going in I think, have myself a drink. Gonna have a drink and watch the shooting.

WES: Allen, do you want to do your . . .

AG: That's a tiger. Korean tiger.

SL: You going to shoot the tiger again?

AG: No, that's enough. We got him . . . well, we might shoot the flowers, you wanna shoot that flower, Bill? Why are we picking all these innocent people? At least I made an awful demon to kill.

WSB: Chinaman ain't innocent, he's got a gun up his sleeve, baby.

SL: Up to now it's been Jack the Ripper, FBI agents, sheriffs . . .

WES: Evil sheriffs, crooked cops.

AG: I started with the Buddha . . . I figure Buddha was empty, so it's alright.

WES: Anybody want to shoot some .357?

AG: What is that?

WES: . . . magnums?

SL: Save me a shot of something, I'll shoot my. . . .

AG: Why don't we all use the same . . . ?

WSB: I'm going in and have a drink.

AG: You gotta shoot the flower, did you make a flower?

WSB: I . . . few shots when we come back out.

AG: We got these flowers we gotta shoot first, Bill.

SL: Take one shot, William, with the .357 first.

WSB: What? OK . . . gimme the .357 I'll do it.

AG: What is .357?

WSB: That gun kicks, boy it kicks heavy.

AG: No good?

SL: That's the outside diameter of the bullet and then the magnum is a longer cartridge.

AG: .357 what? millimeters?

WES: Three hundred fifty-seven hundredths of an inch, I think. There's the difference in their cases. One's a little bit longer, and they put a lot more powder in.

AG: So those are hot, the PMC . . .

WES: Very hot.

AG: As distinct from what? What are you loading it with?

WES: .38 specials. So this gun will take both .38 special and .357 magnum.

WSB: What is this? Alright.

WES: .357.

WSB: What am I shooting, a flower?

SL: The flower you drew.

AG: Which flower?

SL: The one on the left.

WSB: Oh, sure.

[One shot.]

TAPE 6 SIDE B

3/20/92. At Fred's house after the shoot. Cats. Dogs in packs; humans in gangs. Chimney sweeping. Allen sings Blake's "The Chimney Sweeper." The Water Babies by Charles Kingsley. Salman Rushdie. Target review. Still interested in sex? Truman Capote.

WSB: Ruski is living now with Steve and Wes right around the corner. Oh, I'm so glad to have him back, he's an incredible cat. Never has he scratched me or bitten me. And once he was in a fight with Fletch. Real . . . I pick him up and carry him away, he didn't scratch me. Now that's really extraordinary.

FRED: What about the Siamese cat that David Cronenberg gave you?

WSB: No, it's not a Siamese cat, it's a Korat. He's with Udo . . . it's known as Boy.

FRED: Is he still as aggressive?

WSB: He's not aggressive. Nips, little love nips.

FRED: That night we were over for dinner I would have called him aggressive, in fact he's the closest thing to a watch cat that I've ever seen.

WSB: He's doing fine. He's doing fine. That's a Korat cat. They cost. This is a pedigreed one, they cost about seven hundred dollars.

WES: Thailand.

WSB: Peter Weller walked in with this bag. He said "it's alive." And opened it up and I couldn't believe it was a cat, I thought it was some kind of a monkey. And . . . well he's settled down beautifully. And Ruski my old Ruski.

SL: [Calling to a dog] Don't bite, just lie there, just lay down. She's got so much energy and she channels it the wrong ways.

WSB: That is a cat that never bites. Never scratches. Ruski. . . .

FRED: Bubba's really a mellow, affectionate cat. Hey, Bubba.

WSB: C'mere, Bubba. And I have that other cat, Spooner. Jumps into my lap and puts his arms, his paws up around my neck.

FRED: He has a loud purr too.

WSB: Oh man, I really love cats . . . Here he is, come here, Bubba.

FRED: We had him neutered the other day.

WSB: Oh, you have to.

FRED: He was running around, well you . . . we talked about it a couple of times. Sooner or later he was going to run off and get nailed by some larger animal or whatever.

WSB: Oh, no . . . it's essential. I made a great mistake in delaying . . . some idea that cat's shouldn't be neutered, it's nonsense. They have to be. Otherwise in the first place they'll cry around the house, they'll spray all over the furniture. They are unhappy and they make everyone else unhappy.

FRED: They want to go out running around all the time and if he didn't come back . . . would be very unhappy 'cause she's so attached to him so . . .

WSB: That's what I mean. No, it's essential. I had to have the Korat neutered and there was another great . . . the cat that came around. James was screaming, "Oh he's getting another cat now." But when I took him to be neutered two people at the vet wanted to take him. And I gave it to my housekeeper Cindy . . . So three people wanted this cat. Beautiful cat, that's a beautiful cat. Coal-black cat . . . . That dog must weigh about sixty pounds?

FRED: Probably, something like that. She's not big for a shepherd at all.

WSB: No.

AG: What's the virtue of the German Shepherd?

WSB: They're very loyal, intelligent.

FRED: They tend to bond onto one person. They bond with you, the one's I've had would lay down their life for you.

AG: I wonder why that is with dogs. They don't bond with dogs? We've bred a species that just bonds with people?

SL: I don't know, I'm sure there's bonding with other dogs.

AG: That's when they ain't got no humans to bond with, or something?

FRED: Well, when dogs get together they naturally form packs. And their personalities change dramatically; they're capable of doing things they wouldn't normally do on their own.

AG: Just like human beings!

FRED: Exactly.

WSB: That's one of the dangers of the woods is feral dogs.

FRED: I've had friends . . . their livestock . . . dog pack suddenly shows up and kills all their goats.

WSB: I remember a story about a kid that went out hunting and when he didn't come back finally his uncle and his father went out. They were armed only with 9mm pistols and here's the kid up a tree in the middle of a field and the dogs, about seven or eight of them [inaudible] with a single- shot rifle. He'd lost his package of cartridges on the way up the tree. So he had one shot and killed one dog with that through the top of the head. To show how tough they were, they opened up and they shot a number of these dogs. One was found a half mile away shot twice through the guts, and they went and found another a mile away shot. They are tough. They take a lot of killing. This is a 9mm pistol.

AG: What accounts for the transformation of personality of both dogs and humans when they get in packs?

WSB: Well wait a minute that's . . . not possible it's not possible. These dogs it so happened were raised as guard dogs, they were vicious.

AG: But he was pointing out that when dogs in the country get into packs, their personalities . . . We're talking about bonding.

FRED: Even friendly household dogs when they get in packs can do this.

WSB: Sure, yeah sure.

AG: In the city it's all these little kids from poor families are very gentle with their families, when they get out on the street go out there and rob or kill just because they have the pack power.

FRED: To steal a jacket or something like that?

AG: Or just to bash a faggot. There was that one case.

FRED: Or just to shoot somebody, I mean drive-by shooting.

SL: Just to be a member of the gang. A lot of these are initiation shootings; you have to do this in order to be accepted into the group.

[Tape stops. Fred talks about his chimney sweep business. Conversation turns to nineteenth-century sweeps in London.]

WSB: All kinds of cancer . . . particularly scrotum cancer.

FRED: Chimney sweeps would send young boys down the chimneys.

WSB: The middle of the nineteenth century but . . .

FRED: Frequently they couldn't fit . . . would often take most of their clothes off, and so their actual bodies would be covered with soot.

AG: Yes.

FRED: And they had scrotum cancer.

WSB: They had a high incidence of scrotum cancer.

AG: [Sings his setting of William Blake's "The Chimney Sweeper." He sings the whole thing correctly but for a word here and there. I have put in the standard text.]

> When my mother died I was very young,
> And my father sold me while yet my tongue
> Could scarcely cry " 'weep! 'weep! 'weep! 'weep!"
> So your chimneys I sweep & in soot I sleep.
>
> There's little Tom Dacre, who cried when his head
> That curled like a lamb's back, was shaved, so I said,
> "Hush, Tom! never mind it, for when your head's bare,
> You know that the soot cannot spoil your white hair."
>
> And so he was quiet, & that very night,
> As Tom was a-sleeping he had such a sight!
> That thousands of sweepers, Dick, Joe, Ned & Jack,
> Were all of them locked up in coffins of black;
>
> And by came an Angel who had a bright key,
> And he opened the coffins & set them all free;
> Then down a green plain, leaping, laughing they run,
> And wash in a river and shine in the Sun.
>
> Then naked & white, all their bags left behind,
> They rise upon clouds, and sport in the wind.
> And the Angel told Tom, if he'd be a good boy,
> He'd have God for his father & never want joy.

> And so Tom awoke; and we rose in the dark
> And got with our bags & our brushes to work.
> Though the morning was cold, Tom was happy & warm;
> So if all do their duty, they need not fear harm.

FRED: What's that from?

AG: William Blake.

WSB: William Blake.

AG: *Songs of Innocence.* "The Chimney Sweep."

WSB: Now some alert physicians noticed this correlation between chimney sweeps and scrotal cancer.

AG: Now why scrotal?

FRED: Maybe they didn't wash sufficiently. They didn't shower when they went home or when they did, they didn't wash correctly and a lot of the dirt ended up in the dark places. Who knows?

WSB: Who knows?

AG: Actually the chimney sweep's boy was an archetypal bit of exploitation and persecution, you know, like *low* . . . was one of the great classic things, I think Dickens?

WSB: I think the guy with the top hat would put the boy down the chimney.

SL: *Water-Babies.* He started out as a chimney sweep.

WSB: What?

SL: That book *The Water-Babies,* written by [Rev. Charles] Kingsley. The little character of Tom . . . with a really mean master.

WSB: Oh yeah.

AG: What's a water baby?

WSB: Well it's a . . .

SL: It's like a suicide; he jumped in and turned into a little water baby and had gills; it's like a little fairy story.

AG: I see.

WSB: The water babies that I saw were about that long, in my water baby book, about that big and . . .

AG: Foot and a half, two feet long.

WSB: Foot and a half long.

SL: Look like little babies with gills.

WSB: Had gills. They'd dive into the water. Someone tried to catch one. And he dived into the water. *The Water-Babies.*

AG: But that's quite an image of . . . right out of Burroughs. The man in the top hat stuffing a little naked boy down a chimney.

WSB: Yes . . . they had a boy go down there.

WES: At some point they would tie a rope around a goose's foot . . .

SL: Yeah, that was the famous story . . .

AG: Oh, send the goose down . . . .

[Tape stops]

FRED: Well, if you're allergic to cats or dogs, boy you got lots of dog hair around here.

AG: It's just the cat as far as I know, though I used to have cats when I was a kid. I was fond of cats . . . I'm wondering to what extent it's psychological.

FRED: I don't know.

[Tape stops. Picks up with talk of Salman Rushdie.]

FRED: That was one of the times when the world should have risen up and said "Alright this is where we draw the line."

AG: Yeah.

FRED: When somebody can banish somebody from existence because of that, and I felt that they really abdicated the responsibility . . .

WSB: They put themselves in the position of barbarians . . . Can you imagine the pope putting out a contract on somebody?

FRED: Well, in the old days the pope did that sort of thing on a regular basis.

WSB: I know, but not recently.

FRED: But in this day and age only the . . .

AG: It would be considered shocking.

SL: Only Khomeini . . .

AG: Whose gun is that?

FRED: That's a staple gun. That's mine.

WSB: That's a staple gun. That isn't a gun.

AG: Oh, that's for stapling the targets up.

WSB: Yeah, just you now . . . alright this we'll take back with us. Everybody was doing very well. You see what Allen did with my .45 revolver?

AG: That's an easy gun to shoot, but once I got the other guns I was way off.

FRED: Of all the guns that one seems to do the best in just about everyone's hands. It's very user-friendly.

WSB: I'm not talking about the Smith and Wesson. I'm talking about the other one, a single action. With the interchangeable cylinders, they have . . .

FRED: It's not a Smith and Wesson.

WSB: No it's not; it's a Ruger. It has a seven-and-a-half-inch barrel, it has interchangeable cylinders: .45 APC or .45 long Colt.

FRED: The heavy barrel tends to steady the hand.

WSB: Oh man, this is easy. Yeah, it's truly a great gun. No, I didn't bring out the Smith and Wesson.

FRED: Looks like you've been painting again.

WSB: Look, I shot . . .

AG: What happened? You shot a balloon and it splattered . . .

FRED: Spray paint can wasn't it?

WSB: Spray paint can, spray paint can.

AG: Where was the can, up there?

WES: Up with the targets.

AG: And it sprayed all the way out.

SL: It probably had enough propellant in it that it acted like a rocket . . .

WSB: The whole can came out here, and I'm trying to get away . . .

[Goodbyes. Tape stops.]

FRED: Wes is going to help me out of a little computer conundrum.

AG: Oho. You good at that, Wes?

WES: That's part of my . . .

AG: Amazing, alchemy and computers.

WSB: He's good at a lot of things. You know, anything that's mechanical.

[In the car.]

AG: My Chinese roommate [Jack Shuai] is good at that too. Any little thing like . . . I've been in that apartment fifteen years and three of the four burners on the stove didn't work so he was there two days and he took out a little screwdriver, opened it up, said it needed a little more air. Adjusted it very slightly. It took fifteen years for somebody to come along who knew enough about it to do that.

WSB: Jesus Christ . . . I love this with the new grips, feels good. Before that I didn't . . . not to shoot . . . like using the double action, I find that I can really put it in the . . . .

AG: So who would you like to go to bed with at this point? Anyone?

WSB: No one.

AG: Pardon me?

WSB: No one, I'm not interested in sex at this point, very little.

AG: Do you have wet dreams?

WSB: No.

AG: Or dreams.

WSB: What?

AG: Do you have sexual dreams at all?

WSB: No.

AG: Not even that? I seem to be still in the running somehow.

WSB: Well, it's good for *you* but . . .

AG: Well, neither good nor bad; it's just there, you know.

WSB: Bravo, bravo.

AG: Partly because I'm not that interested and so things sort of tend to come to me now.

WSB: Bravo, but I don't . . .

[Tape stops. What follows appears be about Truman Capote.]

WSB: . . . forgiveness for anything that he did.

AG: How'd he get away with it? I don't know.

WSB: Well, he gets away with it because people allow it. Because he demands and he gets.

AG: Yeah, but Gregory didn't do it on that scale. I mean, he was doing it with Jacqueline Kennedy and Jean Stein and . . .

WSB: And who?

AG: Well, all these rich society people. With the millionaires. Joan Rivers, people with giant mansions and apparently he was their darling or pet all during that time. A very high social world where he was behaving this way. With, you know, suicide attempts or overdosing . . .

WSB: All kinds of things.

AG: . . . on valium and whatever. Apparently he was outrageously fucked up in peoples' apartments and . . .

WSB: I'd like to see this. Where is this volume? You got it?

AG: Not with me, no. I have it at home, yes.

WSB: Who wrote it?

AG: It was one of those big things that came around the same time as yours and mine. One of those great big . . . [This is likely *Capote: A Biography*, by Gerald Clarke (1988).]

WSB: I'd like to see it.

AG: And he had an older . . . who did he have as a friend? He had several people who took care of him, ex-lovers or something.

WSB: Yeah, who really looked after him, carried him home and so on . . .

AG: And he was apparently constantly on their case, bugging them. Did you ever read any of his writing?

WSB: Well, of course, I read the Voices of the Rose [*The White Rose?*] other . . .

AG: I read something of his very early that had very good sounding prose. *Other Voices* . . .

WSB: Oh man, and his short stories, "Miriam" [1945], all those were great. *Other Voices, Other Rooms* [1948]. And I read . . .

AG: Did you read . . . remember the last book which is all about society people?

WSB: No, I didn't . . . it wouldn't have meant anything to me . . . I don't care about their . . . unveiling, but [to cat] oh, shut up, what's the matter? So I get . . . yet *Other Voices, Other,* what was the other?

AG: "The Headless Hawk." Was that a story or something?

WSB: Short stories . . . very good.

At home on the couch in the garden, Lawrence, KS, 28 May 1991

TAPE 7 SIDE A

3/21/92. 7 p.m. Truman Capote continued. Recalling the shoot.
Everyone you ever slept with. Looking at AG's photos
from his previous visit (1991). Signing photos, paintings, and targets.
Ron Hubbard. The commandos' instinctive shooting method.

AG: Did you know [Chandler] Brossard?

WSB: Yes, he lived in Morton Street.

AG: Oh, I see he was working at *The New Yorker*. He was always talking about Capote as a beautiful . . . he thought he was good-looking?

WSB: Yes. A beautiful boy.

AG: Working there.

WSB: Yes. And he is first published . . .

AG: Did Dave [Kammerer] ever meet him?

WSB: I don't think so. His first published work was a short story called "Miriam," you remember. Well, it's about . . . this . . . woman . . . who had a sort of ghost girl in her house . . . a familiar. There was such a case described in here. A familiar that no one else can see. But they're very demanding and virtually make life intolerable for the person that they are victimizing or moving in on. She kept asking for sweets and stuff and then . . . people came and searched her apartment. The end of it was these people had searched her apartment . . . then she heard a dull . . . They go out . . . and she heard a dull voice saying . . . hello. Hello.

[Telephone rings.]

AG: Burroughs residence. Hi Jim, just got back . . . very good . . . Here's Bill.

WSB: [Taking the phone] We were just out to . . . a nice shoot . . . Yeah, sure we did . . .

[Tape stops.]

WSB: You know he has his own guns that he shoots and he's a good shot.

AG: Did Bob Wilson have experience with guns?

WSB: Oh, yes.

AG: How come?

WSB: I don't know, he comes from Texas.

AG: Oh, he comes from Texas.

WSB: He did pretty well. But he managed to tear his hand shooting a 45 automatic. You know when that slide slams back you got to be sure to keep your hand out of the way. Here. Oh . . . you don't smoke . . .

AG: Oh no I smoke that . . . grass.

WSB: Sure, 'sgood grass . . . You did very well for someone that doesn't . . . hasn't had any practice at all. You were putting those .45's right into the kill zone from here to the door, which is about practical pistol range. Fifteen feet. Most actual encounters . . . gun encounters take place at ten feet and under.

AG: Ah ha.

WSB: This talk of practice at fifty feet is very unrealistic. From here to the door is a reasonable pistol range for practical purposes. But anyway, you did very well—you kept them all in the kill zone with a .45, that's not a .22, that's a .45 you were using.

AG: Yeah.

wsb: The only gun that to me really has a real kick that's a little bit unpleasant is that .357 magnum. The one that. . . .

ag: That I shot at the end.

wsb: Yeah, that kicks, baby, it really kicks.

ag: You know I opened this package of photographs. What they are is mostly Xeroxes of stuff I took last time . . . not the photographs so much as the contact prints, so I can choose from it. I'm months behind in getting this stuff printed up 'cause I just shoot too much.

wsb: Yeah. I've gotta . . . oh, you've got a knife.

ag: I don't want to hurt my hand.

wsb: Yes.

[Allen's package of photocopies of photographs from his visit of 1991 has arrived.]

ag: You got one of those openers, staple remover?

wsb: No . . . I . . .

ag: They're useful . . . reach inside one of these things, if the staples are not removed, I scratch my hand. . . . You got any [marijuana] left there?

wsb: Oh yeah, take the rest of it. I've got more . . . there's plenty more.

ag: What do you mean I don't smoke? I'm an old hippie [laughs]. I don't smoke much though.

wsb: I do. I smoke quite a bit. It gives me a map of time. It helps me in every way. It helps me to see things, you know.

ag: To see pictures, yeah . . . .

[Allen opens the package.]

WSB: What's that?

AG: It's a long poem that I wrote.

WSB: I want to tell you it's long, hah . . .

AG: It's quite a poem.

WSB: Yeah.

AG: It's a complete account of everybody I ever slept with.

WSB: Oh, for God's sakes.

AG: Written in four hours in the middle of the night.

WSB: I should say that that would be very long indeed. Ha ha ha.

AG: Well, I have the typescript, but they sent me this so I could correct the typescript . . . original. What have we here? Oh.

WSB: Sometimes I don't know if you want to be reminded of everyone you ever slept with.

AG: Well I couldn't . . . one night, after I had that heart attack, I was re-collecting all the people I ever slept with and I said well, if I'm going to write this down I'd better get up now at two in the morning and write it down.

[Looking at the photos from May 1991.]

SL: That's beautiful.

WSB: Isn't that nice?

SL: Just beautiful.

WSB: That's great.

SL: Is this one of yours?

AG: Yeah, that's the . . .

SL: Hm . . . it could be anywhere.

WSB: Could be anywhere.

SL: It's a magical scene.

WSB: It's very magical.

SL: That's good.

WSB: Look at that.

SL: Look at that cat!

WSB: This is out at the lake.

AG: Yeah.

SL: Oh, I love that one of William on the couch.

WSB: Yeah. That's a good picture.

AG: It's not that good.

WSB: Not . . .

AG: Not dark enough there.

WSB: Is that me? Good *God*. I'd never have known myself. Grinning in this sort of hat . . . Like a top hat. That's interesting . . . you know . . . like a young vagabond. That one I don't find particular . . . I look like an old monk or something in that one.

AG: Oh, there are two of those I see . . .

WSB: This is the best . . . that's the real . . . that one, this one . . . that one. This one is strange. That not so special. There's one other in here that . . .

AG: One was on the couch in the wilderness or in the back yard.

WSB: No. This one. That one . . .

AG: Your head's tilted to one side when you're leaning on the balcony with the lake in the background.

WSB: This looks very sort of . . . nineteenth century, like a . . . you got a man with his worldly possessions.

AG: You look like a railroad man.

WSB: Don't you like that one?

SL: Yeah, old conductor.

WSB: The old conductor, exactly . . . The old railroad man with train whistles in the background.

SL: Oh, that's great, look at that.

WSB: Yeah. Now that . . . you see this one first, then this one . . . no wait a minute, I'll tell you the order they go in.

SL: I think that's one of the most beautiful shots of William I've ever seen.

WSB: Wait a minute.

AG: Well, unfortunately it's not very clear.

WSB: Well . . . here, this one, come in this order, this one, the old railroad man, then no . . . well . . . this and that one.

AG: Reclining and very sharply visible . . . on the couch.

WSB: And then that one.

SL: The railroad man almost looks like a character in this other man's imagination.

WSB: Yeah, exactly . . . that's a great view.

AG: Well I'll get you a couple of copies of those, in fact you can keep those.

WSB: Yeah. And I like that.

AG: Yeah.

WSB: That's a great picture. And I like that.

AG: You can keep all these. You keep these, I'll sign em.

WSB: Yeah . . . .

[William and Allen are variously signing art work, photographs, books, and targets from the day's shooting.]

WSB: I think that's nice, don't you?

SL: Look at how great that looks.

WSB: Yes. Real spontaneous, you know.

AG: Is that ink and . . . ?

WSB: Just ink, black ink. Now . . . you know there's the story of the Zen painter who was contracted to do a painting and he thought about it . . .

SL: He's going to take a picture. Could you hold the brush?

WSB: Where's my brush? Gimme my brush . . . that ain't the brush . . .

SL: You want the real thing . . .

WSB: Anyway, so he said, "It'll take me ten years to do this painting." So after ten years were up he sent. . . . an empty canvas, and the emperor said ,"What are you talking about, it's going to take . . . what have you been doing?" And the man takes his brush, *shwew*, quarter of a second. He said, "That has taken me ten years to do." Brion also, when people asked him how long did it take you to do this painting, he would say, well, sixty-eight years, being his age. And remember Genet. They said when did you start to write, he said, "At birth."

SL: While you're signing, you want to go in and sign these gunshot pieces you did today?

WSB: Sure.

SL: And date them, I've got them out right here.

WSB: Why not . . . have you got . . . here . . . I've got . . . this is the easy signing.

SL: Here's a pencil.

WSB: I've got this.

SL: A pencil on these pieces.

WSB: Pencil on these pieces.

SL: This one you'll sign over here by your flower.

WSB: Yes . . . Magnum. Long shot stopper. . . . equinox, 3 . . . 21 . . . 92. . . . *Mas mas mas*, bring more . . .

SL: This character, really plugged him, there's a beautiful group . . . frames it one, two, three, four, five.

[William mumbles.]

SL: Here's your last one.

WSB: Look at that . . . ain't that the *end*?

AG: Ron Hubbard there?

WSB: Yes. Yes. That's L. Ron Hubbard. They pretend he isn't dead. He died ten years ago or eight years ago . . . *sheeit*. They refuse to admit that . . . alright . . . alright hang on. *Message!* à la what the fuck is his name? It's not Applegate . . . it's Colonel Firbanks [(*sic*) Fairbairn, see note 43.] Whatever . . . à la Colonel . . . Remember his name . . . à la . . . Colonel old Shanghai copper . . . *up to eye level and shoot!*

SL: This you did two rounds.

WSB: I know . . . yeah, he's got a broom-handle Mauser up his sleeve. You see, he'd go around like this. And the cop would say . . . Pow! In one year he lost ten officers . . . just give him a little . . .

[SL laughs.]

wsb: Ain't that cute?

sl: Allen, you want to sign yours while we got this out?

ag: Sure.

wsb: So he decided he had to get something practical going and he got that method . . . bringing it up to eye level and shooting.

sl: That's the colonel's method?

ag: Who was this?

wsb: What the hell was his name . . . Colonel . . . Colonel . . . what the hell was that guy's name? Firbank, no not Firbanks. He also devised the commando.

wsb: There was another guy named Applegate, and they sort of got together, you know.[43] He and Applegate, they hit it off right away. . . . Tight grip on the gun, then you bring it up, as soon as it gets to eye level on the target, you shoot, you start shootin'. Yeah. No aiming, nothing like that, there's no time for that. You bring it up and shoot.[44]

ag: What kind of gun was that, that I was shooting? . . . The same magnum?

wsb: Um, yeah, that was the three five seven magnum. .357 magnum and boy that's the . . . s'posed to be the best one-shot stopper. .357 magnum, the best one-shot stopper.

---

43 After the May 1940 disaster at Dunkirk, Winston Churchill called for a new force of small units to inflict terror on the Germans and boost morale at home. Lieutenant Colonel Dudley Clarke had earlier suggested a "commando" force, and his proposal was now implemented. Raids commenced in June of 1940. US Army Lieutenant Rex Applegate was recruited in 1942 by the OSS to teach American intelligence officers to kill in close situations. He trained with British commando officer W. E. Fairbairn (William's "Firbanks"). Applegate's 1943 manual *Kill or Get Killed* is still used by US Marines.

44 Commando instructors teach "instinctive shooting": in a fast-moving, close-combat situation, the shooter keeps both eyes open, focuses his eyes on a particular spot on the enemy individual's torso, and without shifting focus to use the gun sights, quickly raises the gun and shoots.

AG: You mean stopper in the sense of stop somebody.

WSB: Yeah. One shot and he's down.

SL: You can really feel that thing blow out, man.

WSB: Oh man. When you. . . .

SL: It's intense.

WSB: Alright, this is for me.

AG: That's mine. Well, you shot it too, you shot that, you shot that.

SL: Maybe you should both sign it.

WSB: One, two, three, four, five; look, mine, one, two, three, four, five.

SL: First one right in the eye.

WSB: Yeah, OK.

AG: Why don't you circle yours, William?

WSB: No money! Damn your eyes! Damn your eyes! William. William [drawing out the syllables as he signs the target picture] ESSS-BEE-YOU-ARE-ARE-OH-YOU-G-H-ESSS! Threeee, twenty-one, nineteen-ninety-two. There y'are.

One, two, three, four, five for me. No that was the first shot that I did. One, two, three, four, five. One, two, three, four, five. One, two, three, four, five. One, two, three, four, five. . . . You said fire one shot. I fired one shot and hit him in the eye. You took over, and yours went over here. One, two, three, four, five. . . . Oh fuck it. Anyway it's good enough. Take it away. Take it away!

SL: Are they signed?

WSB: We signed the son of a bitch now take him away.

SL: There's one more here, Lord Buddha.

WSB: Just a second now [scribbling].

SL: That's a fun one.

AG: I like this one . . . 'Cause it's got a lot of energy.

WSB: Yeah. Now . . .

AG: Have you read any of my writing on it?

SL: I think that's what makes it, all these motifs. Now this was shot and drawn by Allen.

WSB: Alright, there you are, one, two, three, four, five; one, two, three, four, five . . . now this [writing and speaking:] .45 A B C Ruger revolver, seven-and-a-half-inch. OK? You write your name below that. You've got five shots there, all in the kill zone. And there you are.

Burroughs at home, Lawrence, KS, 29 May 1991

TAPE 7 SIDE B

Looking at photos. Quoting Sara Teasdale. Louis Ginsberg.
Sappho. Witter Bynner. Poets of Greenwich Village 1910s.
Adelaide Crapsey. E. A. Robinson.

SL: Oh my God. Jesus. That's an intense photograph.

WSB: Where's my mouth? [They are looking at photocopies, so the images are somewhat obscure.]

AG: This is the top of your head.

WSB: I understand. What am I doing, just . . . ?

AG: You're painting.

SL: Your face is down in here. Looks like you're bowing to the god of painting.

AG: Couldn't quite get your hand in there unfortunately.

SL: Looks like a full bow, doesn't it?

AG: Well, just painting, just intense . . .

WSB: There's another.

AG: That's upside-down.

WSB: I daresay, same way.

AG: The hands are closer to the . . . Yeah, that's a better one 'cause you can see the whole room.

SL: How'd you get that angle, Allen, through the window?

AG: Yes.

SL: Where were you?

[Allen says something inaudible.]

WSB: That's good; I like that.

AG: Now this is looking at the results.

SL: I like that; that is so characteristic of William viewing a piece, that's a good one.

WSB: That's good . . .

AG: OK turn 'em all over. We're now on twenty-six . . . quietly contemplating it.

SL: William's got such a great profile.

WSB: The picture looks good in here, look at the three-dimensional quality . . . the picture's really coming out.

AG: Yeah.

WSB: In a three-dimensional . . .

AG: Finished your observations of twenty-nine, or just begun? I don't know. Well, making a comment I think . . . you lit a cigarette.

WSB: That's dates it before June 15th cause that's when I stopped . . . came out of the hospital and stopped smoking forever.

AG: What have we got now? Thirty. But you thought that the car dated it, but in twenty years the car will look dated and that'll be alright.

WSB: Possibly . . . . That's not distinguished.

AG: But some of those are nice, there's that sequence.

WSB: I realize that.

AG: The ones painting and the ones rowing I like.

WSB: Yeah, s'alright . . . .

AG: OK. Well, apparently these look alright.

WSB: Fine.

AG: Now this is what? . . . Now this one was the last one in the garden by yourself, I wonder if that will serve . . . it's not in such good focus, but I can blow it up anyway.

WSB: Doesn't have to be in good focus.

AG: How would this be for the Japanese [magazine journalists]?

WSB: That looks very Japanese.

SL: They would respond to that, because of the nature.

WSB: Respond to that very very well. Very definitely.

AG: What should that say as a caption? The couch . . .

WSB: Say . . . say . . . [writing].

AG: Yeah, that's a surprise. I didn't realize that. I must have been standing up or something. I must have gotten up on something.

WSB: All the best paintings are surprises, naturally.

SL: What time of year was that?

WSB: It's got to have been fairly warm.

AG: Summer . . . I think it's May 28, 1991, almost a year ago. It was already spring, summer, when does summer begin?

SL: June 21st or so.

WSB: No, wait a minute.

AG: Funny, all that time and trouble, it's worth it just to get one nice picture like that.

WSB: I've used that old quote from Sara Teasdale: "The things we've never had remain. It is the things we have that go."

AG: Um hm. "The sweetest kiss I ever had was one I did not take." Louis Ginsberg.

SL: Is that your father's line?

AG: "The sweetest . . . "

WSB: Sara Teasdale, now she was a St. Louis lesbian, you know.

AG: Oh, I had no idea she was a lesbian.

WSB: What! Holy shit, man, can you read her poems and not know she's a lesbian?

AG: No, I'm afraid . . .

WSB: Holy mother of God. Requiem for a nun ["Effigy of a Nun"]. "Infinite tenderness [gentleness], infinite irony are hidden forever in her closed eyes, who must have learned in her long loneliness how empty wisdom is, even to the wise."

AG: Mmmm, not bad.

WSB: You think that's written by a straight woman! You crazy man, you think that. Jesus Christ. It's said that she drowned herself in a bathtub.

SL: Is that right?

WSB: That's what I heard. Sara Teasdale, she came from St. Louis.

SL: Did she stay in St. Louis?

WSB: I don't know. She looks like she's on her way to Greenwich Village, baby, to me. Don't you think so?

AG: "The only things we ever have are those we do not keep" . . . .

WSB: "We have lived enough to know the things we never had remain, it is the things we have that go." I used that as the last line in something I wrote about the Beat Hotel. What are you doing? I'm just eating. [Allen is taking photographs.]

AG: Trying to stop time, unsuccessfully.

WSB: The things I have never had remain. The food that I have never had remain. Remain is the food that I have that goes. Well, anyway, yes, Sara Teasdale, the St. Louis nightingale.

AG: Is that what it was? Well "Paterson's principal poet" Louis Ginsberg was a great admirer of Sara Teasdale, and wrote poems on the same theme, including the one I quoted, "It is the ships I never sail that fly the most afar . . . "

WSB: Now wait a minute . . .

AG: "The sweetest kiss I ever had was one I did not take."

WSB: That sounds like her.

SL: Lesbianism was never mentioned by your dad?

AG: Well, I don't think people knew about it in the Poetry Society of America in those days . . . Did you overcook this or is it just naturally soggy?

SL: This was limp when I cooked it, because it was a little old . . . artichokes . . . .

WSB: Sara Teasdale should've gone to New York and had the tail of Edna St. Vincent Millay.

AG: *Really?* Where did you hear that?

WSB: I said she should have.

SL: A match made in heaven.

AG: Did Sara Teasdale ever get to New York?

WSB: I don't know. I know that she was said to have drowned herself in the bath tub. I don't know any of the details. But she was quite a poet.[45]

AG: In my childhood she was one of the main poets I read, because my father grew up with her, or on her.

WSB: He did what?

AG: Grew up poetically with that school of poetry and that kind of poetry.

WSB: Yeah, sort of real manic lesbian poet . . . a thousand . . . "When nothing is left, the old year dying, why are you bringing me down to the sea? The tide is low and the wind is high . . . nothing is left but the old year dying, why did you bring me down to the sea . . . a thousand wings sweep out of sight . . . " sometimes I lose it. But she had a good sense of rhyme you know, and all that. The requiem for a nun ["Effigy of a Nun"], boy, "infinite tenderness, infinite irony are hidden forever in her closed eyes, who must have learned too well in her long loneliness how empty wisdom is, even to the wise."

> [Infinite gentleness, infinite irony
> Are in this face with fast-sealed eyes,
> And round this mouth that learned in loneliness
> How useless their wisdom is to the wise . . . .]

AG: Very good.

WSB: Very good. Very lesbian.

AG: Well, I'm sure that heterosexuals have the same insights occasionally. Or do they?

---

45   Sara Teasdale was courted by the poet Vachel Lindsay (a Ginsberg favorite), but married Ernst Filsinger in 1914. They moved to New York City's Upper West Side in 1916. She won a Pulitzer Prize for her book *Love Songs* in 1918. In 1929, she filed for divorce. After the divorce she reconnected with Lindsay who was by then married. Lindsay killed himself in 1931. Teasdale took an overdose of sleeping pills in 1933.

SL: Heterosexuals? Insights?

WSB: That isn't the point. There's a certain poetry . . . and once you read a fucking line of it, you know it's written by a lesbian. You know . . . the great lines of Lesbos, of . . . Sappho herself. Of course, there's Byron's lines [in "Don Juan"] "Lesbos where burning Sappho the lesbian nightingale loved and sang. The isles of Greece the isles of Greece . . . eternal sunshine bathes them yet but all except their sun has set."

> [The isles of Greece, the Isles of Greece!
> Where burning Sappho loved and sung,
> Where grew the arts of war and peace,
> Where Delos rose, and Phoebus sprung!
> Eternal summer gilds them yet,
> But all, except their sun, is set.]

As for burning Sappho the lesbian nightingale, she wrote this great little poem "it is the middle of the night. The something something sets in the Pleiades, and time passes, time passes and I lie down alone." [Fragment 8.]

> [The moon is set. And the Pleiades.
> It's the middle of the night.
>   Time passes.
> But I sleep alone.]

AG: That's the famous Sapphic fragment.

WSB: Yes, yeah, the lesbian nightingale, baby. She lived on the island of Lesbos. Which is still there, a pretty big island.

SL: Are they all lesbians on Lesbos?

AG: Tourist lesbians.

WSB: I don't know . . . I've never been there.

AG: I've been about thirty miles away. It's right off the shore of Asia Minor.

WSB: Yeah. It's one of the larger islands. It's not like the place I was in . . . Thasos was small.

AG: That's amazing you know Sara Teasdale by heart.

WSB: St. Louis.

AG: What was her story around St. Louis? Was she known by the literate people as being . . . was she alive when you . . . yeah, she was alive in the twenties . . .

WSB: S'pose so. I know nothing about her life. Nothing whatever. I got her poems and read them.

AG: But where did you get her books from, or who? Was that when you were there still?

WSB: Yeah, sure.

SL: Was she like taught in schools?

WSB: Yeah. No, I don't think so. I know nothing about her, except that she . . .

AG: Where did you hear that she drowned in the bath tub?

WSB: I don't know. I'd like to know more.

SL: You'll have to check her out.

AG: There is a biography of her.

WSB: What finally happened to Witter Bynner?[46]

AG: He was living in Taos or Santa Fe.

WSB: Santa Fe, sure. I know that.

AG: And died there about maybe ten years ago or longer.

WSB: Oh more than that.

---

46 Harold Witter Bynner (1881–1968), American poet.

SL: Maybe in the sixties.

WSB: Must be more than . . . [He died in 1968.]

AG: And he left behind a certain amount of money.

WSB: Yeah, the Witter Bynner Foundation.

AG: And that gives a prize to the American Academy of Arts and Letters. And I think Antler got it one year.

SL: Where is Antler?

AG: Milwaukee.

WSB: You know that Witter Bynner was a complete alcoholic; he was drunk from morning till night.

AG: Did you ever know him?

WSB: No.

SL: But your mom took you to his health clubs, right?

WSB: When I was an adolescent, I went in to Santa Fe with my mother and my boyfriend . . .

SL: And your boyfriend.

WSB: Yes.

SL: Really? I didn't know that.

WSB: Well he wasn't much of a boyfriend. At any rate, so she had known him I think in St. Louis.

AG: Hm.

WSB: I had a book of his poetry that I wanted him to sign. Here I am, a boy of sixteen and I wanted . . . "Red leaped the moon from behind the black rim of night. And soon it was silver forever and there was no change." Big deal. And . . .

AG: What poem is that, by Bynner?

WSB: Witter Bynner.

AG: What was the first line in that, I didn't . . .

WSB: "Red leaped the moon from behind the black rim of night and soon it was silver forever and there was no change." What was another . . . ? Oh. "I threw the dice with death. I won. But death only smiled" . . . some kind of a toad winked its eyes. "Then I asked shall death belittle are we much my brother said, oh beloved who shall care?" Stuff like that, pretty romantic stuff for boys of sixteen. Anyway we got to the house, we rang on the door. My mother was there, prepared to front for me and I had a book of poems. But he wasn't there or was out. Out cold [laughs]. Out, out, out, out.

SL: Did anyone come to the door?

WSB: No. No one came to the door.

AG: He was a very consequential person at one point or other in Paris or New York, with Pound and others I think.

WSB: He wasn't much of a poet.

AG: For a while. But he was a consequential personage in the literary world of his time . . . and my father had a correspondence with him.

WSB: And?

AG: About poetry, you know, back and forth. And I remember seeing one letter. He was a member I guess of the Poetry Society of America.

WSB: I think he was.

AG: Which was Mary Carolyn Davies, if you remember her, from the Village, Witter Bynner, [Joseph] Auslander, Alfred Kreymborg was the big hero.

WSB: Who?

AG: Alfred Kreymborg, ever hear of him? He ran little magazines in Greenwich Village in 1917 or 1920 that Hart Crane, and everybody else . . . and he lasted into the fifties. [New York poet anthologist 1883–1966]

WSB: At some point . . .

AG: The best of Greenwich Village . . .

WSB: So quaint all this . . . and so . . . you know, way back there, nostalgic. God almighty.

AG: My father used to take me to the Poetry Society.

WSB: Winter Bynner, Sara Teasdale . . .

AG: How about Louise Imogen Guiney. You know her? [1861–1920]

WSB: No.

AG: And Adelaide Crapsey? [1878–1914]

WSB: No no, I don't know these people.

AG: Gary Snyder and Philip Whalen had the Adelaide Crapsey Admiration Society.

WSB: Oh for Godsake.

AG: [Laughing.] She wrote the cinquains, remember "these silent things, the bandage on the brows, the lamp light." ["Cinquain" was her term for a Haiku-like verse form that she invented.]

WSB: What?

AG: Cinquains! Like extended haiku. "These be three silent things . . . "

WSB: Oh yeah.

AG: "A bandage on the brow, a moth at evening, the lips of one just dead."

[TRIAD
These be
Three silent things:
The falling snow . . . the hour
Before the dawn . . . the mouth of one
Just dead.]

WSB: Oh yeah, I've heard that.

AG: That's Adelaide Crapsey.

WSB: Yeah, well. Who is that poet who said, "come and receive the something youth . . . this is not for you . . . drug takers."

AG: The laureate . . . Louise Bogan.

WSB: Exactly.

AG: I used to know lots of Edwin Arlington Robinson [1869–1935].

WSB: I know a lot of that, that's very good. Like "there are mistakes too monstrous for remorse to tamper or to dally with. And familiar as an old mistake . . . as we wept."

[There are mistakes too monstrous for remorse
To fondle or to dally with, and failures
That only fate's worst fumbling in the dark
Could have arranged so well.]

AG: What is that first two lines from, the same?

WSB: It's from the thing he did on the Arthurian legend. "There are mistakes too monstrous for remorse to tamper or to dally with I do not know I do not know." This is some old king. And then, "God knows where with full address and foreign air with news of nations in his talk and something . . . in his walk appeared and stayed and held his head as one by kings accredited." And then there are various things . . .

AG: What was the first line of that?

WSB: "The man Flammonde from God knows where!!!!!!!"

AG: Your pronouncing is funny . . .

WSB: "With firm address and foreign air appeared and stayed and held his head as one by kings accredited." And then . . . nature . . . what is it? . . . "Nature will rarely give the power to be, the power to be Flammonde and live." And then . . .

AG: I remember "meanwhile we do no harm for they that with the Gods have striven."

Burroughs at home, Lawrence, KS, 28 May 1991

TAPE 8 SIDE A

3/20/92. 9 p.m. to 10 p.m. Morning 3/21/92. Edith Sitwell. Cats. All my love goes to animals now. James Shirley. Great American Mysteries. The Crispo case. Richard Elovich. John Healey from Mexico City. Joan's shooting.

SL: What about Dame Edith Sitwell? [1887–1964]

WSB: She wrote something about . . .

AG: Something about her vanity.

WSB: Dame Edith Sitwell, what a bitch she was.

AG: She was nice to me.

WSB: Was she?

AG: She was nice to me and Gregory. She defended us from being attacked by *Life* magazine.

SL: When was that?

AG: We went to Oxford in 1956 or 7, '57 and met Auden and met Quentin Anderson, Quentin Stevenson, Dell Morey and Edith Sitwell, and saw her perform *Façade* at Oxford. And then she invited us to lunch in London at the Sesame Club, a ladies' club. And we said, "May we own you?" And she said, "Oh, you have me." Very nice.

WSB: Oh she was a nice . . .

AG: But then *Time* magazine two years later wrote that we had pandered to her and tried to offer her marijuana and she said, "Oh, no I always break out in spots."

WSB: No, not marijuana, heroin.

AG: Heroin or something like that.

WSB: Because people get allergic reactions to it.

AG: Yeah, but they were mixing everything up. So she wrote them a very peremptory letter saying she would not have admitted such a reporter to her company as she did two excellent poets from America whom she admires.

WSB: Oh, great.

AG: Oh, she was really nice.

WSB: She was quite an old . . . yes, quite. She was sort of one of the patrons of . . .

AG: Oh, Denton Welch.

WSB: Denton Welch.

SL: Would you like strawberries or raspberries for dessert . . . or both?

AG: Both.

WSB: I want raspberries. [To cat:] Oh my beast, my Spooner. Oh, I love my Spooner beast. Oh my beast. Um. I love you, I love you. All of my love goes to animals now.

AG: Well, the two of you make a nice couple, I must say.

WSB: Look at that. Look at the way . . . that's Toughs. Now look at him, the way he puts his paws up to me. Yes, my beast. . . .

AG: That's the most affectionate of them?

WSB: Well, no, Ruski is more affectionate . . . but I *love* this, mm mm. God, my God . . . you disturb him somewhat. Come on. Come on. Come on, baby. I love you. I love my cat. I love my spoony cat, I love my spoony cat. You see, he is giving out *pure love*. Look . . . Oh God, my Spooner. I love him. He's disturbed by what you're doing.

AG: Well I ain't doin' nothing to him now . . . .

WSB: You wonder what sort of feeling, what sort of love is coming from this cat. Look at that, look at the way he loves me. . . . Oh my cat . . . My Spooner . . . . Oh how I love you love you love you love you. Mm. It's alright, it's alright, Spooner, it's alright, Spooner. He's a little nervous, he's a nervous cat.

AG: That's 'cause I'm moving around a lot.

WSB: No, the cat has always been a little nervous like that. I don't know what. He was a full-grown cat when he first came here. Well, not . . . a year old perhaps. And he's been here for about two years.

SL: Raspberries have a very short shelf life.

WSB: Mm. Spooner, my Spoonsy! Someone give him a little more food, cause he's . . .

SL: Spooner? To distract him?

WSB: Spooner beast. Spooner. He knows . . . he's very affectionate when he wants food. Damn right he does.

AG: Mm. A certain perfume.

WSB: Of raspberries. Like old . . . barns in the summer.

SL: The raspberry eaters.

[Tape stops.]

AG: Very nice set up here.

WSB: Oh yes . . . this is great.

AG: Well, you got this all by yourself, you have the house, you have your solitude. You got people, a lot of people coming in to help.

WSB: That's right, yes.

AG: Good people, intelligent.

WSB: I need that. And they made it possible for me to bring Ruski back . . . that means so much to me. My Ruski.

AG: When Steven and Wes moved here and got the house they made it possible for you to bring Ruski back?

WSB: Yes.

AG: A ha.

WSB: [I'll] never let him go. My God, I love that cat.

AG: Scepter and crown must tumble down and in the dust be equal made with the four crooked sides and six spade . . . death lays his icy hand on kings, little kitties, they sprout wings. [Allen is riffing on "Ajax: Dirge," by James Shirley.]

> [The glories of our blood and state
> Are shadows, not substantial things;
> There is no armor against fate;
> Death lays his icy hand on kings.
>> Scepter and crown
>> Must tumble down
> And in the dust be equal made
> With the poor crooked scythe and spade.]

WSB: Well, you see . . . this [book] is interesting.

AG: American myths, yeah, that's right up your alley. *Great American Mysteries* by Joe West, published by Globe Communications in Boca Raton, Florida. 1991 . . . . I think you've had that book around since the summer, haven't you?

WSB: Oh yes.

AG: I think I remember seeing it. I was trying to read up on that case and he got away finally.

WSB: No. *He* got out of it but the other . . . that actually did it did not. He's in jail now, got about twenty years, I guess he's still in jail. Serves him right. What did they want to murder some harmless Norwegian faggot for? It's terrible.

AG: A guest in the nation no less.

WSB: Yeah, look at this. There's the guy. Anthony Andrew Crispo. That's the art dealer.

AG: Right. Is he still in business?

WSB: No, well all sorts of things . . . the Internal Revenue left him broke and he went to jail for about eight years, six years.

AG: Crispo?

WSB: Yeah, for tax, tax charges. Well they knew that he was in on this murder, that's why they were so rough on him. It serves him right. All that nonsense, killing people and hurting people . . . There's the guy, he was very handsome.

> [In 1985, the burned body of a Fashion Institute of Technology student was found in Rockland County. The victim had been shot in the head, and the gun was found in the gallery of art dealer Andrew Crispo, whose associate Bernard LeGeros was charged with murder. The defense claimed that Crispo had made the victim kneel and the defendant shoot. Crispo was not charged and did not testify. Trial publicity, however, encouraged another man to come forward to report having been assaulted at the gallery. "This time, Crispo was charged with kidnapping, sodomy, assault, coercion, and unlawful imprisonment. But in the end, the same man, Crispo's henchman Bernard LeGeros, took the fall . . . " Crispo was later jailed for tax evasion, released, and a decade later jailed again for attempted extortion. "He continued to be the bogeyman of New York City's gay world. He was . . . what was meant when older gay men cautioned younger gay men about Bad Things That Happened when hooking up . . . "
> — Choire Sicha, *New York* magazine, April 1, 2012.]

AG: What was he doing with them anyway? Just trying to make a living as an art[ist] . . . the kid I mean.

WSB: He wanted to crash the art scene. He wanted to be in with Crispo and Warhol, you know. He was just a little snobbish faggot.

AG: Well, he wasn't quite little; he looked like he was a good masculine type.

WSB: Well, I didn't say little, I mean little in the sense . . . eyes blue, hair blond, height five feet eleven, weight 135 pounds. He was very slender. Age twenty-six. Norwegian student.

AG: Was he into masochistic stuff? 'cause apparently they got him down on the floor or something.

WSB: I think more or less yes. He wanted to get in with these people, and they killed him. He was the son of a sea captain in Norway. I think I've been in the town, it's a seaport town, what is the name of it?

AG: Bergen?

WSB: Bergen. I was in an old seafarers' hotel there with ships, pictures of ships . . .

AG: Beautiful town, I was there.

WSB: Right on the harbor, fog . . . I would have liked to have been a seaman. I could see that. I can relate to that. And they show him.

AG: But they tortured him quite a bit before they did that. They threatened him.

WSB: Well, anyway. "With a laugh, Crispo replied, 'You're going back to Norway in a fucking box.'"

AG: Who reported that?

WSB: This is the . . . I think this is the account of the young man that *did* go to jail. Bernard was his name. And his family hired this old lawyer. Here he is crippled with arthritis. But he said that the young man Bernard was under the evil influence of Crispo, owner of a prestigious gallery on the most expensive stretch of real estate in the world on Manhattan's East 57th. Now Crispo himself was a foundling. He was brought up in a Catholic nunnery. Then he became an art dealer, how he got where he. . . . well it's in here. He became very successful.

AG: I wonder how he and Shafrazi got along?

WSB: I don't know.

AG: They probably knew each other.

WSB: They probably did, certainly. Crispo. I'd like to ask other New York artists if they knew this guy.

AG: Raymond did.

WSB: Who? Raymond Foye. Yeah. Well, I'll tell you who else did was Richard Elovich. Because he was for a while a doorman at Limelight.

AG: Crispo was?

WSB: No, not Crispo, Richard Elovich.

AG: Yeah, so he knew . . .

WSB: Well, he knew who he was by sight.

AG: Richard is doing very well, you know. He's got quite a career as a performance artist.

WSB: I'm glad to hear it.

AG: You know about that?

WSB: Well, I know about . . . well, I saw he was in the paper for giving out needles.

AG: That, ACT UP . . . but also he very often has performances at St. Mark's and at the Kitchen and he's quite an author and actor and performance artist, sort of like happenings. And the ACT UP stuff is an extension of his theatrical work. He also went to Hazelden, he was strung out, I think it was junk. And you know he worked for Jasper Johns for a while . . . and he was strung out on alcohol or I think junk.

WSB: Yes, I know . . .

AG: A long time . . .

WSB: On junk and speed balls and stuff . . . a heroin addict.

AG: About three years ago when Peter [Orlovsky] was taken to hospital nearby freaked out and kept for about four weeks, Richard came and gave Peter a little talking to, sort of encouraging him to go into a rehab program. He was very good about it, I must say. Very gentle and very firm and concerned, he really developed marvelously.

WSB: Yes. I don't think . . . for a while he was almost insufferable. When I saw him in Paris, I don't know, he was so manic, he made both me and James so nervous.

AG: High on coke or something?

WS I don't know, I just remember he was almost impossible to be around.

AG: Well, he's very moderate now.

WSB: Oh, I know, because I've seen him subsequently. He visited here and was very nice and reasonable and everything. Yeah, I was quite impressed with him.

AG: One, two [taking a photograph]. Let me see what this is . . . half a second . . .

WSB: You have the light behind you.

AG: Yes. OK, one, two. OK very good. I set this up last night, aimed it focused it. One, two, OK.

WSB: Another sort of surprising thing that turned up here . . . well, I'll wait till you're. . . .

AG: Was what?

WSB: Well, someone turned up from Mexico, John Healey. Now John Healey was the manager of the Bounty in Mexico City. It was his apartment that this terrible thing with Joan [the shooting of Joan] occurred.

AG: 210 Orizaba.

WSB: No, not 210, it was the Bounty.

AG: Oh, I see it wasn't in your apartment.

WSB: Oh no, no . . . it was in his apartment.

AG: Oh, all along I thought it was at Orizaba.

WSB: No, above . . . there was an apartment house above the Bounty run by this Mexican . . . great Mexican woman.

AG: Was Healey there when that happened?

WSB: No. Well, he was around, but . . . anyway he was really drinking. I thought, well, he's dead years ago. But it turns out that he got off alcohol and has a house in Porto-Vecchio or something like that on the coast.

AG: Porto . . .

WSB: Something . . . anyway, he had a friend in Wichita that he had gotten off . . . helped to get off both booze and heroin. And they came to visit here. Now Healey's about my age, a little younger, about seventy-seven, seventy-five.

AG: Good health?

WSB: Yeah, well, he's alright he stopped drinking years ago, won't touch a drop. And I was thinking these people, oh God he's gone years ago, from liver trouble, whatever. And he told me about some other people, what had happened to various people. John Crowley was coming down to visit him from Alaska . . .

AG: Who was that?

WSB: John Crowley, you wouldn't know him. He was around the Bounty for a while. And he was coming down to visit John from Alaska, driving down. And was killed in an accident on the way.

AG: On that visit.

WSB: No, nothing to do with that visit. This happened some time ago . . . and various other people . . . what had happened to them, as many as he could remember. I would have some more tea now.

AG: I'll make sure this water's hot, yah. Should I wait for it to whistle, or . . . ?

WSB: Yes. Well, yeah . . . there's nothing in there? No, no no no, I need a new one. Oh, we never use . . . oh, that's fine, yeah, great.

AG: Put it in?

WSB: Yeah, put it in there. Fill it up, fill it up with water. With hot water . . . yeah, that's fine.

AG: Yeah, the water's hot now.

WSB: Mm hm.

AG: What did he do to clean up the mess after the shooting? I thought it was in your apartment or Joan's all these years.

WSB: No. No, it was not.

AG: So did he have any part in the explanations to the police?

WSB: Well, he was called as a witness.

AG: Did he say anything about all that? Or had he read *Queer*?

WSB: I don't know, I don't think so.

TAPE 8 SIDE B

3/21/92 10:15 a.m. Murder Along the Way: True Crime in America's Suburbs. *William Kunstler's cases. Johnson heiress case. Mortimer and Lita Hornick. Guns. Bands influenced by Burroughs. Houdini and Thurston the Great Magician.*

AG: *Murder Along the Way: True Crime in America's Suburbs* [by Kenneth Gribetz. Penguin, 1991.]

WSB: It's . . . interesting. He's a pretty good writer too, this guy. There's one case in which Kunstler was the defense attorney.

AG: Yeah, he's good.

WSB: Kunstler? He said, "Up from New York, stormed Kunstler like the shaggy lion he resembles, screaming 'frameup.'" But it didn't wash. I think the guy was guilty as hell, no doubt about it.

AG: Kunstler's very good at…remember the Larry Davis case?

WSB: Which one was that?

AG: He was a black guy that the police had used as an informer. Or had busted and turned him. And a big guy and finally he didn't want to do it anymore and he went to . . . he was going to go to the police or went to the police to tip them off about some double-dealing that the narcs were doing. So they organized a police posse and broke down his door and shot him in his bed . . .

WSB: Shot him in his bed?

AG: . . . or tried to shoot him in his bed.

WSB: Did they kill him?

AG: He killed somebody and he got out. They were very inept. He got out and on the way killed somebody, killed one of the cops. The cops claimed that they had come to . . . just to talk to him or arrest him or something . . .

WSB: [Chuckles] Indeed.

AG: So Kunstler reconstructed the invasion of the house and proved that he was lying in bed without a gun and that the bed was riddled with holes, the door had been busted down and he had witnesses and he reconstructed it completely to show that they had just been inept and that . . . I think they had shot each other actually.

WSB: Absolutely . . . yes, I remember that case.

AG: And he got a cop killer off. So he was...

WSB: It was a real mess, that . . .

AG: Davis was re-tried for another bust that he had, maybe possession of a gun or something, and is in jail, but he got off on the murder trial. And that was the heaviest...'cause all the newspapers were playing it as "cop killer Davis, black cop killer Davis." The most worst kind, you know. And it was quite a reversal. And none of the newspapers acknowledged that there was something fishy about the police story really. I mean, they just said . . .

WSB: Well it reeked to high heaven . . .

AG: It was a jury trial.

WSB: Well, the police have done too much of that sort of thing. They have a license to kill anyone, particularly uppity informers.

AG: Yeah.

WSB: And it's just too raw. In this case, however, the guy was guilty. It was a funny . . . an odd case. 'Cause he was found with a . . . with his pants down, fucking a girl that apparently he had stabbed and then, oh, it was . . . [inaudible] So a lot of it hinged on the fact that they couldn't find the knife. Well now Kunstler said it was impossible for him to have just . . . they finally found the knife in the car, in the police car, and Kunstler said it was impossible for anyone with their hands cuffed behind their back to have reached the knife and then kicked it under the seat. However, a cop did this, showed that it was possible.

AG: So that didn't destroy Kunstler's story?

WSB: Well, that and other things . . . it was just...wait a minute . . . "after only forty-five minutes of deliberation, jurors returned a guilty verdict."

AG: After what? How long?

WSB: Forty-five minutes. I guess it was pretty . . . That was the one. There's some queer killings in here. People who killed a queer, an old queer and . . . they nailed him. To steal something that . . . a ring that he had, they thought it was worth something was only practically a five and dime ring . . . worth about fifteen dollars. It was just costume jewelry. [Leafing through book.] And . . . one . . . he claimed he was trying to help the girl in the parking lot . . . He was guilty.

AG: You know Jim Bakker? Apparently he got a divorce from his wife.

WSB: Who?

AG: You know, Jim Bakker, the evangelist who went to jail.

WSB: Oh yes.

AG: Apparently he had a divorce. Now on top of everything else, eternal love has failed. . . .

AG: How did Kunstler get him out of that jam?

WSB: He didn't. "Gone was William Kunstler's hope of deflecting the trial, the real evidence in the case, by creating a scenario for a frame-up. In the end, the jury did not believe Amer Zada's contention that he had only been trying to help the girl, not kill and rape her. Neither that disingenuous cry of innocence, nor the attempts by Kunstler to instill ideas that a murder weapon had been contrived and planted, that the witnesses against Amer had been corrupted, that the cops were racists, and that the entire case was nothing but a frame-up, none of it washed."

AG: Well, I wonder . . . who is the guilty person? Zada?

WSB: Zada. He's a sort of Turk.

AG: How do you spell that?

WSB: Z-A-D-A.

AG: The thing is that Kunstler does examine those cases very carefully and he generally doesn't take them if he's going to lose them, or if he doesn't think that there's some real case there.

WSB: I don't see why he'd take this one.

AG: Who's writing, the prosecutor?

WSB: It's written by the prosecutor, yeah.

AG: Yeah, well. . . . What'd he get, twenty years?

WSB: Yeah.

AG: That was in New York.

WSB: Well, it was upstate somewhere. I don't know. It wasn't in New York City.

AG: Um hm. [Long silence.] OK, I'm gonna clean up the kitchen.

WSB: Alright you Calico beast, my little beast.

[Tape stops.]

WSB: . . . weekend there.

AG: John Giorno and Les Levine and you.

WSB: Yes. Now her name was Johnson and she married a psychiatrist called Victor who was known for his reckless lobotomies. Well then . . .

AG: She was the heir of the Johnson baby powder . . .

WSB: Yes.

AG: Johnson Pharmaceuticals.

WSB: She also had a huge apartment right by the League of Nations. It was a sort of a whole floor.

AG: Oh, in the same building as Truman Capote and Kennedy and everybody.

WSB: Huge, huge place . . . Well, she claimed that . . .

AG: Who was she a friend of that you spent the weekend there?

WSB: She was a patron of John Giorno's and Les Levine's. And she had a huge guest house where we stayed. Well anyway, she claimed that Victor was trying to murder her and had hired a mafia connection to do it.

AG: Victor her husband?

WSB: Yes.

AG: Ooh. And was still married with her and living there?

WSB: Yes. What happened with that case, it was complicated . . . I don't think he was convicted.

AG: Oh, this was after you left.

WSB: Oh, yes, yes, I just knew her briefly. And he had gotten...I don't know whether it was a divorce, but he had gotten that apartment and some large sum of money, plus the fact that he was a practicing psychiatrist. But according to her, he wanted more, he wanted all of it. I don't know whether there's anything in this. I have just the vaguest memory of him.

AG: So Johnson's Wax or Johnson Pharmaceuticals I wonder.

WSB: Johnson's Pharmaceuticals.

AG: That's something you'd look up, what year was this?

WSB: Johnson's baby powder and all that . . . hmm . . . James would know. It was about fifteen years ago.

AG: I assume the patronage has stopped by now [laughs].

WSB: Well, John had nothing . . .

AG: Nothing to do with it.

WSB: I hear you had a date with Lita Hornick.

AG: Yeah, I see her all the time.

WSB: Oh yeah.

AG: She's very nice actually.

WSB: She's very nice. You know her husband Mortimer...

AG: Just died [snaps fingers] like that.

WSB: Like that, of a heart attack.

AG: And she will too now 'cause she has the same symptoms I have, congestive heart failure. And she refuses to go on any kind of diet, so she's constantly [pant, pant, pant] and overweight.

WSB: She also had a series of accidents. Her course...for that that she was on. And then she . . .

AG: She burned herself . . .

WSB: With rubbing alcohol. She put rubbing alcohol all over herself and then lit a match or a cigarette or something [and was] burned. It seems to me, you know, real self-destructive.

AG: There's something very funny about her, she's extremely generous but in a very good way, with good people.

WSB: *Kulchur* magazine.

AG: She supported John, she supported *Kulchur* magazine, and she supported all sorts of people.

WSB: Some of my earliest, early work, before *Junky* and before *Naked Lunch* was published in *Kulchur*. Oh, I thought she was very nice.

AG: She takes me out to supper at the Four Seasons, once at the Four Seasons . . .

WSB: Have you ever been to Lutèce?

AG: Yeah, with her.

WSB: Wasn't it great?

AG: Yeah. Ever been out with her?

WSB: Yeah, I've been out with her and Mortimer.

AG: Sometime when you're in New York, let's go out with her again.

WSB: Yes. It really was unbelievable food . . . well it costs a hundred dollars a person.

AG: Yeah, well, she's still at it, she takes me out, you know, twice a year.

WSB: And I noticed you see, he had a monthly account. So when you're finished there's no tipping, nothing like that. He just gets up and walks out; it's all on his account, the service and everything. Yeah, the food was incredible. I had venison, which I like, and then some incredible hors d'ouvres and I think some kind of special sorbet. And the wine was also incredible. He said, "Let's have some more of that cheap wine" [laughs].

AG: Who said that, Morty?

WSB: Morty. Well you can imagine how much that cheap wine was costing, about a hundred dollars a bottle.

AG: Last time I went I had this . . .

WSB: Unbelievable wine . . .

AG: So I asked the *maître d'* if you could get salt-free. He said, "Of course, monsieur" [laughs]. And they really did a good job.

WSB: Oh yes.

AG: Vegetables and some grilled veal that was really great. No salt.

WSB: Anything they do has got to be first rate for those prices. You order some strawberries, you know those little *fraises des bois*, wild strawberries. They examine each berry to be sure there is no green spot or no mushy spot. Every berry has to be perfect. Well, that's what you're paying for.

AG: The berry examiner [laughs].

WSB: Examine each berry. [AG walks over to the kitchen sink.] Well, I was surprised and very pleased to see how well you did shooting, Allen.

AG: Wait a minute now. What did you say?

WSB: I say I was surprised and very pleased to see how well you did with the shooting.

AG: Oh, well, well . . .

WSB: You weren't shooting .22s, you were shooting .45s.

AG: Yeah, but that's an easy gun apparently.

WSB: Yes.

AG: The next one . . . I couldn't get any . . .

WSB: That small one.

AG: The small one I couldn't get any handle on.

WSB: That's a tough one, that three five seven magnum, that really kicks.

AG: What's the name of the long one that we did?

WSB: That's the Ruger .45.

AG: The one I shot the Buddha in the heart with so excellently.

WSB: It's a Buddha . . . it's a...

AG: Buddhist .45 [laughs].

WSB: It shoots either the .45 APC that is the automatic cartridge, or the .45 long Colt, which is the classic peacemaker old west gun.

AG: That was that .45 long Colt that I was able to shoot with.

WSB: Yes . . . well, it's the ,45 long Colt and the .45 APC . . . are about the same ballistics. I can't tell the difference . . .

AG: Which did we have in our hand there?

WSB: We had the APC. And then you also...

AG: What does APC mean?

WSB: Automatic pistol cartridge. And you also did very well with the .45 auto. That is the army gun. It was the army gun for eighty years until they dis- . . .

AG: That was the one that kicked a lot?

WSB: No, it doesn't kick very much. The only one that kicks is the three five seven magnum, that's that short-barreled one. The one that Wes bought . . . for a very good price at $225.

AG: How much does the APC cost?

WSB: What?

AG: That looks like a more expensive gun.

WSB: The Ruger?

AG: The long-barrel.

WSB: Long barrel, seven-and-a half-inch barrel, let me see that cost I think . . . It's got two cylinders so I can use either the long Colt or the APC, which is a good feature.

AG: Two separate cylinders that can be interchanged?

WSB: Well, all I have to do is...yeah, it's the same caliber, but the bullets are shaped differently, so I have to have a different cylinder. I think that gun, new, brand new, which I bought, cost about three hundred.

AG: Um hm. Well, that's my gun. It's a little big to carry around in New York.

wsb: Well it's no pocket gun. I've got a pocket gun, I should have brought it along. .25.

ag: Well I don't want one . . . I'm sure to kill somebody...I mean that's the reason I don't have 'em ['cause I have a terrible death wish?].

wsb: [Laughs] Well, I do too. Let me show you . . .

ag: I just wouldn't trust myself with one of those monsters. [Sings] Brought out my hairy monster, da dum da dut da du. Brought out my hairy monster. You know that song?

[Tape stops.]

ag: Hah? Oh, that's the one you just change the handle, or rubber handle.

wsb: Yeah. It's a five-shot.

ag: What's that called, what's the name of that one?

wsb: Well it's made by Taurus.

ag: Taurus. Right, made in Brazil or something.

wsb: Also, the identical gun is made by Colt and Smith and Wesson.

ag: Yeah.

wsb: Now here is the real cop .25.

ag: Now that's an excellent looking . . . that looks like it's handy. Very serious too.

wsb: [Quickly, to himself] one, two, three, four, five, that's right . . . one, two, three, four, five, six, seven and one in the chamber is eight. And one more down there, nine shots.

ag: It's loaded huh?

wsb: Yes, it's loaded.

ag: Is there a safety on it?

wsb: What? Yes. It's on safe. I'd have to flip that down.

AG: Well, just don't point it at my machine [laughs].

WSB: [Click.] See that? That means it's ready to fire.

AG: [Woefully] *Woaohhh* . . .

WSB: All I got to do is cock it and shoot.

AG: Well let's not.

WSB: [Click] Here's the . . . feel how light it is. It is loaded, remember, but it isn't just going to go off spontaneously.

AG: Um hum. That's a very small gun isn't it?

WSB: Yeah.

AG: And it carries seven bullets.

WSB: No, it carries nine.

AG: Nine. Beretta.

WSB: Yeah.

AG: So who uses these?

WSB: Mmm. Anyone who wants to carry a very small, very conceal-able gun. But of course it doesn't have anywhere near the power of a .45, it's a .25.

AG: But that's enough to kill you with that.

WSB: What?

AG: The right shot would kill you with that.

WSB: It's placement. Yeah. In the head or in the heart. Oh yeah, a lot of people got killed with the .25.

AG: Just a little heavier than the .22, the Beretta.

WSB: Yeah.

AG: Black, black solid thing like that.

[Tape stops.]

AG: *Naked Lunch* was shown here in town at the Opera House theater. Had a full house, said Bill. People seemed to enjoy it . . . it was well-reviewed here. Although the reviewer didn't quite know how to take it. Sort of a dumb review.

[Tape stops.]

AG: . . .reviewer say? I don't remember. . .stupid, puzzled.

[Tape stops.]

AG: . . . dead ten years ago and still advertising as if he were still alive . . .

WSB: She was a fugitive from the FBI.

AG: [Did you ever have any?] direct communication with him?

WSB: No, he won't . . .

AG: So I asked this kid . . . very interesting . . . to make a list of all the bands that had been influenced by your work.

WSB: Oh. Very good.

MICHAEL: Is that why you were saying Ministry?

AG: Yeah. So it was . . . he's saying there are two kinds. Some are literate and conscious, and some have indirect influence. So the cut-ups, originally, both Cage and yourself, something of Dylan, something of the Jefferson Airplane, and something of the Grateful Dead very early. Then of pre-punk: Lou Reed, Patti Smith, Jim Carroll, Steely Dan, Frank Zappa.

WSB: Yeah.

AG: Then of the punk seventies, eighties: Richard Hell, the Clash, Lydia Lunch, Chris Stein of Blondie. From the post-punk, new wave: Sonic Youth, Butthole Surfers, Laurie Anderson, Hüsker Dü, and Bob Mould, who came out of that, Nick Cave and Diamanda Galás. That's what I remembered . . . who is she, Diamanda Galás? Do you know?

MICHAEL: She's that woman that kind of operatically screams . . . John Giorno puts her on his albums.

AG: Sound. Performance. Then there's also Cabaret Voltaire, Throbbing Gristle, which is Genesis's origin, Psychic TV, that he became . . .

WSB: That's also Genesis.

AG: Yeah. And the Swans, English [*sic.* American]. Then Tom Waits, Soft Boys. D'you know them? They cut up *The Soft Machine* and *The Wild Boys* and got the Soft Boys. A guy named Robyn Hitchcock. And Nova Express band. And the Cure. That's England, then the Smiths. Did you ever hear of them?

WSB: No.

AG: Then of punk and post-punk, Siouxie and the Banshees. To some extent the Sex Pistols influenced, Fugazi, "Desolate Fugazi's" Cop Shoot Cop, in the Lower East Side [laughs] . . . name of the band . . . Bongwater, that's Kramer's band.

WSB: Don't know it.

AG: Madonna to some extent.

WSB: Yes.

AG: Bad Religion and Transylvania, they're from New Jersey. And from England Throbbing Gristle and Cabaret Voltaire.

WSB: That's familiar.

AG: Then in German, Einstürzende Neubauten, Nick Cave. And recent, Ministry, do you know that name?

WSB: Oh yeah.

AG: Who are they, Ministry?

MICHAEL: I think there are three of them and he does this real pounding screaming . . . in fact I could . . .

AG: It's recent industrial.

MICHAEL: Yeah, yeah, post . . .

AG: Then Consolidated, you know them? A band called Consolidated.

MICHAEL: Nope.

AG: And Nine Inch Nails, and then to some extent, the U-2. That's quite a . . .

WSB: That's quite a list.

MICHAEL: Nine Inch Nails is great.

AG: You know the Sonic Youth?

MICHAEL: Do I have them?

AG: I mean do you know them.

MICHAEL: Um hm.

AG: So Thurston Moore and Lee Ranaldo of Sonic Youth want to produce a record of me, using a lot of these bands, the newer bands, to write music for my poems. And this kid is organizing it all.

WES: Are you going to do it?

AG: Yeah.

MICHAEL: 'Cause James could tell you a lot more about . . . they have approached William several times.

AG: The Sonic Youth?

MICHAEL: Um hm.

AG: Well, they are big, Bill, they're worth doing. But I'm going to start with them now, 'cause I met them and have been working with . . . a little.

SL: They're pretty intense.

WSB: They good?

AG: They're very good and they're very popular. Very smart. Lee Ranaldo gave me a whole packet of his poetry and I met Thurston Moore at St. Mark's at the big beatnik reading.

MICHAEL: What's he like?

AG: Big tall fellow, young-looking.

MICHAEL: Is he about thirty by now?

AG: He looked to me like twenty.

WSB: Is he taking his name from the Thurston . . .

AG: No, his name is Thurston Moore.

WSB: Thurston is a very famous magician. He's the one that made an elephant disappear . . . He was good. He was a great illusionist.

AG: Did you ever meet the Sonic Youth people?

WSB: No.

AG: They're on Giorno Records and they're on the Willner record, your Willner record.

WSB: But I did see Thurston make the elephant disappear.

[Michael laughs.]

AG: When?

WSB: Nineteen . . . late 1920s. I went to a performance. And he was famous . . .

AG: What city?

WSB: St. Louis.

AG: Ah ha.

WSB: I also saw Houdini.

AG: You saw Houdini! In St. Louis too?

WSB: Yes.

AG: Now what . . . in a big theater?

WSB: Big enough.

AG: Was crowded?

WSB: Of course it was crowded, naturally. Both Houdini and Thurston were sellouts wherever they went.

AG: Ah ha.

WSB: Naturally.

SL: I was wondering when I came in why you were saying "Ministry."

AG: I had asked him [David Greenberg] a week ago to check around and find out which bands had been somewhat influenced by Bill, directly or indirectly, and…'cause he was right up on top of all these bands. He's been hanging around with Lee Ranaldo and the other people from Sonic Youth. Actually a very intelligent kid who's a good poet and he's also running the Sunday afternoon poetry reading at CBGB Gallery.

SL: Gallery?

AG: They have a gallery next door to CBGB's.

SL: Art gallery?

AG: Art and performance, they have a lot of poetry. I've performed there and he's just lined up Huncke and Huncke's friend to read there and he's arranged a reading for Peter [Orlovsky] and for Eliot Katz and for Lee Ranaldo and he's really crackerjack.

MICHAEL: That's great.

AG: Yeah.

Burroughs at gun/pawn shop, Lawrence, KS, 18 March 1992

TAPE 9 SIDE A

3/21/92. 12:45 p.m. Watching Naked Lunch *at Liberty Hall. Allen and William comment during the film. Conversation after the show regarding characters, actors, and plot points. Mailer's a double agent.*

AG: Ornette Coleman and the London Philharmonic. Somewhat abstract title style, it isn't as organic as your own painting. Modern I guess, sort of minimalist . . . "Based on the book by William Burroughs." Applause. Directed by David Cronenberg. "Yay, bravo," says Bill.

WSB: Yay.

AG: Yay for "Nothing is true, everything is permitted, Hassan-e Sabbah." Where's that from, "The Mark Inside"?

WSB: Me.

AG: I mean what book is that?

WSB: *Naked Lunch.*

AG: [To the tape recorder:] That was the epigraph to the book . . . the one mark. . . .

WSB: About the rube.

AG: Oh yeah, the rube section.

[Film audio: "Exterminator."]

AG: But he says it very deadpan, that "exterminator." 'cause there's an exclamation point at the beginning of *Exterminator!*

WSB: You make yourself heard. [William worked as an exterminator in Chicago. The title of the book is meant to represent the cry of the exterminator in the apartment halls, to make residents aware that it's time for "the service."]

AG: Yeah, you want to be heard, you gotta yell. Have you seen the final cut version of this, like this?

WSB: Yeah, sure.

[Film audio: "You want I should spit right in your face? You vant you vant?!"]

AG: That's the end of the book, immediately . . . Now there's that character Martin [laughs] smoking. Am I really a wimp like that?

WSB: Well, I don't know.

AG: Come on now, fess up, you see me as a wimp. He's got bumps on his face! [Kerouac character].

[Film audio: "Guilt, guilt is the key . . . "]

AG: "Somebody's stealing my roach powder, somebody's got it in for me," that's Cronenberg's invention.

WSB: Sure is.

AG: See now, you would have said that with some amusement rather than this serious . . .

WSB: We must deal with what's in front of us.

AG: I giggled to the little soprano saxophone, Coleman was quite good, for sound . . . There's that pressed tin wall, you notice?

WSB: Um hm.

AG: Now that's your own dialog, I remember that, chapter one.

[Long stretch of unrecorded tape follows. Recording resumes in the car, driving home after the show.]

JAMES GRAUERHOLZ: . . . seeing it for the second time. . . .

MICHAEL: That it made more sense to me, because the first time I was confused as far as the plot. And this time it does make sense.

WSB: It makes sense.

MICHAEL: It is a linear story.

WSB: Oh, absolutely, absolutely.

MICHAEL: It seemed really disjointed . . .

AG: More linear, but I still didn't quite get . . . I've seen it three times now . . .

MICHAEL: I'm so glad I got a chance to see it again, at the movies.

WSB: I too . . .

MICHAEL: Because on video I just don't think it'll be the same. It'll be smaller than it is.

WSB: No, I wanted to see it this way.

AG: Had you seen it this way before, in a theater, Bill?

WSB: Yes, of course.

AG: Oh, OK.

JG: In that same theater, in November. A private, pre-release screening.

WSB: Same place, yes.

AG: So it does . . . you said it does improve on re-seeing the second time.

WSB: Yes, it does.

AG: So what elements seem clearer?

WSB: Well, just the way it all ties together.

AG: Well, it's obvious, every time he takes that black meat the type-writers turn into bugs.

[Laughter]

AG: And start talking to him [laughs]. And telling him what he's doing. But remember, the black meat was originally given to him by Benway. But on the other hand, the hallucination began before the black meat . . .

JG: With the bug powder.

AG: With the bug powder and not even taking the bug powder himself. 'Cause he hadn't taken the bug powder when he was busted.

MICHAEL: No, yeah, that's the very first time he took it, Joan gave it to him.

AG: Yeah, so maybe he *started* nuts. Or he started by hallucinating at the very beginning with the powder, turned into the bug without him having gotten high. And demanded to be fed. The typewriter bug virus demanded to be fed the . . .

JG: "Rub it on my lips."

AG: . . . the substance.

JG: Well, the first time to me it appears . . . it strikes me that he's co-opted at the end. He gets his Clark Nova [typewriter] back, the Clark Nova's been tortured and is on the point of death, and the last words of Clark Nova to him are, "Remember, all agents defect and all resisters sell out."

WSB: Right. Yes.

JG: And so when he finally achieves the goal of the whole routine, to find Benway, and you know, check that out, he's co-opted by Benway, and has been in the process of being co-opted all along.

AG: I know, but he was . . . the Clark Nova, who apparently belonged to the CIA, no . . . was it the CIA or was it the mugwump typewriter that talked about the CIA?

JG: The mug-writer was saying. . . . [laughter].

MICHAEL: Mug-writer.

AG: The mug-writer. So on one level it's the CIA sending Lee out to get close to Benway and penetrate Interzone Corporation and find out who's at the top and it turns out to be Benway. And Benway sends him on a journey to Annexia.

JG: Yeah, wants him to . . .

AG: Although I'm really a little disappointed from the very beginning that Benway didn't turn out to be the head of the CIA.

JG: Yeah.

AG: 'Cause that would have been an obvious move.

JG: To me . . .

AG: Did that ever occur to you, Bill?

WSB: What?

AG: In relation to the movie, that Benway would have been an appropriate head of the CIA?

WSB: He must be at least a triple agent.

AG: Yeah. Well, Mailer's a double agent, 'cause he's penetrated the CIA imaginatively and at the same time he hasn't destroyed it, but found it's just human.

JG: In fact, he was honored and spoke to an in-house gathering at the CIA.

AG: Really.

JG: Yeah, he went a couple of months ago; everyone was there and he actually met all these people and got to hear what they thought.

WSB: What did they think?

AG: Where'd you read about that?

JG: A big story in the *New York Times*.

AG: Really? Oh, I missed that.

WSB: Of course . . . I wish I had . . . Do you have that still? Because it had disappeared . . .

JG: I gave it to you; it's somewhere in William's house.

AG: Oh, let's see if we can find it. I want to read it. I missed the *Times* on that one.

WSB: It was interesting, and disappeared when I . . . those things ought to be . . .

JG: Norman sent William a nice note saying that he was sorry that he couldn't . . . he knew about the invitation to come do a story with William and he regretted that he couldn't do it, he had so much work to do.

AG: What is the story?

JG: Well, he was in the pool of persons, you know, a very short list of people that we would agree to have out for this kind of a project.

AG: Oh, to have him come and talk with Bill.

JG: Yeah, do a piece about the movie. And it was a nice idea but I think . . .

WSB: I didn't expect him to.

JG: Me neither.

AG: Well, you never can tell, he does all sorts of interesting things.

JG: It was very nice note saying . . .

WSB: Very nice note.

JG: Says "we'll do something together yet before we're sent to the barn" [laughter].

WSB: Yes, a nice note.

AG: Last time I saw him he said, "You know we see too little of each other. We should get together." First time he said that in many years. I'll be seeing him at the PEN Club banquet later this month, or early April I guess it is.

JG: I think at the end when Fadela rips off her face and she's Benway and Roy Scheider does that speech . . .

AG: Yeah, kind of campy speech at the end . . .

JG: That to me, I get the feeling that that . . . see that . . . that's the scene that to me . . . I don't fault David Cronenberg for not doing the movie in a . . . I don't think he should have done it differently than he chose to do it . . .

WSB: No.

JG: But when Benway finally gives that wacky speech I mean that to me is the flavor of the novel more. "Oh, this little thing, ha ha, Fadela, she must be on the rag."

AG: Yes. No, the words are good. The acting sometimes didn't have enough of a sort of corn-liquor [laughs] energy.

JG: It's funny if you stop and think, suppose Peter Weller, instead of dead-panning the talking asshole and the "I was a queer, bobo we called her," instead of dead-panning that if he had really camped it up . . .

AG: Not camped, no, no, vigor.

JG: But I mean if it had been a hysterical attention-getting thing, it would have been Ken Russell.

AG: Not quite . . . you know I had read that to my class before . . . four days before not knowing it was in the movie, and it was funny, full of humor, outrageous humor. This way you don't get the outrageous humor of the voice. Doesn't have to be gay or queer or anything.

JG: No, it's a different . . . different. . . .

AG: But I particularly objected to the tonelessness of "The Market," that Martin reads.

JG: Yeah, "The Market" when he's reading. . . .

AG: [Oh, I can't stand it.] He didn't pronounce it with any kind of color in his voice.

JG: You know who had some great line readings, delivering . . . line deliveries was Ian Holm.

AG: Who's that?

JG: That's Frost, Tom Frost.

AG: Yeah. Yes, yes.

JG: He's in the street and the typewriter crashes at his feet and he says, "That's my mujahideen, for God's sake!" [laughter].

WSB: Oh boy [at a distance]. Oh there's my poor cats . . . come on, get out of the door . . . there's my Calico . . .

JG: Now you've seen *Naked Lunch*, Udo.

UDO: Yes, I'm very glad. . . . .

AG: Good way to see it . . . it'll be in Europe.

UDO: It will be opening in Europe the day when I leave here. The 21st . . . um, 24th.

JG: Germany?

UDO: Also in Germany and Switzerland. It's meant to be . . .

JG: There was a very big opening last weekend in Paris.

AG: Really? How'd it do?

JG: I don't know how it's done this week but it was just a smash, you know, everyone couldn't wait to see it. . . . Thanks for coming out to the movie.

AG: Oh yeah, well, that was interesting. I understood it a good deal more now, but it still seemed a little, I don't know . . . for one thing a bit garish.

JG: You know I was thinking while I watched it, in a way David has taken William at his word on a couple of things that . . .

AG: He's constantly quoting him and paraphrasing him and fragmenting him.

JG: When William wrote this introduction to *Naked Lunch* he said, "I awoke from the sickness at the age of forty-five. I had no memory of writing this book."

AG: Right.

JG: But that was kind of a put-on. William remembered writing the book; that was just like a thing. Then of course in the introduction to *Queer* he says "I'm appalled by the realization that I would never have become a writer if it were not for Joan's death." A couple of things like that, and a few others, and David [Cronenberg] takes them literally.

AG: Well, he pieces it together like a jigsaw puzzle.

JG: Yeah.

WSB: Yeah, that was a put-on.

JG: You remember writing *Naked Lunch*, don't you?

WSB: Of course I do. No, I'm talking about various kinds of memory.

JG: Allen, did you ever see the nine-page statement that William made as the introduction to Ira's book, plus a few pages of questions and answers?

AG: Well, did he use that? Ira sent me the sort of interview.

JG: That I and William did for the press.

AG: Yes.

JG: 'cause in there William talks about Kiki, says the real Kiki . . .

AG: Wasn't as effeminate . . .

JG: Wasn't proud of helping me to be a writer, he was just . . .

AG: There as a friend.

WSB: I wasn't a writer. Well, I was a writer but . . .

JG: Sure you were.

AG: You'd published a book, Bill, after all.

UDO: I was wondering where was that, the shooting of Joan . . . ? [Microphone jostled, remainder of Udo's remark unclear.]

JG: The shooting of Joan? Basically I think David couldn't resist.

AG: But twice.

JG: When he looked at the life story and the book and all the other books, I think he just couldn't resist doing something with that theme, it's just kind of a meta-event.

AG: But twice, which is a bit much. But it shifts the attention from the politics and the structure and imagination to Bill as person. And to Bill's biography, rather than to the imaginative structure, although . . . So then it becomes like a psycho-history of Burroughs or William

Lee, rather than William Lee's fabulation. In that way I thought it was a bit intrusive. Same with . . . I thought it was a little intrusive with Paul Bowles.

JG: They were very . . . I must say Jeremy and Hercules were privately nervous about . . . when they had the first draft, which is very similar to the movie from the very first draft. They were nervous about what would Paul think, whom they'd just been working with on that . . .

AG: Well, they know Paul, so apparently they were . . . You know this book that I've got about Tangier here . . . have you looked at it?

JG: I haven't seen it yet.

AG: Here. It has a lot of that stuff about Cherifa in the market, about years of passionate ambivalence.

JG: Who says that?

AG: I mean, that kind of . . . it's her ambivalence, Jane Bowles's ambivalence is very clearly indicated there. And you know, described at great length, chapter after chapter. And her horrifying degeneration into paralysis, psychological paralysis followed by physical paralysis. And the business of finding the shamanistic thing in the plant, the poison packet in the house plant. That's in here. Apparently it's Ahmed Yacoubi [painter and lover of Paul Bowles] that found it. You know about that?

JG: I remember that.

AG: You know that story Bill, about supposedly Cherifa having planted some poisonous magic packages?

WSB: Know it? Everybody in Tangiers knew it.

AG: Yeah. And apparently it was Ahmed Jacobi who discovered it.

WSB: Well, huh . . .

AG: Who found it, according to this book.

wsb: Well, yeah . . . that is questionable. That's the other book, not the Green book. You haven't read the Green book?

ag: This is in this book here.

wsb: Michael?

michael: Yeah.

wsb: Do you have the Green book? [Michelle Green, *The Dream at the End of the World: Paul Bowles and the Literary Renegades of Tangier* (Harper Collins, 1991).]

jg: What, the [title unclear]

michael: I think we have it, yeah.

wsb: I think you have it, yes.

ag: I'd like to look at it and get the provenance.

wsb: I liked it. I thought it was very, very funny and . . .

jg: I'd actually like one of these.

ag: You can get it very easily. Burroughs is featured in it.

jg: Well, we gave permission for. . . .

wsb: This is considered the best and the whole thing revolves from beginning to end around Paul and Jane Bowles.

ag: A lot of it, but actually there's more than that. It's a long history of Tangier. It begins . . .

wsb: No, I'm talking about the Green book.

ag: Oh, well, this is all of Tangier from historical times . . .

wsb: Oh, well this had a lot else too of course.

[Long pause in conversation.]

ag: Well, congratulations, Bill, actually that was quite good, such a far out piece of imaginative fantasy.

WSB: That's it, yes.

AG: To get on screen with the talking asshole. It's quite a feat. And it's certainly going to be a cult film that people will be seeing. But I haven't seen many films. Are there many films that are that far out and that weird?

WSB: Well *Brazil* was pretty far out and weird.

JG: There are a lot of films. Period.

AG: But the combination of drugs, homosexuality . . . some good prose . . .

JG: No. That's all unusual.

AG: So that's impressive. [Francesco] Clemente thought it was a little garish.

WSB: Garish is not the word that I would use, what does he mean by garish?

AG: Sort of exaggerated, or too colorful, not ordinary enough; there's a certain ordinariness in the book too.

WSB: Well, remember that a film cannot use more than a tiny fragment of a novel.

AG: I like the thing that you said about, "What have they done to my novel? They haven't done anything. It's still up there on the shelf for people to read." Quoting whom? Steinbeck?

JG: [Raymond] Chandler. In the introduction to Ira's book. "How do you feel, Mr. Chandler, about what they've done to your novel?"

WSB: It's not the question; they're two different media.

TAPE 9 SIDE B

3/21/92. James recalls the genesis of the movie.
Allen's character in the film Heart Beat. *How WSB became a painter.*
Corso in Godfather III. The Exorcist *(film). The history and character*
of the Ugly Spirit. Brion Gysin. Hostage to the Devil.

JG: Well, William, it's been a long haul with this movie.

WSB: Hasn't it?

JG: Think back over it. Back to 1984, when you met David in New York.

WSB: Met David in New York on my birthday.

JG: It was in the summer of '84 at this telephone right here that I took the call from Jeremy Thomas and he offered the basic deal terms for an option and I said OK basically.

WSB: Yes.

JG: And that's right around the time we went with Andrew Wylie and Andrew helped to fix that up. It was in January of '85 we went to Tangier with Jeremy and Hercules [Bellville] and David.

AG: That long ago?

JG: Yes.

WSB: Yes, indeed.

JG: Then David came here in was it February '86 that he was here, Michael, for William's birthday?

MICHAEL: '86?

JG: Yeah, you met him didn't you, on the birthday?

MICHAEL: Or '87?

JG: Maybe '87. Anyway it was December '89 that he sent the first draft. Finished the first draft. And the first draft is very close to what you see on the screen.

AG: Who wrote the draft?

JG: David. David wrote his own script and all the revisions. After the Tangier trip I sent him a copy of the letter to Ginsberg, you know that book.

AG: Now where did he get the relationship of Jack and me, from biography?

JG: Well he read Ted's [Ted Morgan's] biography, surely. I know that because the water glass rolling on the floor wasn't hit by the bullet, is a detail from Eddie Woods's testimony of the shooting.

AG: Eddie Woods, did he die in Amsterdam?

JG: Different Eddie Woods.

AG: Bill said he saw somebody from the . . . the guy whose house it was at.

JG: John Healey.

AG: John Healey.

JG: Remember him, the bartender at the Bounty?

AG: No, I didn't know him.

JG: He was sitting right where I am now. . . . Well, Allen, I can think of two movie characters now that are at least loosely based on your biographical persona. That's this one and the one in *Heart Beat*, Ray Sharkey's part.[47]

---

47   *Heart Beat* (1980) was a film by John Byrum based on Carolyn Cassady's memoir of that title, starring Sissy Spacek, Nick Nolte, and John Heard.

AG: Yeah.

JG: Which I remember . . .

AG: Both of them are wimps! I'm going to go down in history mythologically image-wise as a wimp! *Har har har!*

JG: I remember in '78 when William and I went to LA to do a story on that movie.

AG: Which one? *Heart Beat*, yeah.

JG: Somewhere along the line I picked up the word that having seen the script you were so put off by the Ginsberg character that you asked them not to have your name . . .

AG: Not about me, about the *whole* thing. But particularly, the one line I objected to was, "Waiter, there's a turd in my soup."

JG: Right.

MICHAEL: I have never seen that film.

JG: Oh, it's fine.

MICHAEL: Do we have it?

JG: It's rentable. "Waiter, there's a turd in my soup."

AG: Well, I thought it was terrible. I just didn't want to have anything to do with that kind of commerce, that's all. I just want to be pure as driven snow. And they offered me twenty grand.

JG: To use your name?

AG: Absolutely. I said, "Absolutely not."

JG: You did the right thing. And you know what the worst thing about the movie is?

AG: What?

JG: It's based on Carolyn's stories.

AG: You see what they did was they bought her thing cheap in order to be able to exploit Kerouac.

JG: I know. I know. But the problem is . . .

AG: You know, to exploit Neal's name and Jack's name.

JG: I know, but the problem is that the story that she tells, and I've nothing against Carolyn, but the story she tells, and you can see it now that her whole book is out, is the idea that . . . you know the distaff side of the Beat generation. Here she is picking up, raising the kids, cooking and cleaning, and trying to live a decent life and go along with these kooky sexual experiments. Meanwhile Neal dies and then Jack dies and she goes out and turns on the lawn sprinkler and that's the last scene. And it's all about surviving; all these crazy poets come to a bad end.

MICHAEL: Well, that's one side of it.

JG: It is. Joyce Johnson did that very well in her two books.

WSB: I thought there was some very good acting in that.

AG: In *this* movie.

WSB: No, I'm talking about *Heart Beat.*

AG: Oh really?

WSB: I thought that the portrayal of Neal was great.

JG: Nick Nolte.

WSB: Nick Nolte was so amazing. I was sitting having lunch with these people and it was like Neal was sitting there beside me. That depth. Kerouac no.

JG: Yeah, but the half pint of whisky that Nick pulled out of his boot and drank during lunch was more like Jack than Neal.

AG: Yeah. Actually, my view . . .

WSB: No, but I got the feeling of Neal being there whenever I dealt with Nick Nolte.

JG: What is your view, Allen? I want to hear that.

AG: Well, I thought that both Neal and Jack for *Heart Beat* were better looking in real life and better spoken.

JG: Hm hm. I don't doubt it.

AG: And Nolte's pursing his lips quite often as I seem to remember was . . . showing torment or something by moving his mouth a bit . . . I mean Neal was a lot more in command of his own body, I thought.

UDO: Kerouac looked to me like Philippe Mikriamos from Paris.

AG: Ah huh.

WSB: Which one.

AG: In *Heart Beat*.

WSB: In *Heart Beat*. Well, I don't think I ever saw the whole film, now James and I were out there . . . But all I can say is that I felt that Nick Nolte was very convincing as Neal.

JG: Let's rent it. I'll go rent it and we'll watch it.

AG: Did you actually see the movie?

JG: Let's watch it.

AG: Bill?

WSB: No, I don't want to see . . .

AG: No, had you actually seen it ever? Did you actually see the resultant movie, ever?

WSB: I saw some of it, yes. But Kerouac's a very much more . . . a harder part to play than Neal. More complex, more . . .

AG: Yeah. I thought the guy who played Kerouac in *Naked Lunch* was really not very . . . really ugly. Moles on his face and everything.

WSB: Grey and pasty-looking.

MICHAEL: Those guys were so cardboard though, in that movie. They're just barely characters.

AG: Well, I can't complain about myself, myself. But Kerouac certainly was much better looking and better spoken. You know, you need an actor with more elegance of mouth, and handsomer. Handsomer!

JG: I think the guy that plays Tom Frost, the Paul Bowles take-off, I think he's a brilliant actor.

AG: The acting is good, though he's a little more like a pudgy businessman rather than the thin . . . but then he's a different character. He's an agent of some sort who's capable of coming in with a gun, and Bowles is. . . .

WSB: Also that bit about lip-synch.

AG: That was very good

WSB: Very good.

AG: De-synchronization.

WSB: I didn't catch that in the first movie.

AG: Oh, that was one of the best, most memorable things I thought, but I saw it twice already.

WSB: Yeah, I really got it this time, brilliant . . .

UDO: This I got. I missed much of the dialog, seeing it for the first time, and so I'll see it again as soon as I hit Switzerland then it'll be played at the end . . . looking forward to that.

JG: It's a little mumbly, there's a lot that I . . .

AG: You know what was mumbly was the talking asshole. If you don't know the text, I suspect that people wouldn't quite get that low tone monotone, a few words, will miss some of the connections.

JG: It's an interesting choice because when you look at *Queer* and those routines from *Naked Lunch* . . .

AG: Oh, it's a great choice to put in . . .

JG: But I mean in the actor's choice of Peter reading it that way. I mean I can't fault him at all. But I always imagine, when I see Bill Lee sitting in the Bounty bar and trying to impress Allerton and he comes in and he takes off his sunglasses and says, "hard day at the studio, yes, you know, dry-hole gulch." You know then the story about the old prospector and pushing aside the maps and all the dust . . . "I ever tell you about the man that taught his asshole to talk?" I mean it's like a conman rap barker . . . shill . . .

AG: It begins that way.

WSB: W. C. Fields, carny, carny.

JG: [W. C. Fields voice] "Pretty soon his asshole started talking at all hours of the day and night. Hear it for blocks away, he killed it with his fist."

AG: You want to be loved just like other people.

JG: He's like sleep-walking through the . . .

AG: It's a monotone. It's like he's doing it hypnosis-like in that other . . .

JG: That's it, he's being projected to say it.

AG: I didn't think that he gave it enough color, because that could have been absolutely uproarious in the movie. With that night, driving along and occasional flashes of . . .

wsb: That was very good, that scene with the movement and the Arabs by the side of the road. That's very typical of driving into Tangier, you pass people, even a camel here and there.

jg: "Homosexual. I still remember the panic that froze my lymph in my glands when that baneful word first seared my reeling ears . . . "

wsb: "Reeling brain," my dear.

jg: "Reeling brain. I was a homosexual. A curse, been in the family for generations. The Lees have *always* been perverts." I mean . . .

ag: Could have been more color.

jg: It's a different . . . but then that wouldn't have been the Bill Lee that is the subject of this story. This guy is sort of a Kafka character, you know? Sort of caught up in this . . . without knowing . . . I'm going to rent *Heart Beat* in case you guys want to look at a few minutes of it. Just for fun. I've done a lot of research into the Mexico City thing in particular, I don't mean the shooting, I mean the whole scene. And I just am fascinated by William's personality as a real person. To have a kind of a life-like story.

ag: I would be more interested in seeing one of the imaginative works done well. Closely . . . close to the structure.

jg: That's what Gus [Van Sant] and I are doing on *Wild Boys*, also.

ag: That'll be interesting.

jg: Did you ever see my treatment for *Wild Boys*?

ag: No.

jg: You would like it.

wsb: I think so, yes. I like it very much. It's a Peter Pan, a queer Peter Pan.

ag: What's the name of that theater we went to?

JG: Liberty Hall. And the manager-projectionist who helped us is Jeff Johnston.

MICHAEL: He's the manager.

JG: He manages the films portion. David Millstein's the owner and Tim Griffith's the guy who helped us. But Jeff Johnston's is the one who actually helped us, the cineaste who runs the joint.

UDO: How did you get the print?

JG: I called Fox and when they said that they never never never never never release a video, I said well I can understand that but this is pretty important and you've got some unused prints I happen to know [laughs], about sixty. No, actually I was lucky, I can't take the credit. I lucked out. It turned out that the assistant of the director of the print distribution department, Angela, is a huge fan of William. And she took it on personally to make it happen. And I promised her that she could have a book signed. She hinted that she wanted that and I said absolutely.

AG: Michael, how do you spell your name again?

MICHAEL: My last name?

AG: Yeah.

MICHAEL: E-M-E-R-T-O-N.

WSB: It's me . . . *me.*

JG: Michael Emerton, M-E.

MICHAEL: William, that note you wrote me was so cute. "Dear ME" . . . . Dear me.

JG: Dear me. [Quoting the movie]: "For God's sake! That's my mujahideen!" . . . Ian Holm was good.

WSB: I love that scene. You've seen *My Own Private Idaho* haven't you, Allen?

AG: Yeah.

WSB: Yeah. I love the scene with what's his name . . . Udo Kier with the lamp . . . that dance he did with the lamp.

JG: "Sitting on a bullet, thinking of power."

WSB: He was great.

AG: He looked like the guy in this film.

WSB: He did, yeah.

AG: Are they the same people?

WSB: No.

JG: Which guy in this film?

AG: The slimy . . .

JG: No, that's different but . . . Hans?

AG: Hans is combination of Alan Ansen and Dutch Tony . . . . When did you and Bill meet? What year?

JG: Me and William? I met . . . OK I see what your question is. I met you in May 1973 in New York . . . . And William and I met on February . . . 12th or 10th 1974.

WSB: Yes.

AG: That was the day you came to see me? And I sent you right over there.

WSB: Then I rented that loft from Mike Balog.[48] It was a huge thing about a hundred feet really.

AG: The loft.

WSB: The loft.

---

48   Michael Balog (1946–1987), painter friend of William and James.

AG: Where was that? 77 Franklin or something.

WSB: No, no Broadway.

JG: 452 Broadway.

WSB: 452 Broadway, my dear. There was a very sleazy sort of Jewish cafeteria underneath us and [it] went right through the building.

AG: I remember that. I couldn't remember where.

WSB: You know what happened to Mike Balog? He committed suicide, with a .22 rifle, which is rather a difficult task. But he did. In Los Angeles.

JG: In Los Angeles two years ago.

WSB: The last time we saw him he was in a very run-down loft . . .

AG: You rented the loft from him?

WSB: We rented the loft.

AG: He owned it, or . . . ?

JG: He rented it . . .

AG: You sublet it from him.

JG: He actually sublet it from Debbie.

AG: Really?

JG: Debbie who worked for Bob Rauschenberg. And he was around that Rauschenberg Lafayette Street . . .

AG: Debbie . . . ?

JG: Can't remember her last name. But I remember Debbie was the landlady.

WSB: I met him at Bob Rauschenberg's.

JG: The first time.

WSB: I think so.

JG: That's in '65 with [David?] Prentice and . . . But he was so depressing the last time I saw him, I remember. He was in kind of a concrete loft on Lispenard Street, totally dark, water running down the stone walls. There were these weird sculptures that he was trying to make, welding things, but he didn't really know how to weld. He was so alone. And he was getting psychotic. And I remember I used to hang out with him at the Ocean Club, him and Ralston Purina.

WSB: Yeah.

AG: Really?

JG: Brought him back to the bunker one time, got high. He was just so kooky; he'd smoke a joint and just be absolutely weird. Benign, but weird. Then after . . . you remember that.

WSB: Something about . . . oh, yes. Now what he was making, in the loft on Broadway, were these things that he made from broken plywood. And that is what gave me the idea, later, of shotgun blasts *through* plywood. I don't know how he did it. He broke them with hammers or something. I said, oh God, look at the way they . . . they look like cities and things.

AG: Hm hm.

WSB: So I just fired a blast with a shotgun through a piece of plywood and I looked at it and I says, Jesus, this is work of art!

AG: Ah ha.

WSB: That began my painting career, so I owe in a sense my painting career to Mike Balog, who committed suicide. I heard that from Earl McGrath, you know, what had happened to poor Mike Balog.

Well, yes, he was . . . I don't know what happened to him after we last saw him.

JG: He moved out to LA and he was just in a very weird space and finally did that.

WSB: He was terrifically self destructive.

JG: Very.

WSB: Apparently so.

JG: Well, Allen I promise you that if Gus and I can get our *Wild Boys* project off the ground, and I do think we will, it will be . . .

AG: I want a role.

JG: You can have a role.

AG: I want to be the. . . . what do I want to be? What's in *Wild Boys*?

JG: A lot of characters.

WSB: I could act. . . . the colonel.

JG: You could be the colonel? He's got a pretty big part.

AG: Give Gregory a part, he's always great on film. Have you seen him in *The Godfather*?

JG: Oh no, I haven't that's the . . .

AG: *Godfather III.*

JG: He's in it?

WSB: No.

AG: Have you seen that, Bill?

WSB: No, I haven't seen the film.

AG: Gregory has a brilliant one-minute role.

WSB: What did he do?

AG: They're bickering at the board meeting for the Vatican bank. And the Godfather's taking over the bank. And it's all been arranged in advance and suddenly at this very staid board meeting in like a little chapel in the Vatican or something, an unruly stockholder rises up and gets the microphone, with sort of salt-and-pepper hair and not dressed like the other stockholders and says, "Wait a minute! Look at that guy, he's got the map of Sicily on his face. He must be the Mafia or Catholic, or both!" [General laughter]. Then they shut the microphone off on him and he's listed as "Gregory Corso, unruly stockholder."

WSB: He's well-cast, of course.

AG: And he made up his own lines. And apparently, he says, it's the first time "the Mafia" has been mentioned in the movies with that word.

JG: Oh.

WSB: Really?

AG: Yeah, that's what he says . . . the Mafia prevented it all those years. And you know he was living in Rome and hanging around in the Giordano Bruno Piazza, where Giordano Bruno was burned. It was just the place where junkies and Americans and like the bohemian Euro-Italo-American bohemian. . . .

WSB: We'd get all the Vatican gossip from Pierre Rochette. He visited me here.

AG: Yes. I never met him.

WSB: Oh well, he's . . .

JG: Really? He went to Moscow with Gus Van Sant and Francesco Clemente not long ago.

AG: Yeah, I heard. Clemente knows him.

wsb: He knew E. M. Forster.

ag: Really? Did he convert him?

wsb: No. He knew E. M. Forster, he knew . . . wait a minute . . . well, he baptized Clemente's children.

ag: Hmm!

wsb: And he also knew Durrell. Lawrence Durrell.

jg: His mother was a social maven and Durrell would often visit her salon.

ag: So what has he done, Bill, has he converted you to the faith?

wsb: No. No. He has not. I think that they have so much bad karma that they haven't dealt with. . . . the Holy Inquisition . . .

ag: Right.

wsb: Now . . .

ag: Well, the Inquisition there and in America . . .

wsb: No, I'm talking about the Inquisition, the Inquisition. They've got these exorcisms. I say these spirits may be the remains of tortured souls from the Inquisitions. Is there any wonder that they shrink from the name of Jesus Christ? That they're scalded by holy water?

jg: Hm. Great idea.

wsb: Yeah. An idea that would be very unpalatable to most priests.

ag: How would [Rochette] take such an idea?

wsb: I don't know.

jg: He took it . . .

wsb: He didn't get it.

JG: He took it alright.

WSB: He didn't get it!

JG: Oh, he didn't?

AG: How would he take such an idea?

WSB: I don't know. I simply don't know.

JG: He would analyze it.

AG: What's he do about the politics of the church if he's so intelligent? . . .

WSB: He says that he feels they're wrong on homosexuality.

JG: They're wrong on abortion.

WSB: Wrong on abortion.

JG: Wrong on birth control, let's put it that way.

WSB: He has to be sort of careful or they'd boot his ass out of the church.

AG: Yeah.

WSB: I never said anything about that idea to him. This is an idea that I got after reading a lot of exorcism material.

JG: Write it to him, he would love to entertain it. But I just want to comment that he said to William, he says, "I can neither give you extreme unction, which doesn't have to be given at the point of death, but can be given." William was still recuperating from this . . .

WSB: Bypass.

JG: The first operation actually.

WSB: No, it was the second.

JG: It was before your actual . . .

WSB: Are you sure?

JG: No, I'm not. I thought it was in the spring, it was April.

WSB: I'm not sure.

JG: But he said, "I can neither give you extreme unction nor exorcise you until you have been baptized."

AG: Right. Yeah.

WSB: That's correct.

JG: And I said, "Well, William, want to get baptized? You got a priest right here, he can do it."

AG: Yeah.

JG: Not too late, you can pull a Tom Eliot, Graham Greene.

AG: Did they get baptized at the very end?

JG: Not at the very end. Eliot became converted to the Anglican church in his thirties . . .

WSB: Oh man . . . yeah, the Anglicans, sort of a watered-down Catholicism.

JG: Oh yes, it's the campiest. The Anglicans get to wear fancier dresses.

WSB: I know they do. *Campier* dresses. But now [under his breath] what was I talking about?

JG: Exorcisms, demons.

WSB: Yes, exorcism and demons. Well, it was after that . . . I hadn't gone as far in my looking in to the whole matter of exorcism . . .

JG: Till after he said that.

WSB: Till after, exactly.

JG: William, do you remember going to see *The Exorcist* with me in Times Square?

WSB: Of course I do.

JG: Do you remember how it was supposed to be such a scary movie, there was such a word on it. And we were sitting there and it was in the afternoon and the curtain started going up, and then like it started showing that, you know, Georgetown and it said "The Exorcist." And somebody went [screams], screamed in horror. Really cracked up the whole audience [laughter].

AG: Was that any good?

WSB: Oh it's . . .

JG: The first one's great.

WSB: Very good indeed, very good. She has this trick of turning her head all the way around.

AG: Yeah, I remember I've seen that.

WSB: Then she spit all over the priest. Well, this actually happens, you know, in exorcisms, these people spitting . . . but the thing about it is they can spit up buckets full. You know, more than they could possibly contain. That's one of their tricks, spitting up buckets full of stuff that looks . . . like spaghetti full of hair!

AG: Oh God!

WSB: And has a foul odor. Buckets full!

JG: What do they do with this stuff after the possessed one's spit it up?

WSB: They take it out and dump it somewhere.

JG: I think they should be studying it; they should turn it over to scientists to examine it.

AG: Flush it down the toilet or something.

WSB: Oh, you could . . .

JG: Then you'd have a possessed toilet [general laughter]. Devil in your toilet.

WSB: [to cat] My beast, yes, you're so affectionate.

UDO: You're all wet.

WSB: Comes from outside where it's raining. So I would discuss this with Pierre, I didn't have the information at that time.

AG: Well, you'll see him again.

WSB: I will I hope. I like him. He's nice. You should get and read that book, that exorcism book.

AG: Yeah. I've got it written down what it is.

WSB: Yes. It really is worth reading every fucking word. Every fucking word is interesting. It's fascinating to me.

AG: Well you're a specialist in that area.

WSB: Exactly.

AG: Exorcism and shamanism, and you have a special interest in it. So! With the ceremony that we saw, did you get any glimpse of the Ugly Spirit or what that was historically or biographically?

WSB: Well, I know what it is. I have known for many years.

AG: The nurse, your governess, or..?

WSB: No, no, she was just a very minor [figure] in this. The first person who really *showed* me the Ugly Spirit was Brion Gysin. He was the one that said, "The Ugly Spirit shot Joan because," and I never found out why. "For Ugly Spirit shot Joan because." This Brion wrote out in a sort of trance state. And he said it was written in a sort of a nineteenth century script, like the Boston Brahmins in this messed up era. There were some great characters at that time, sort of the end of the *fin de siècle.*

AG: So the phrase "Ugly Spirit" was from him, but did you ever locate the specific quality or character or historical personage or . . . spirit?

WSB: Well no, it's very much related to the American tycoon. To Hearst, Vanderbilt, Rockefeller, that whole stratum of American acquisitive evil. Monopolistic, acquisitive evil. *Ugly* evil. The *ugly* American. The *ugly* American at his *ugly* worst. That's exactly what it is.

AG: But then that's the character that has possessed *you.*

WSB: Yes. Certainly.

AG: So would that be a family thing from Burroughs? Or from Ivy Lee or, Ivy Lee built up?[49]

WSB: No, not necessarily.

AG: That it would apply to moving your hand with Joan? [The unsteadiness or moving of his gun hand that resulted in her death.]

WSB: Well. Anyway, now you're . . .

AG: That's how Brion was locating it, that way . . .

WSB: No, he said, "Ugly Spirit shot Joan because." The because broke off there . . . shot Joan because . . .

JG: I think you're on to something.

AG: Well, in the preface to *Queer* you spoke of it as the Ugly Spirit that entered you and depressed you beforehand and after . . .

WSB: Yes, certainly.

AG: And his phrase was "the Ugly Spirit shot Joan because," and that

---

49 William's maternal uncle Ivy Lee was a pioneer in advertising and a public relations man for the Rockefellers.

it's a case of your possession. So I was wondering, with the shaman, did you get any glimpse of the action or operation or persona of the Ugly Spirit in you when he was exorcising it?

WSB: Well yeah, he said it was the toughest case he'd ever handled. And for a moment he thought he was going to just lose.

AG: Then I remember yesterday you were saying, when he was talking about it, "He had to face the whole American capitalism, Rockefeller, the CIA."

WSB: Yes. Yes.

AG: J. P. Morgan, ITT [chuckles] . . .

WSB: All of those things. Hearst. Particularly Hearst.

AG: Hearst the word man, the original image-manipulator.

WSB: Yes. Precisely. [If] they say something is true, it is. He said, "We don't report the news, we make it!"

AG: Yes.

WSB: I've seen the film a number of times. *Citizen Kane* . . . . Well, Orson Welles had a lot of trouble from that.

AG: Never recovered.

WSB: Not direct . . .

AG: Well, the film . . . He couldn't do anything in Hollywood after that.

WSB: Right, that's right.

AG: Probably Louella Parsons or somebody got after him.

WSB: Well, that's what the shaman said, he didn't know what he was up against. He didn't expect the strength and weight and evil intensity of this spirit, this "entity," as he called it, an entity. The same way the priest in an exorcism has to take on the spirit. Some of them are not strong enough. Some are killed. Then there was one there where the priest fucked the guy, fucked the priest.

AG: The guy or the spirit?

WSB: The spirit fucked the priest.

AG: In the body of the guy who was . . .

WSB: Oh no, no . . . He jumped on the poor priest and fucked him up the ass. He said, "You are my sow, I will ride thee!" And the priest . . . well he finally won, but he had a hell of a time and he died about a year later. The spirit fucked him up. Fucked him literally, literally and figuratively.

AG: That's in *Hostage to the Devil* by Malachi Martin.

WSB: Yes. See if I can find that particular case.

Burroughs at Steve Lowe's house, Lawrence, KS, 19 March 1992

TAPE 10 SIDE A

3/21/92. When William was Allen's therapist. Reichians of New York.
William's psychiatrists. The shaman has to see the spirit.
Chained to the couch for narcoanalysis. Rushdie.
Mexico City junk. Kerouac's Tristessa. *Matt Dillon wants to film*
the murder of Kammerer; Lucien wouldn't want it.

JG: Did you used to sometimes be sort of like a psychiatrist and have Allen tell you stories?

WSB: Oh yes, yes.

JG: Where did you guys do that? Was that on Morningside Drive?

WSB: No, 115th Street.

AG: My room or the room I shared with Hal Chase . . . for a long while. I would lay on the couch and Bill would sit at my . . .

WSB: Your head . . .

AG: By the window into the courtyard, I seem to remember. And I would put my head on the pillow and just look up at the ceiling and talk . . . free associate mainly . . .

JG: Did he listen? Or guide. . . .

AG: A little guidance, but mostly questions once in a while. But mostly what was on my mind and I had to break the ice and talk a bit.

WSB: Yes.

AG: He did that with Jack also, but in the other room. Where did you do that with Jack?

WSB: I don't remember.

AG: I think in the front room or something like that.

WSB: Yeah. . . .

JG: Had you read Freud or any psychiatric . . . Was what he told you about it the first exposure you had to the concept of psychoanalysis?

AG: No, I was at Columbia, remember, you know, Freud, Marx, Darwin, that was the dominant intellectual stuff. And I had seen many psychiatrists in relation to my mother.

JG: Oh yeah.

AG: And I had no general . . . I had read Kraft-Ebing for the sex parts.

JG: Pathology.

AG: And I knew something about Freud, though I didn't read Freud specifically because . . . though I had read a little Reich . . . no no, I hadn't read Reich by then. Could I have gleaned Reich? Let's see. Had I read Reich? I'm not quite sure.

JG: It's interesting, because . . .

AG: '46 I read Reich, or '47.

JG: In the letters of William there are Reichians mentioned. There was a guy named Benny Graf, for example. Turned into some kind of an informer, but he was a Reichian . . . was there Reichian therapists?

AG: There were Reichian therapist then, Dr. Lowen, Alexander Lowen was around, though not in '45, not during that time. It was '46, '47 that I met . . . When I was living on 92nd Street I met a whole group of Reichians, Norman Schnall, Vickie Armature with whom I was busted, through Huncke. Friends of Huncke who lived up on West End Ave and 93rd Street or 92nd Street. I was hanging around with Neal, or Neal was hanging around between me and Jack in my room there. And . . . must have been '46 '47.

JG: Do you know how William got exposed to Reichianism?

AG: I think he had read *The Mass Psychology of Fascism*. How did you get exposed to Reich, Bill? Remember Norman Schnall and . . .

WSB: I read Reich way back when, and I made an orgone accumulator . . .

AG: I'm thinking about '45 '46. Not '47. The orgone accumulator I think you made in Texas or later, but . . .

WSB: In Texas down Kells's place.[50]

AG: Yeah, but I'm thinking of '45 '46.

WSB: I don't remember that. I was aware of his work for a long time.

AG: When did you read *The Mass Psychology of Fascism*, or look at that?

WSB: That was of no interest to me; I was only interested in his techniques, not his theories.

AG: Yah.

WSB: I was interested in the theory . . . the discovery of the orgone, and his whole cancer theories. But I was not interested in his social theories.

JG: [*The*] *Cancer Biopathy?*

WSB: [*The*] *Cancer Biopathy.*

JG: The meaning of the orgasm.

WSB: Yes. All that I was interested in, but I was not . . .

AG: *The Function of the Orgasm.*

WSB: *Function of the Orgasm*, but I wasn't at all interested in his social theories.

---

50 Kells Elvins, an old friend with whom Burroughs invested in cotton farming in Texas in 1946.

JG: What about Reichian therapy, the massage and the character armor stuff, did you ever have that?

WSB: No, I never had it.

AG: I did.

WSB: And I was not too . . . I thought it was sort of getting off on a line that was not too interesting to me.

AG: When did I go to a Reichian, Bill, it was '47, '48? Something . . . it was after '46 certainly it was '47. I went to a Reichian in Newark, Dr. Cott . . . . So but that's much later . . . but around that time Alexander Lowen was the major guy that this actor Norman Schnoll was going in to get breakthroughs. They were talking about the word breakthrough. And Vickie Armature had something to do with it.

JG: Did you ever meet any of William's psychoanalysts? Federn or Wolberg? [51]

AG: I knew Bill when he was going to Wolberg.

WSB: Wolberg is apparently still alive and Ted Morgan I felt it was very [unclear] of him, going up to see any of these people.

AG: Ah huh.

WSB: Now Wolberg refused to see him.

JG: Eissler.

WSB: Eissler.

JG: Eissler refused to see him.

AG: Now who's Eissler?

---

51 Paul Federn (1871-1950) was a disciple of Freud who fled to New York in 1938. Burroughs entered analysis with him in 1943. Federn referred William to Lewis R. Wolberg (1905-88), a US-trained psychoanalyst who treated William using hypnoanalysis and narcoanalysis, 1944–46.

JG: George Eissler. [(*sic*) Kurt Eissler][52]

WSB: Eissler was the psychoanalyst I saw in Chicago.

AG: Oh, long, long before then.

WSB: Yes.

AG: '42 '43?

WSB: No, it was '43, around there. So he talked to Eissler and Eissler said, "Well now, you know the patient is not going to be violated." And so Ted asked him, even if the former patient agrees? And in he said in some cases yes.

AG: Hui!

WSB: In some cases yes . . . if the man, if the man agrees that he's still . . . He didn't want anything to do with it, in other words. Nothing to do with it at all.

JG: Was Eissler the first psychiatrist that you ever saw?

WSB: By no means.

JG: Really? Who was?

WSB: Wiggers.[53]

AG: Oh, Wiggers, in New York in '41 or '40 . . . ?

WSB: No earlier than that. '38.

JG: '38, in New York. You came down from Harvard to see him?

WSB: No, I was out of Harvard.

---

52 Kurt Robert Eissler (1908–99) trained in Vienna, fled to Chicago in 1938, and was cofounder and long-time director of the Freud Archive. William pursued analysis with Eissler in 1942–43.

53 Herbert Wiggers (1907–53), William's first psychiatrist, had William committed to Bellevue Hospital in 1940 after he cut off the end joint of his left little finger in despair over his lover, Jack Anderson.

JG: Oh, working for Massek, Givaudan, & Van Dolen.

WSB: Van Dolen, Givaudan, & Massek.

AG: What are they?

WSB: The advertising agency that I worked for [in 1941]. Anyway . . .

JG: How come you went to see Wiggers?

WSB: Well, I wanted to see a psychoanalyst and he was recommended.

[Here, there seems to have been an erasure of some minutes of recorded material.]

WSB: . . . good spirits. Many of the . . .

AG: As the shaman was saying, and as you were saying, and as Blake says, you can't exorcise or beat Satan, except you see him clearly. Or see his system, or his rationale, the way he thinks, what he thinks that he's doing. Or see his outline as Blake says. Or glimpse him or see him so you can put him in the fire as the shaman says.

WSB: Yes, exactly. The shaman has to see a spirit.

AG: But do you have to see the spirit in the shaman too? To directly see it, see who it is and where it came from?

WSB: No. It isn't as personal as that, who it is and where it came from. It's been there. It was always there.

AG: So it might be a complete stranger who you'll never know who it was or where it came from.

WSB: Very likely, it probably is.

AG: Ah huh.

JG: There's a scene I was curious about, William, I think it was . . . was it Jack Kerouac? Maybe it's *On the Road*. He has that you have some chains in your room and he's saying, "These chains, those are for when I'm in my narcoananlysis regression." Remember that thing about he'd take you down through eight personalities and you'd be a raving lunatic?

AG: No no no, a Chinaman at the banks of the Yangtze mud.

JG: Chinaman at the bottom . . .

WSB: No. He put these chains on around my feet when he was . . . through hypnosis was regressing me through the various . . .

JG: Oh, he actually did put you in chains.

WSB: Oh yes, yes.

JG: Just your feet?

WSB: Yes, yes.

AG: Why?

WSB: Because I could become violent and attack him.

AG: OK.

WSB: Yes.

AG: Right.

WSB: Now remember, in exorcisms they always have two assistants there, strong assistants, like the young man, the young fireman, they're often ex-policemen, in case the possessed person, that is the spirit in him, becomes violent and attacks the priest.

AG: That's what R. D. Laing used to do. Provoke the neurotic aggression, or spirit, and then . . . but he always had it in an environment where he was protected . . . *Dharmapala*.[54]

WSB: By a strong . . .

---

54 "Protector of the law": in Buddhism, a wrathful guardian deity.

AG: And that's what the function of the Vajra Guards for Trungpa, 'cause he was handling stuff that was so explosive that people were likely to freak out . . .

WSB: Absolutely.

AG: So he needed somebody to protect the environment. *Dharmapala*, door guards.

WSB: And they have unbelievable strength too. I mean even a little girl can be extremely dangerous to the priest unless he has these two assistants, usually.

JG: Well, did you ever get violent with Wolberg?

WSB: No, but I could have.

JG: What drug did he use to regress you?

WSB: Barbiturates.

JG: Barbiturates?

WSB: No, no, he used nitrous oxide.

AG: Oh, he did?

WSB: Yes.

AG: I didn't know that. I thought it was just hypnoanalysis.

WSB: No. I can't be hypnotized.

AG: But his specialty was hypnoanalysis. He wrote a book on it didn't he?

WSB: I know he did.

AG: So he used nitrous oxide. How interesting. I had no idea. You didn't mention that then, I don't remember.

JG: How did he apply it?

AG: 'Cause I dug nitrous oxide.

WSB: This way [sniff]. So I could take as much as I needed.

AG: Then . . . so . . . I see.

WSB: Nitrous oxide.

AG: I did a lot of that with my dentist, with a notebook in my pocket.

WSB: In other words, you've got to be very careful with that stuff. If you don't mix the right the mixture of oxygen, it can cause brain damage very, very quickly.

JG: Wolberg treated you this way approximately how many times? Dozens? Hundreds?

WSB: Hmmm yeaaah . . . twenty, thirty.

JG: Wow. And so do you remember getting really wild and getting some deep stuff out behind the nitrous?

WSB: Some pretty deep stuff, but it was reassuring to me to know that I couldn't attack him. I'd do something awful.

JG: Chains!

AG: That's pretty normal.

WSB: Also . . .

JG: I'm trying to visualize . . . yeah?

WSB: Dr. Reik [Theodor Reik, who wrote on masochism] said that deep analysis requires a great deal of courage on the part of the therapist and the patient, because if the patient is encouraged to express all this aggression that he has . . .

AG: Or she or whatever, panic . . .

WSB: He can often attack the therapist.

[Tape stops.]

JG: . . . Federn did, that's right. [This refers to Federn's suicide in 1950.]

WSB: Yes. His wife had died and he had a well-advanced cancer in a vital organ.

JG: And he chose suicide.

WSB: Chose suicide, which was considered by the psychoanalysts as a rational act.

JG: Yeah. And it was he . . . did he send you to like this one whose name escapes, and then that one sent you on to Wolberg?

WSB: I just forget. . . . the details. Who was the other fella, his name escapes me . . . Dr. something or other, he's good, he was good.

JG: Not . . . this isn't Eissler.

WSB: No, no Eissler's way back there in Chicago.

JG: OK.

AG: What was Eissler's first name?

JG: Kurt.

WSB: Kurt.

AG: Any relation to Hans Eissler the musician-composer, German?

WSB: I didn't ask him [laugh, sigh].

JG: We don't know.

WSB: Don't know.

AG: I gotta stir my soup before it burns.

JG: OK. I'm gonna make a quick run. I'll be back in a minute.

AG: . . . tape . . .

JG: I'll bring you tape, a catalog for Steven, maybe a copy of my *Wild Boys* treatment for you, while I'm thinking of it. It'll be fifteen minutes. Well, you know it's fascinating to me, these things, and why William started them and why he stopped them, into the next one . . .

AG: I have some of it on here [the tape recording], not all.

JG: Yeah, I know. It's hard for him to bring it back. [German accent:] I suspect zat zer iss some evasion, some block in ze mental . . .

AG: What do you think about that business about the capitalism . . . surprise.

JG: Not that! (laughs)

AG: No no not that, aaa!

JG: OK . . . [Door slam.]

AG: Now what am I doing? . . . So life goes on in the United States among the beatniks.

UDO: I started with *On the Road* . . .

WSB: [From a distance] Dr. Spitz!

AG: Spitz.

UDO: [correcting their pronunciation]: Schpitz.

AG: Dr. Schpitz, OK.

WSB: Spit it out! I was just . . . I said Doctor Spitz, that was him.

AG: OK we'll have it for . . .

WSB: Dr. René Spitz![55]

AG: Oh.

UDO: René Schpitz.

---

55   René Spitz (1887–1974), Austrian psychoanalyst, practiced in New York 1940–43.

WSB: Yes. Good man he was too.

AG: What were you saying?

UDO: I started reading *On the Road* in 1962, in September about. And at that point I never even dreamt about meeting any of these guys.

AG: The funny thing is that '63 we already knew each other . . .

UDO: '62.

AG: So we already knew each other almost twenty years. Kerouac. So it was quite ripe. Almost . . .

UDO: And you see in 1963 I went for the first time to Paris and I lived behind the Cafe Odeon. And so I was walking about the quarter, rue Gît-le-Cœur and everything, but I didn't have any idea . . . of the hotel I didn't have any idea.

AG: Well, it's just a hotel actually, it's nothing special, just a . . . I always thought it was kinda silly to call it the Beat Hotel, because it's more romantic as 9 Rue Gît-le-Cœur, frankly, "there lies the heart," the original name. I don't know who started calling it that. Either Brion or maybe . . . [56]

UDO: Was it you?

AG: Oh no, I would never be so vulgar, my dear [laughter]. No, I mean it's too self-referential and too . . . actually it was probably Harold Norse, if anyone. [Yelling to William] Who started calling that place the Beat Hotel, Harold Norse?

WSB: I don't know, who did?

AG: I always thought it was a bit corny.

WSB: Anyway . . . the hotel was a sort of old . . . awnings, all of that. All I know is now. . . . [This is speech at a distance, unclear and covered by simultaneous chatter from AG and Udo.]

---

56 "The Beat Hotel was named by Gregory Corso" (Miles, personal communication, 2 July 2018).

AG: Yeah, he did write . . .

UDO: This was published in German.

AG: Really?

UDO: Many years back.

WSB: 9 rue Gît-le-Cœur.

AG: He also wrote a book . . .

WSB: [Now back in the room, shouting, apparently about Salman Rushdie's problem] Ignorant stupid barbarians!!! Can you imagine the pope putting out a contract on somebody?

AG: Ah ha.

WSB: This reveals themselves as a thousand years back, and it's barbarous, it's barbarous. Has anyone said this?

UDO: Not in print.

AG: I don't think anybody has said it right out like that, 'cause everybody doesn't want to be politically incorrect.

WSB: Oh shit.

JG: And get a contract on them.

AG: I did. I have a poem about it.

JG: A lot of people . . .

WSB: Well you . . . yes, yes . . .

JG: It's obvious that Islam is a religion that, whatever else can be said in its favor, has a lot of aspects that are just deeply rooted in the fourteenth century or something.

WSB: Or whenever it started, but yeah . . . but more than that, much more than that, it's a thousand years back and . . . this is incredible. It's barbaric. Can you imagine the pope or the president of the

United States putting out a contract on Gorbachev?

AG: Well, we put . . .

WSB: I don't say that they haven't done it.

AG: They put out a contract on Saddam Hussein. And they once put out a contract on Gaddafi . . .

WSB: Listen . . .

AG: And they once put a contract on Castro.

WSB: Oh yeah, that went on for years.

AG: But apparently there's a public contract out for Saddam Hussein.

WSB: Yeah, but they never got him. They fought a war to get one person; they kill a hundred thousand civilians, and they don't get him! For Chrissakes, why didn't they nail this bastard? Maybe they wouldn't have had to fight the war.

AG: Um hm.

WSB: Gross incompetence, gross incompetence.

MICHAEL: So would everybody like soup to start?

AG: I'll have some.

WSB: Which kind of soup . . . ?

MICHAEL: Chicken soup.

AG: My old chicken soup.

WSB: I think I'll wait . . .

AG: You don't have to eat it.

WSB: I want to wait for goulash.

MICHAEL: Does everybody want to wait till salad afterward?

AG: You mean salad later?

MICHAEL: Salad after or before?

WSB: I'll have salad afterwards.

MICHAEL: OK. So Udo . . .

UDO: A little soup, yes please . . . .

MICHAEL: Is it OK?

WSB: Just cool it off a little bit, babe . . . .

[Talk of film financing turns to the Chinese bug spray/drug dealer in the *Naked Lunch* film whose line is "no glot, come Fliday."]

AG: Where does that phrase come from originally? Was that an actual thing?

WSB: Yeah. Sure.

AG: Where?

WSB: OK, it's a real . . . Mexico City, he said come back Friday 'cause the Chinese used to be pushers. So then they found there were so many informants and deadbeats, that they quit . . .

AG: Quit selling it to the whites.

WSB: Yeah. So when you came they said, "No glot, come Fliday." Which means come no time.

JG: Suppose you said, "But this is Friday."

WSB: Come next Fliday.

JG: Or Fliday after that.

AG: Dave Tesorero ["Old Ike" in *Junky*], I don't think I met him.

JG: Old Dave.

WSB: Old Dave!

JG: Dave Tesorero, he was Esperanza's boyfriend.

AG: Oh, yeah, I didn't meet him. He was in Mexico City, right.

WSB: Right well sure. He was my supplier for many years and he got a morphine scrip [prescription] going; it didn't cost much and we split that and that kept me going for about six months. And we would go and get a big hunk of morphine. It's about eight or ten grains a day. And we'd split it up. Oh, it was a great feeling when I had a whole month's supply of morphine.

AG: There was enough in his . . . How many people had to share that?

WSB: Two. Just me and him.

JG: Didn't he ever cut Esperanza in on it?

WSB: Well, that was up to him, if he cut her in, it's nothing to do with me.

JG: So the deal was he got the scrip, you paid for the dope, and you split it down the middle.

WSB: That's right. That's exactly it. Simple as that.

JG: Pretty practical. After all, it was legal, and once he got it . . .

WSB: Yeah, sure it was.

JG: Did you know Esperanza or any of that *Tristessa* scene?[57]

AG: Yes. I went with Jack to Tristessa's house.

JG: You did?

AG: Yeah. With Gregory, I think, Gregory and Jack and I . . . Peter . . .

JG: Or Lafcadio [Orlovsky, Peter's brother] or one of the boys?

AG: No, I think it was me and Gregory.

WSB: She said that you just sit down on the curb and die.

---

57   *Tristessa* is a novel by Jack Kerouac, published 1960, recounting his affair with a woman in Mexico City whose real name was Esperanza.

JG: Where was the house you went to?

AG: I don't know but it was somewhere in the Tenampa district . . . the Plaza Garibaldi, somewhere in that direction in Mexico City.

WSB: I remember that.

AG: Between the Zócalo [plaza] and the main square downtown . . . .

JG: How long did Jack live with Esperanza?

AG: Well, he . . . [in the novel] *Tristessa* . . . it's a matter of missing her one day. A whole day spent in her house watching her family and the chickens and the . . .

JG: The whole love affair is just one day in the house?

AG: Well, most of the writing, or half of it was that.

JG: You know there's a screenplay going around.

AG: You ever read that, *Tristessa*, Bill? Have you ever read Kerouac's *Tristessa*?

WSB: No, I've not.

AG: You might like that.

WSB: What is it?

AG: It's about Esperanza.

WSB: What is it?

AG: *Tristessa* is about Esperanza. It's a description of the place where she lived with her family and it's very well-detailed.

WSB: Her name is hope. Esperanza of course means hope, as you know.

JG: And Tristessa means sadness. . . . Although the actual word for sadness is tristeza. E-Z-A.

AG: I read it this year, it was very good.

WSB: Sounds like . . . did she live on . . . I remember once I went over to see her to get some morphine. And I had to go up almost a ladder, very steep thing with a little loft there . . .

JG: Same place you went to?

AG: I went to this tiny room with her family on the third floor of some sort of strange apartment that had glass floors or something.

WSB: What?

AG: Glass . . .

WSB: I know exactly what you mean . . . glass stuck in the . . .

AG: Where they. . . .

MICHAEL: The hotel we stayed in, in Mexico City, do you remember with the glass floor?

JG: The Majestic had glass floors . . . . Well, Matt Dillon is supposed . . . was invited to play I guess Jack's part in a script of *Tristessa*. And he told me that there's a character that he thinks that has to be William. And I said well that's quite possible but it's not from Jack's book, because William does not . . . as far as I can remember there's [not] even the slightest reference to William in Jack's book.

WSB: Yes. Not in that book . . .

JG: Not in *Tristessa*. Actually I want to see the screenplay.

AG: Might be Garver, you think so?[58]

JG: Could be Garver. Is he in the book?

WSB: Yeah.

AG: But Garver was in that book.

---

58 Heroin addict and dealer Bill Garver appears as Bill Gains in *Junky* and as Old Bull Gaines in Kerouac's *Desolation Angels* and *Tristessa*.

WSB: Oh he was, yes. I don't want to be Garver. He was too dreary.

JG: Well, if Matt thought it was you, and he knows your life story . . .

WSB: Well, anyway. I would have to be sort of . . . you know . . .

JG: Well, I want to see the script actually, along the lines of what we were talking about before.

WSB: Me too.

JG: Maybe there's another turd in the soup. I'm not censorious, I just want to . . . to make a picture of him . . .

WSB: I'd like to see it . . . [and take it from there] that I can get me teeth into [laughs].

JG: You know what Matt's really interested in?

WSB: What is he really interested in?

JG: He's fascinated by the story of Lucien and Kammerer.[59]

WSB: Oh God.

JG: That's what I said when he told me.

WSB: You know, sort of . . . I know Lucien wouldn't want it . . . nobody wants it, really. Now I don't think it's at all that terribly interesting. This obsession, and here he wasn't that . . . it was ludicrous. The more I look back, I realize how ludicrous . . .

---

59 David Kammerer was killed by Lucien Carr in August of 1944. A feature film about that incident and the circumstances that led to it, *Kill Your Darlings*, was released in 2013.

TAPE 10 SIDE B

3/22/92. Breakfast conversation. Calico cat reminds William of Jane Bowles and Joan Burroughs. [Transcript is truncated here since the remainder of the side is taken up with fragmented, mundane conversation of little interest.]

AG: I'm still trying to figure . . . something about the cat . . . can you tell which cat that is?. . .

WSB: Is it Calico? It probably is Calico, yes, I think it's . . .

MICHAEL: Calico Jane.

WSB: Calico Jane. Calico Jane from Panama. She reminds me of Jane Bowles and *Two Serious Ladies* [Jane Bowles novel, 1943], and of Joan my wife.

AG: Who does, Calico?

WSB: Yes Calico . . . Calico Jane, Calico Jane from Panama. She is the daughter of Ginger and she was born in that corner. Right there was she born. As a child, as a kitten, she was sort of catatonic. Nobody wanted to take her. She was just limp.

MICHAEL: She was so cute.

WSB: And I finally put her up in the house. I realized that she was getting better when she finally got up and learned to scratch me . . . . What day is this, is this Saturday or Sunday?

SEVERAL VOICES IN UNISON: Saturday.

WSB: I thought it was Sunday. [Tape label says 3/22, which was a Sunday.]

Cut-outs in front of Steven Lowe's house, Lawrence, KS, 19 March 1992

TAPE 11 SIDE A

Lucien and Dave hijinks. The seven deadly sins. Gelek
Rimpoche on anger. Kerouac on anger. The Gettys. Christopher Isherwood.
Trungpa Rinpoche. James's dream. Robert Bly. Edward Dahlberg.

JG: I'm sorry, I got a little mixed up. You're walking with Lucien and Dave comes along.

WSB: No, I am not . . . I am walking behind Dave and Lucien.

JG: And they come to like a fruit stand.

WSB: Yeah.

JG: And there are bats?

WSB: No. Lucien does some little thing, batting at the awning or something. And Dave comes along and he has to do something too. Some childish thing. So he kicks and knocks a . . .

JG: Cantaloupe.

WSB: No, no, just a box of something. The guy comes out and says, "What the fuck's the matter with you?" Quite rightly. And Dave has to give him a dollar or something. But I thought, Jesus Christ, he's just got to do some stupid thing because Lucien . . . you know, get one-up on Lucien with this stupidity. They'd get themselves thrown out of hotels and all these *stupid sophomoric* pranks that Dave went along with, trying to be, you know, Lucien's age. It was grotesque. It was *absolutely* grotesque and unsightly . . .

JG: [Unsightly tricks.]

WSB: Yeah. These are unsightly tricks.

JG: Hm hm. Before God, these are unsightly tricks.

WSB: That's from *King Lear*. "Sire, these are unsightly tricks."

JG: Yeah. Well . . . but it sounds like Lucien . . . as it happens with the young . . . Lucien could have gotten away with batting the awning.

WSB: Yeah, but Dave couldn't.

JG: Kicks over the whole . . .

WSB: Well, no, I didn't say that he made more damage, but . . . he had to *do* something . . .

JG: Naturally for attention.

WSB: To be *with* Lucien and it was horrible. I remember that moment, he's got this blank expression on his face, and he's gotta go and kick something over in order to stay on a level with Lucien.

JG: Well, Lucien wrote more recently after he got the gluttony Christmas card.

WSB: Oh yes, my gluttony Christmas card, yes.

JG: And he wrote back and he said, "If you've got one of sloth, I'd like to have it, because that's the sin I have been preoccupied with lately."

UDO: Sloth?

JG: Sloth.

WSB: Laziness.

UDO: Ah.

JG: It means laziness. Actually the original sin was called axidy [(*sic*) acedia].

WSB: Called what?

JG: [Acedia], and it meant loss of faith, loss of purpose, loss of spirit.

WSB: Sloth . . . laziness.

JG: That's a modern definition but it applied to priests, you see. Not priests, but I mean monks, people in a monastery. And they would read and copy manuscripts all day and they were very prone to this sin of [acedia]. Sort of like heartsick and empty.

WSB: Not doing anything is the point. There were obviously a lot of secret drinkers in those monasteries.

JG: No doubt.

WSB: They have a stash behind the Virgin Mary. I'm quite sure of it, because they made liqueurs. Lots of liqueurs, see, came from . . . Benedictine came from a monastery.

JG: Right.

WSB: And all these liqueurs that they made.

JG: Chartreuse.

WSB: Chartreuse, yeah. Each monastery had a certain liqueur, and don't tell me they didn't nip at it along the way.

JG: Sure.

WSB: Course they did.

JG: But it was sinful to nip too much.

WSB: Well yeah. It isn't sinful *per se* to drink liqueurs or wine.

JG: No. But if they use it to like hold their . . .

WSB: To excess it becomes gluttony. It becomes gluttonous, my dear. And slothful, both gluttonous and slothful. Yeah, it's terrible.

JG: Pride, anger, envy, lust, gluttony, greed, and sloth.

WSB: Yeah. The worst sin is anger.

JG: Technic . . . yeah?

WSB: Cause it gives rise to so many other sins. It gives rise . . . is very closely linked and related to pride and to envy. Pride, envy . . . um . . . not too much to sloth.

JG: Pride, anger, envy, lust, gluttony, greed, and sloth. Pride is the cardinal sin.

WSB: Well, pride, yeah, that's the cardinal sin.

JG: It's always the first one on the list.

WSB: Is it, yeah. Well, pride of course and anger because . . . pride, you're necessarily subject to anger. Oh, absolutely.

JG: Well, I think the sin of pride as is meant by the people who named it, has to do with . . . sort of let's say the kind of thing of *you* get upset about when you see mankind like bulldozing the Amazon to put up a Hilton.

WSB: Yes.

JG: The pride is the pride of not submitting or acknowledging higher powers. When I make myself God and like I'm the center of the universe, that's pride. Not so much pomp and circumstance as standing up and you know . . . there is nothing that I need to respect, I am the king baby of the universe.

WSB: Yes, that's it. But also all forms of nationalism and group glorification are manifestations of pride.

JG: True.

WSB: Whether it's yourself or your group or your nation, your country, it's the same . . . sort of very bigoted, stupid and closely related to anger. Yes, it's a bad sin. . . .

JG: Yeah, very bad one.

WSB: No doubt about it.

AG: Anger. Gelek talked a lot about anger, remember?

WSB: Who?

AG: Remember Gelek Rimpoche mentioning that would be the one addiction that would be a difficulty at death? Anger.

WSB: He talked about it?

AG: When you talked to Gelek Rimpoche.

WSB: Oh yeah.

AG: The question . . .

WSB: Oh yes, he said that anger is much worse than . . . um . . .

JG: Opiates.

WSB: Opiates, which can be seen as a form of sloth.

AG: Oh, he said that?

WSB: No. *I* said that.

AG: But he said that the difficulty of facing at the moment of death . . . the original question was would our addictions be a difficulty at the very moment of death, or after.

JG: Yeah. Would it be a spiritual disadvantage.

AG: What was your phrasing for that?

WSB: Well, I asked him just that and he said, "It's not so bad." He said, "Anger is much worse." Anger is the worst to carry over, much worse than opiate addiction. [To the cats] Alright my children, go out, I suppose . . .

AG: Which cat is that?

wsb: Fletch.

jg: What'd you say?

wsb: Because he'll eat somebody else's food.

jg: Oh, Michael's doing the food. That really gets me through the heart.

wsb: What?

jg: About anger. Because I'm not really intrinsically an angry person, but I have a lot of bursts of anger.

ag: Well, we all do, my dear, come and join the club.

wsb: Everybody is riddled with these things.

jg: And I always . . . but the thing is . . .

wsb: Unless they're fucking saints.

jg: I always feel the anger as a burst.

ag: Oh no, the thing is to take an inquisitive, curious interest in the anger.

jg: Yeah.

ag: Just examine its current, you know, dispassionately that I'm angry and then what did it? Realize what you're angry about . . . one way. That's the Gelugpa analytic way.[59]

wsb: Yes, yes . . . .

ag: But the question that the Tibetans make is of simply noticing it. In fact their view is you don't have to do anything about it. All you have to do is notice it. Because adding the dimension of noticing the anger immediately evaporates about 80 percent of the heat and the pus.

---

59 Gelugpa is the branch or school of Tibetan Buddhism in which Gelek Rimpoche was trained and was a lineage holder.

JG: I'm pretty good at that.

AG: That about right, Bill?

WSB: Well, yes.

AG: I liked his way of saying . . . you know, the rising of it and its occurence, you don't have to do anything about it, merely to notice it is sufficient to dissolve most of it.

WSB: True.

AG: And that's really a kind of very interesting tantra, you know, just one little extra dimension of awareness of the surrounding of the thought. Kerouac had a really good line on that, I keep quoting that over and over now. "Anger doesn't like to be reminded of fits."

WSB: Of what?

AG: Anger doesn't like to be reminded of fits. F-I-T-S.

WSB: F-I-T-S.

AG: A fit of anger.

WSB: A fit of anger.

AG: Anger doesn't like to be reminded of fits.

WSB: Of its own fits, you mean.

AG: Well, yeah, the short poem, anger doesn't like to be reminded of fits.

WSB: Yes.

JG: I like it . . . . That a fit is an unsightly, out of control, embarrassing thing.

AG: Yeah. A very funny line in *Mexico City Blues*, Blakean in a way. That's the one thing I actually got . . . had my focus sharpened by Gelek Rimpoche as a sort of shaman himself.

WSB: As what?

AG: That's the one point that I got sharpened, my focus sharpened with Gelek Rimpoche . . . . I was thinking of calling Gelek. You got the energy?

WSB: Who?

AG: Gelek Rimpoche . . . .

WSB: You know how rich people hate to lend money or give money to somebody. The richer they are, the stingier they are.

AG: Well . . . but certainly give people . . . everybody gets stingy to give money to people on the skids.

WSB: Not everybody. They give money to their institutes and stuff like that, but they hate to make a personal loan or a personal gift, as a rule. Not always, not always. The father of John Paul III, he was quite generous, he gave three hundred dollars a month to Brion.

AG: Really?

WSB: Yes, yes. We talked about it.

AG: That's right.

WSB: What?

AG: Yes.

WSB: He was pretty good, pretty generous with . . .

AG: That's the one that's the junky?

WSB: Well, of course, yes.

AG: Not the old-old man.

WSB: The old-old man is long gone.

AG: Who bequeathed the museum, the old-old man?

WSB: Well, he started it, and I think Getty III showed us around there. He was terrifically gentlemanly and a great person. He showed us around the museum. It's quite a museum, they had some really first-class stuff there. They have . . . it's there still. It was something started probably by the old man. The old man apparently was not too bad. He was pretty generous. The whole family had all these troubles. Let's see . . . I think one of them was stabbed by his wife with a barbecue knife and killed.[60] And then there was a scandal of Paul Getty Jr.'s wife dying of a . . . as I told you . . . a massive overdose of heroin in Rome.

AG: Yeah.

WSB: And he had to get out and stay out.

AG: Get out of England?

WSB: *Italy*, this is in Italy . . .

AG: Yeah, right, right, right . . .

WSB: So anyway, there's those two and then the kidnapping of the grandson. And junk.

AG: He paid on that too.

WSB: Well, how much? Who paid? Nobody knows. The kidnappers I don't think got anywhere near what they asked for. They probably got about five hundred thousand.[61] Anyway, they say that the old man helped on that, but there was quite a lot of money scattered around. So, that was a hell of a thing. Then now in this . . . stroke . . . terrible, terrible just awful. I mean, well, we shot up heroin together. He was generally very nice. He invited me to lunch.

AG: I met him once. Forgotten where now.

WSB: I met him first in London, then New York. He was living with

---

60 George Franklin Getty II, oldest son of J. Paul Getty, took an overdose of pills and stabbed himself with a barbeque knife. He died next day in the hospital, 7 June 1973.

61 On 10 July 1973, J. Paul Getty III was kidnapped by Italian gangsters who demanded $17 million. His grandfather held out, and J. Paul Getty III was finally released in December upon payment of $3.4 million.

Harry Smith for a while.

AG: Aha, no I didn't know that.

WSB: Yes. That was the time I met him in New York, and . . . for lunch, that's the last I saw of him . . . Oh no, then we saw him in California, at the museum.

AG: And he showed you around. He knew his way around? The young fellow . . . he knew his way around the museum in terms of . . .

WSB: Oh, certainly. This is before his stroke.

AG: Right, right.

WSB: Yes, of course he knew his way around. Exactly. And that was when I bought some very good heroin and we split it . . . . Brion knew him quite well too. . . . . Yeah, I've seen him ten, fifteen times maybe. And then he was at a party in New York in Steve Lowe's loft, you remember, when Trungpa was there.

AG: Oh, really.

WSB: Of course, weren't you there?

AG: I don't remember.

WSB: Steve Lowe's loft in New York, just off Broadway, there's a little street there, almost at Canal.

AG: This Steve Lowe here.

WSB: Yes!

AG: I remember he had a little loft somewhere around Bleecker or somewhere like that.

WSB: This was a big loft . . .

JG: Howard Street.

WSB: On Howard Street it was quite a big loft . . . and then . . .

JG: You were there: It was the night that he made that partridge.

WSB: Yes.

JG: And you . . . and Christopher Isherwood and Don Bachardy came over, you . . .

AG: Touched the dust at his feet and he said, "Oh no, don't do that."

JG: Yeah, you attempted to kiss his . . .

AG: No no, to touch the dust at his feet.

JG: To touch his feet, right.

WSB: And Paul didn't like it at all.

JG: You mean Christopher.

AG: Christopher didn't like it.

WSB: No, *Paul* didn't like it.

AG: Paul Getty.

WSB: Paul Getty. Trungpa tried to touch the place of his ear . . .

JG: Oh, that's another matter.

WSB: And he didn't like it at all. Getty didn't like it.[62] You see, I had given a reading and I think Trungpa as well. And then we came down to Steve Lowe's loft . . .

AG: Oh was this after that big reading we all did together?

WSB: Yeah, Howard Street. On Howard Street. And he cooked up some partridge pies and stuff and Trungpa was there. And he tried to touch the place . . . the ear. And Getty didn't like it, Paul didn't like it at all. And . . . well, that was the occasion.

AG: I have a very dim recollection. I remember the reading and I

---

62 The kidnappers had cut off J. Paul Getty III's ear and sent it to his parents.

remember the . . . at Loeb Auditorium.

wsb: Yes.

ag: I think it was Anne [Waldman], myself, you, and Trungpa.

wsb: I think so, yes. It was certainly you and me and I'm sure Trungpa read. Then we all went down there.

ag: Yeah. But the party I've sorta forgotten.

jg: That was a different night from the partridge.

wsb: This was on Howard Street.

jg: They were both on Howard Street.

wsb: Yes, that's right, both on Howard Street.

udo: How old is this Getty now?

jg: Thirty-five.

udo: Thirty-five.

jg: That was the first time we ever saw Trungpa, William.

wsb: What?

jg: That was the first time we ever saw Trungpa.

wsb: Oh, I don't think so.

jg: It was in '75 in the spring. And that's when he said that you come out to . . .

wsb: Naropa.

jg: Naropa. And we said OK. And we went to Naropa in June '75 and then you had another talk with him and he invited you to do a retreat in Barnett, Vermont, Tail of the Tiger, now Karmê Chöling.

wsb: Yeah.

JG: And we had the celebrated discussion of whether you could take a typewriter or not. And he said, "No, no, a carpenter doesn't bring his tools." Anyway you insisted at least in bringing a notepad.

AG: Yeah.

JG: You did in August '75 spend one week. I guess it was just one week, in a retreat hut.

WSB: Ten days.

JG: Ten days at Barnett, Vermont.

WSB: Yes, I know that. There was another occasion . . .

JG: It was the spring of '75.

WSB: Wait a minute, hold on, I'm trying to remember.

JG: OK.

WSB: Oh, Allen took me to meet Trungpa, and he was living in New York in an apartment. And we talked a little, it was kind of not very animated and he did however remember having met Bruce MacManaway.

AG: Right.

WSB: That I met in England. So . . . and later he told Allen he had thought me a man like a stone!

AG: No no, no no, he said, why is it . . . this was after Lucien said, "Fuck you."

WSB: Yes.

AG: . . . At one of his things. He said, "The people you bring are like stones."

WSB: What?

AG: Like stones. Hard as stones.

WSB: Who?

AG: The people you bring.

WSB: Oh, I thought you said . . .

AG: 'Cause there was Harry Smith, who he slapped . . .

WSB: He said about me . . .

AG: Lucien, who said fuck you . . .

WSB: . . . I was a man like a stone . . .

AG: No . . . generically . . . talking generically.

WSB: Well, anyway . . .

AG: Tough customers.

WSB: This was before, this was before the party.

JG: Before the reading?

WSB: Oh yes. Yes.

JG: OK. So that is the first meeting.

WSB: Well, I guess so I'm not sure . . .

JG: I remember the reading at Loeb Auditorium . . . after we came back from New Orleans in April '75.

WSB: I read there, a long piece about the Mayans.

AG: Um hm.

JG: Yes. Did we use the slides with it? Was that . . . ?

WSB: No, that was not . . . When we used the slides was the one in Toronto.

JG: And in Barnard? That little Barnard reading.

WSB: Yeah. Particularly in Toronto I remember . . .

UDO: What kind of slides?

WSB: Well, slides showing . . .

JG: Pictures of Malcolm McNeil's artwork of the abandoned. . . . .

WSB: Yes. Sort of illustrating what I was reading about. I thought it would work better than it did. I . . . you know, it's alright . . .

JG: It actually worked pretty good.

WSB: I think it did, yeah. Nothing to . . . you know, nothing cataclysmic or overwhelming but, alright.

JG: Remember that first summer at Naropa, William?

WSB: Yes, we killed a brown recluse.

JG: [Laughing] That's what you remember best.

WSB: No, that isn't what I remember best, but I remember we stayed in the Emerson or some . . .

JG: That's right, the Emerson Apartments.

AG: Ninth Street. Which Anne dreamt of as the Remembersome Apartments.

JG: The Remembersome Apartments, I like that. Yes, we did, the apartment had dual sinks, we were like college students, both wash before their eight o'clock class. And there was a giant brown recluse in one of them and we did kill it, that's right. First thing.

AG: How'd you approach it?

WSB: I didn't, James did.

JG: The recluse?

AG: Yeah, how did you kill it?

JG: I killed it with a tennis shoe.

AG: Oh.

JG: And I had a vision there in that apartment of an angel at the foot of my bed. I'd drifted off into a half sleep and . . . don't you remember that story, William? I saw . . .

WSB: What kind of an angel?

JG: Um . . . It was guy all in white [chuckle]. It was a guy all in white and it was just a traditional angel.

WSB: Got wings?

JG: Um . . . no . . . may have been like a robe or something.

WSB: And a robe, a white robe.

JG: Yeah.

WSB: What did his face look like?

JG: Cute.

WSB: Got a halo?

JG: No.

WSB: Mm . . . Mm . . . Interesting.

JG: I wrote it out.

WSB: Yeah.

JG: It was the afternoon of that day that Robert Bly visited.

WSB: Yes. I remember the occasion.

JG: His rap was fine.

WSB: Well, I don't . . .

AG: Yeah, I remember when Bly visited. Now Bly was funny. He said that he thought Bill was evil or something.

JG: He said there was no love in you.

wsb: Oh fuck. . . . He's one of those opinionated people who's always pissed off at someone. He's very much like the one who was in the first issue of *Big Table*.

ag/jg: Dahlberg.

ag: Edward Dahlberg.

wsb: Dahlberg. The same sort of cranky person who feels everybody . . . I got him . . . he showed up in Paris and I got him a dentist or a doctor and he said I was awful.

ag: You got him a dentist or a doctor?

wsb: Yes, certainly.

ag: And he repaid your kindness with this . . .

jg: Surliness.

wsb: With surliness and talking badly about me. He showed up there. Dahlberg . . . he'd say anyone that . . . no one that doesn't read the classics can be considered seriously as capable of an opinion, kind of . . .

jg: Yeah, but you know I'll tell you something about Ed Dahlberg . . . about his writing. That he wrote an autobiography called *Because I Was Flesh*. And it is really quite something, especially the first half. Because, you see, he grew up in Kansas City and his mother was one of the female barbers. She had a barber shop. She was a lady barber in Kansas City at the turn of the century.

wsb: Yeah, that's OK.

jg: Right down town and it's pretty interesting stuff.

ag: That's quite good, yeah, I remember that part. That's what was published in Big Table, wasn't it?

wsb: I think so. A section of that. I remember that . . . .

TAPE 11 SIDE B

3/22/92. Breakfast conversation at William's. English gangsters and other Tangier expats. Barbara Hutton. David Herbert. Manusi runs amok. Rubio and the Grand Rabbi. William reads Dr. Wolberg's notes on a case of hypnoanalysis. The ultimate secret of the Ugly Spirit. Brion was a shaman. Jacques Stern was a bubble demon. Are you the patient Wolberg was talking about? Allen prepares to depart. Brion named it, the shaman caught it, but it's still hanging around. The shaman is coming on Tuesday to bless the house.

WSB: Billy Hill owned all the bookmaking shops in London. He used to show up at the Parade Bar in Tangier.

AG: Did they talk about their exploits?

WSB: No they didn't.

AG: I think that book by Iain Finlayson does talk about the Krays.[63] [*Tangier: City of the Dream.*]

WSB: The Kray brothers and Gypsy Hill, who was the wife of Billy Hill. She ran a Whiskey au Go Go place on Mexico Street.

AG: In the Green book . . . that woman named Green that wrote on Tangier, does she talk about the Krays?

WSB: No. She's talking more about the high society in the mountain, and this woman that collected animals. Daphne du . . . Maurier [*sic*] or something.[64]

---

63 The Kray twins were organized crime figures in 1950s-60s London. Ronnie Kray went to Tangier c. 1960.

64 William is likely recalling Daphne Fielding, one of whose social set, Countess Phyllis della Faille, collected animals.

AG: Did she have much about Barbara Hutton?[65] Apparently she was a mess.

WSB: She was. Not completely, she'd pull herself together now and then.

AG: Apparently she was on a lot of drugs.

WSB: Mostly alcohol, a horrible mixture of alcohol and barbiturates. You know, pills. Much better someone should take junk than a horrible mixture like that. Well, they get so sloppy. They can't walk. She married about . . . how many . . . there was two in Tangier, there was this young man, was a nice young man, and he was living with Barbara Hutton, and she set him up in a riding stable. He was a sort of a riding master, and gave him about $100,000. She was very generous. Then there was [Baron Gottfried] von Cramm, a tennis star, who was queer. . . . She was married to him for a while.

AG: Why would she want to marry a gay guy?

WSB: Can't imagine. See, she was that way, she married people, it was ridiculous. Then there was this man who ran a . . . he was a Vietnamese who ran an . . . antique store or oriental artifacts store in Marrakesh. So she paid to have him go to his embassy and get himself registered as a prince. She claimed he was a prince. And Lord Herbert told her, "Listen, Barbara, he's not a prince, and he's just taking you." And she said, "You are ruining my life! Get out!" He said, "Well alright. Go ahead and marry him then." Which she did. He lasted about several months or a year.

AG: Was she there when we were there in '61?

WSB: I know the house. The house is a huge house. I know just where it was. But she was popular with the natives.

---

65 Woolworth heiress Barbara Hutton (1912-79) occupied a mansion in the Kasbah after divorcing her third husband, Cary Grant, in 1945. Her lavish entertainments put Tangier on the international high-society circuit. She was married and divorced seven times and is notorious for spending down a fortune estimated at $900 million.

AG: Did she spend a lot of money?

WSB: She spent a lot of money. She contributed very generously to charity. She put out a lot of money for hospitals and distribution of food, stuff like that. You know just, charitable. So everybody liked her.[66]

AG: Did you ever meet her?

WSB: No, no.

AG: You were never invited?..

WSB: No, No. I was never invited because I was looked upon as a pariah.

AG: Did you ever meet [Lord David] Herbert?

WSB: I finally at the end [laughing], at the end of my stay, when I was ... became sort of famous ...

AG: This was what year?

WSB: Well, that would be ...

AG: After *Naked Lunch* was published?

WSB: After *Naked Lunch* was published and I was getting quite famous. Then the English colony decided, well, we'd better pay some attention to this person. He's getting to be a personality, a personage.

AG: Yeah. So did Herbert invite you to his house?

WSB: I was just leaving. I had my ticket and everything. And he said an old friend of yours, Graham Eyres Monsell, who I knew at Harvard, who later became a lord, he's here and would like to see you again and I said, well, I've got my ticket, have to leave.

AG: So you never got up to his house. He was sort of eccentric.

---

66 Hutton funded a soup kitchen that fed up to a thousand people per day (Green 16).

WSB: Never got there. I did get invited to the Honorable David Idiot [laughs] as Brion always called him. David Eliot. And he was the one that was living with his boyfriend, ex-boyfriend, a Kray twin. He came to Tangiers and was taken up by the Honorable David Idiot. He was a fickle, willful young man. And he fell out with David Idiot. But he invited me to his house and they had this absolutely perfect English meal. That is, lamb, roast potatoes, mint jelly, Brussels sprouts, and an English pudding, a sweet pudding.

AG: Over-cooked Brussels sprouts or well-cooked?

WSB: They were properly cooked. They didn't imitate all the faults of English cooking. He had a big house on the mountain.

AG: Did Brion get around to see all those people? Barbara Hutton and everybody?

WSB: He was sort of only on the edge because Brion was always alienating people by his sharp tongue, and by his not kow-towing to them at all. He managed to alienate David Herbert some.

AG: Apparently not hard.

WSB: It wasn't too hard but . . . Oh well he said, that "all I ask of people is . . . that I invite to my house . . . is that they be themselves." He would not stand any sort of pretense, anything like that. He would say, "It's second-rate. Out. Don't come again."

AG: Well, he set himself up as a social arbiter for the upper classes.

WSB: He did. For years. He's still alive. He's certainly in his eighties.

AG: You know he's written a book about it.

WSB: I know. I read it.

AG: And Rupert Croft-Cooke finally wrote a book in the late sixties or something.[67]

---

67 Rupert Croft-Cooke (1903–79), English author of fiction, nonfiction, and screenplays, relocated to Morocco in 1953 after serving a prison sentence under the "indecency" laws used to prosecute homosexuals.

wsb: Yeah, well, he was second-rate.

ag: This book by Finlayson also deals with Croft-Cooke too.

wsb: I read it. I read Croft-Cooke's book.

ag: He mentions me as some sort of a rag-tag beatnik poet or something.

wsb: Who does?

ag: Croft-Cooke.

wsb: Oh yes. He was a real snob, you see.

ag: Remember that time I once kissed him in the Mar Chica [bar]. He reacted as if I was a vampire.

wsb: Thrust a snake in his face.

ag: I must have been drunk. I don't know why I did that.

wsb: He was pretty horrible. He was a real snob. And Lord David Herbert didn't *have* to be. He was top-notch and he knew it. Still is.

sl: Did you see him when you were there on that trip with Cronenberg?

wsb: The only person we saw was Paul. Paul Bowles. And he was sort of recuperating from an operation. I was surprised that he accepted our invitation to have dinner. "Cause he usually doesn't go out . . . .

Oh, get out from there. Get down from there, small beast. Come on, jump into my lap. Come on, beast. Oh shut up. When they make that noise they're about to scratch.

ag: I remember you were a very fearsome piece of work when you'd get drunk and get high on majoun and wave that machete around. Very bad-mannered that way.

wsb: Yes, well, it was long ago.

ag: Peter and I used to get a little . . .

WSB: You won't see me waiting in the shadows. I'm very careful with weapons.

AG: Nor rusty *pistolas.*

WSB: Yeah. You can't be too careful.

AG: I've never been very wild, never drunk, never got into very bad habits. I've been a wimp all my life.

WSB: Well, that's good.

AG: I wonder if I'll have to pay for it in my next life.

WSB: The worst drunk I ever saw was . . . what was his name? He was sweet when he was sober but he was a nasty . . . but my God I went out with him one night in Tangiers and he got drunk. He pulled out a knife, "Anything that gets in my way gets this!" And he's *weaving* from side to side from one end of the street to the other waving this knife [laughs]. For *God* sakes would you put that thing away before we get hurt. Before something awful happens.

AG: You used to wave that *machete* around. Isn't that the same thing? Saying what you'd do exactly, if you were to run amok or you ran across somebody running amok.

WSB: That guy that ran amok, Manusi was his name. Everybody could see it coming. He was a real walking time bomb. The last time I saw him, he said to me, "Why does the American embassy have wires in my head?"

AG: Oh-oh. Like my mother.

WSB: Also he had lost weight and he had that sick look of schizo-phrenics. Mentally ill. Even the smell. They have a certain smell.

AG: Sour.

WSB: Sour. Like mouse piss.

AG: What was his name?

WSB: Manusi.

AG: Italian American or what?

WSB: No, he was Arab, man. [*Manusi* is of Sanskrit origin: woman.] Very fanatical. He said to Dave Woolman, "You like little boys: *Allah doesn't like that.*" And they said, Jesus Christ, man, that guy is dangerous. Well, he had a big butcher knife and he went amok in the Socco Grande, where I would normally have been, except that I stopped to have a drink, a coffee, with someone. And then I heard the shutters going down. Shop shutters. And that means trouble. And that was when he started. He started there. He killed one, two, three, about four people. And he went right past the embassy, which was then in the native quarter.

AG: Right, I remember.

WSB: And the embassy officials pulled their Marine guard in and shut the doors. He [the Marine] had a .45. He could have stopped him, but, you know, you stay out of things. Then he got all the way down on the Avenida d'España before the Moroccan police sort of surrounded him and shot him in the stomach, not killing him. And then they said, "What's the matter?" And he said, "Well I've got an evil spirit." That was his excuse. So they sent him to jail for twenty years. But there was a big escape from that jail, and Manusi was one of those who got away . . . . So I don't know what finally happened to Manusi.

Then there was my little boyfriend. Rubio. Blond. A red-haired boy from the Rif . . . . And he was called Ginger. Well, Ginger went and stabbed the Grand Rabbi of Tangiers.

AG: Wow.

WSB: In the stomach.

AG: Over what?

WSB: Just crazy, you know. He saw him as an enemy. This was a great personage. He used to sail around like a ship; he had a beard and this grand manner, he sailed around. And well he recovered. All the Jews were out there praying for him in front of the Spanish hospital. And Ginger went to the nuthouse they had in Tangiers. It was run by a Belgian doctor. It was a very humane place. No beating of the inmates or anything like that. Then he was moved to Rabat. And I sent him some money.

AG: This was after you knew him.

WSB: Yes. Been to bed with him a number of times. And he got out . . . after a couple of years. And he's now the sage of the Socco Chico. However, he'd lost a leg from an infection. Then I heard from him, fairly recently, in the last couple of years, that he was in Florida at some friend's; an American friend had taken him to Florida for treatment. And invited me down there to have a Moroccan meal. And I talked to him on the phone.

AG: How old was he by then?

WSB: Forty, or . . .

AG: You knew him when he was a kid.

WSB: Yeah. I think he wanted me to call up and talk to his patron, and I talked to the man. You know, just to corroborate that we did know each other. He sent me his picture. And so on. I hope he's alright.

AG: That's a long relationship.

WSB: Yes. Fraught with . . .

AG: Fraught with peril. Did he ever say why he stabbed the rabbi?

WSB: No, he said, "Well, one of those things," [laughs] one of those things. Well, there's a lot of anti-Israel feeling.

AG: Ya.

WSB: They didn't think of Jewish Americans as being Jews. But they thought of *him* as being a Jew. So I don't think the authorities . . . they were inclined to take a lenient view in other words.

AG: [James] gave me this yesterday . . . . Have you seen the notes from Dr. Wolberg?

WSB: *No!*

AG: Well, writing circa 1947, would you like to hear that? Should I read it to you?

WSB: What is it?

AG: It's Dr. Wolberg's notes.

WSB: Oh no. This is very . . .

AG: It's *very* interesting, actually. Speaking of the Ugly Spirit or whatever.

WSB: Wait a minute, this is *interesting.* [Reading]

> He had been unable to bring this up through several years of psychoanalysis. The analyst believed that through the medium of regression, it would be possible to return the patient to a period of his life where he would be able to remember and to live through a traumatic experience which might account for his homosexuality.

That was just oversimplification.

> When I saw the patient, it was apparent to me that he was markedly disabled in his relationships with people. He had been seeking a means of circumventing his anxiety and, through reading, had become convinced that were he able to uncover a secret in his past regarding some traumatic injury that had been inflicted upon him, it would explain and remove his fear of people, particularly women.

> It was apparent to me that during his long period of psycho-therapy, he has successfully evaded relating himself closely with a psychiatrist, and has spent most of his time attempting to enucleate elements in his past history which seem to account for his difficulty. He had become progressively more and more frustrated as he discovered that his memories and accounting of early difficulties had very little ameliorating effect upon his anxiety and present interpersonal difficulties.

He had become convinced that all the early incidents that he had produced were merely cover memories and that deeply imbedded within himself there was a memory so traumatic and so devastating to his conscious mind that it had success-fully evaded all attempts at probing. He therefore wanted help in hypnosis in order to get to the bottom of his difficulty. It was possible to induce a fairly deep trance, and through the medium of automatic writing in a regressed state, the patient was able to recapture an experience in which he had witnessed his parents having sexual relationships. He lived through the frightening experience of encountering for the first time the sight of the female genital organ, which he con-ceived of as mutilated. This incident aroused deep fears of castration and a horror of observing female genital organs for fear of being confronted with the possibility that he too might become castrated.

This is a typical Freudian . . . wait a minute.

In recapturing this early traumatic event, his living through the emotions relating to the event exhilarated him tempo-rarily. However, it did not alter in the least his customary character pattern, nor did it make it possible for him to give up his fear of women. The result was that he insisted that what he had recaptured was valid, but that there was prob-ably something even deeper than this which, if enucleated, would immediately remove his anxiety.

AG: Hallucinated or what?

WSB: Enucleated [to enucleate is to remove the nucleus of a cell, or to isolate and remove a gland or tumor from its surrounding tissue].

AG: Oh, isolated in such form . . . related to a nucleus.

WSB: Here, while the goal of recapturing early memories had suc-ceeded, we had failed to produce any change is his neurotic structure. From the therapeutic standpoint, this case had to be classified as a failure. Even though the failure was not the fault of hypnosis but rather the product of the generally mistaken notion that recapture of early traumatic memories can bring relief to a character problem.

AG: That's a very funny thing. You know what its implication is, in a way, is that you *have* no early trauma, you *have* no Ugly Spirit, that you're chasing a will-o'-the-wisp in looking for a . . .

WSB: Final . . .

AG: . . . a final cause or a final trauma, that you did have some trauma with seeing your parents.

WSB: It wasn't my parents.

AG: Who was it?

WSB: If anything it's related to the governess and her girlfriend.

AG: Apparently at that point in the hypno-analysis the recollection of the *parents* making love was impressive for a moment.

SL: Maybe just the recollection of being born.

WSB: The birth trauma, that was [Otto] Rank.

AG: But as far as *he's* concerned [Wolberg], you did have something happening with the parents.

WSB: Not . . .

AG: But that wasn't so bad. However, you still had the feeling that there was something even *worse*. And had this persistent feeling of some very early experience.

WSB: Yes.

AG: And he's saying the case is a failure because you can't find this early experience because maybe it doesn't exist or something. It would be a very funny way of dealing with the Ugly Spirit [laughs]. The ultimate thing is that you just had this [laughs] *conviction* of original sin.

WSB: Yes, well. It's interesting. Where did this come from?

AG: James.

WSB: I know James, who's . . .

SL: Peter Sayles.[68]

AG: Swales.

WSB: Swales. I understand that Wolberg is dead. Three years ago [Wolberg died in 1988]. He would be a very old man, certainly almost ninety. Eissler's still alive. Kurt Eissler, who is now head of the Psychoanalytic Institute in New York, and he is an orthodox Freudian and will allow no deviations from the dogma laid down by Freud.

AG: Did he . . .

WSB: A lot of people have said that these so-called memories of . . . early sexual memories are sort of an invention of the analyst rather than the patient. And the patient, feeling that the analyst wants to find such a thing, provides it to him. It often refers to nothing.

AG: Yeah.

WSB: So many people, thousands of people, particularly people who are living in, you know, tenements, see that kind of thing all the time [people having sex].

AG: It would depend on the degree of isolation from real life or sexual life or barnyard epithet activity, whether or not it would be impressive if you had somebody from which the sex was hidden a great deal or made very secret, then all of a sudden he burst in on his parents fucking and stark naked during a menstrual period with blood all over, and the woman underneath, and the guy screaming

---

68   Dr. Wolberg's notes are being read here from an unpublished paper by Peter Swales, "Burroughs in the Bewilderness: The Haunted Mind and Psychoanalyses of William S. Burroughs" (Grauerholz 3).

and the lady screaming, it might be quite a trauma if they'd never been told about the birds and the bees!

WSB: Well, that's true of course. And remember most of Freud's patients were middle class, very inhibited, Viennese. Middle *upper* class. Because it was expensive.

AG: But I remember seeing my parents. Didn't even see them. I once stumbled into . . . I think I told you during that psychotherapy that we did when we were together . . .

WSB: Yes.

AG: In the closet, I was rummaging around in the summer, Coney Island or Rockaway or somewhere and I saw the Vaseline, the K-Y, the genital Vaseline whatever, and a douche or something. Condoms.

WSB: Yeah.

AG: And was quite shocked!

WSB: Well I wouldn't wonder.

SL: You saw the sex kit.

AG: Well, whatever it was, all the apparatus.

WSB: Yeah, the apparatus, the paraphernalia.

AG: It sounded like an operation or something. "He inserts his penis into her vagina." Remember that was his explanation?

WSB: At any rate. Then Eissler said that this . . . he denied that this was true [the fake memories, and insisted rather] that Freud was right. Sort of like the pope, he'd become sort of a pope. He refused to see Ted.

AG: Ted Morgan? [William's 1988 biographer.]

WSB: Ted said, he said, "Well I can't reveal anything." And then Ted said, "Can't you even do this if the patient himself gives permission?"

And he said, "In a certain case no."

AG: And in this case he felt . . .

WSB: He felt it would be detrimental.

AG: After all the years, detrimental to your, what, sanity?

WSB: Not to *me*. But to psychoanalysis.

AG: Oh. In what way?

WSB: Here's this sort of notorious person, of sort of bad character in the eyes of ordinary society, and he was psychoanalyzed for many years. It casts aspersions on the treatment, don't you see?

AG: Notorious but at the same time you were an honorific person. So that would mean then, his estimates and his notes would make you out to be some sort of . . . impossible.

WSB: Listen, he felt the whole thing was too hot to touch. He wanted to have nothing to do with it. He wanted no reference to treatment. That's all . . . .

AG: So this thing of Wolberg's: "Whereas the conclusion was there was probably something deeper than this, the vision of the parents making love, which, if enunciated, would immediately remove his anxiety." [69] So a deeper secret. Presumably the secret of the Ugly Spirit or of the possession. But he is saying there is no further trauma.

WSB: Yes, he couldn't have handled it.

AG: And do you still think there was some specific event?

WSB: Of course there was.

AG: That was not reachable.

---

69   William thought the sex scene recovered under hypnosis had involved not the parents but his nanny and her girlfriend. However, he believed there was a deeper trauma, perhaps involving the nanny directing him to perform oral sex on her boyfriend. The nanny left the Burroughs's employ when William was four years old (Morgan 33-34; Miles 24-25).

WSB: Not with such means, no.

AG: And would the memory of the event be necessary for exorcism?

WSB: No, not necessarily.

AG: Or memory of the feeling. In other words, did you get anything from the shaman's sweat-lodge ceremony in that realm?

WSB: That was much better than anything psychoanalysts have come up with. Something definite there was being touched upon. He did more than . . .

AG: So what could it possibly be, you got any idea if it's a definite event?

WSB: It's the means, the moment at which the spirit gained access.

AG: So the ultimate secret would be that moment when the spirit gained access.

WSB: Well, presumably if you see it at the moment it gained access, then it'll be dropped.

AG: Dissolves.

WSB: This you see is the same notion or same . . . exorcism, psycho-therapy, Freudian psychotherapy, shamanistic practices, getting to the moment when whatever it had gained access. And also the name of the spirit. Just to know that it's the Ugly Spirit. That's a great step. Because the spirit doesn't want its name to be known.

AG: So Brion was the one that actually named it.

WSB: Yes, yes.

AG: What year was that?

WSB: Well, it'd be 1959.

AG: In Paris.

WSB: In Paris, yes.

AG: How did that question rise then?

WSB: Well, he saw it.

AG: So Brion was a kind of shaman.

WSB: He was a shaman. A very potent shaman. And he told me, also, he said the worst possible influence on you at the present moment is Jacques Stern.[70]

AG: Um hm.

WSB: That he's a bubble demon. A little green demon. Well, he was, but also he had moments when he wasn't, I mean, it's like . . .

AG: I remember.

WSB: Gregory said the same thing. He said sometimes he's sort of a little kid and at other times he's . . . there's something really evil and nasty.

AG: I remember he was very generous with me; once lent me a hundred ten bucks to go to America when I was leaving. And then maybe . . .

WSB: Then he'll start screaming.

AG: Twenty minutes later he says . . .

WSB: Start screaming at you, "Why you con!"

AG: "Money off me!"

WSB: "Getting money off me!"

AG: But then when he got ill, twenty years later, I sent him a couple hundred dollars when I heard he was broke. And I got a very nice note

---

70 Jacques Loup Stern (1932–2002), writer of French aristocratic and Jewish banking wealth who met the Beats in Paris in 1958. Afflicted with polio circa 1949, he was thereafter reliant on a wheelchair. Of the Beat group, he was closest to William, with whom he shared many interests, including heroin.

from him saying that it was very rare that anybody had ever repaid him.

WSB: That's true. Well, you remember that was the time when he was thrown out of the Chelsea [Hotel]. Then he went to that welfare hotel on Washington Square. And he just sort of sneaked up to the room without telling . . .

[Allen laughs.]

WSB: And they threw him out. He arrives in front of my house, when I lived down the Bowery, with all his possessions in great plastic garbage bags. There he is, sitting on a broken wheelchair.

AG: So what'd you do?

WSB: Well, I had to take him in.

AG: Yeah.

WSB: And fortunately, this guy named Maurice Wade who lived on Prince Street whom I heard from recently . . . . He carried him up there. And then I tried to find somebody or some way of taking him . . .

SL: Placing him somewhere.

WSB: Placing him somewhere. And I would place him with someone like some woman who knew him from before and had an apartment. And two days later I got a telephone call. "I can't stand it anymore. I have a family, I have a child, and he destroys the furniture and builds fires in the ashtray. I just can't have it." So after about three of those I just gave up and went to Boulder . . . .

SL: What happened to Jacques Stern? Where is he now?

WSB: I don't know. Then he turns up in a . . . he had an expensive apartment on 57th Street . . . .

SL: Gramercy Park?

WSB: Gramercy Park. He had a house there for a while.

AG: That's the last I saw of him . . . . He'd recovered his money or something.

WSB: No, but he had all of these vicissitudes.

AG: Yeah.

WSB: One day he's out in the street and the next day he has a huge apartment somewhere. And then he had this other apartment and then he claimed that his girlfriend Wendy broke in with a CIA man and tortured him to reveal God knows what. And he did indeed have some cigarette burns on his back. He called me, said desperately, "Please come." And then finally when we left and I'd given him what money I had, sort of about twenty dollars, and we both concurred that there was nothing he couldn't have done himself, his injuries and ripping the telephone out of the wall . . . Oh, the place was a shambles . . . .

AG: What year would that be, mid seventies or something? Late seventies?

SL: Yeah. The party at Gramercy . . . we were there in '75.

WSB: Well, he was . . . he stayed at the Gramercy Park Hotel for a while and then I went to see him. I had dinner with him there once and he seemed quite rational.

AG: Quite what?

WSB: Rational. So then I went, and I noticed that the lock on his door of the hotel room was broken. And I said, Oh God, here we go again. And once again he had this story of someone having broken in and it was obvious that he had broken the lock himself. And a day later he was asked to leave the hotel . . . And he then became friendly with Stewart Meyer and we saw Stewart a number of times and the last time I heard of him was through Stewart, that he had married again. So the woman was looking after him and he was in pretty good shape.

AG: Yeah. That's what I heard recently. I think Gregory saw him or heard from him lately.

wsb: Oh, I must ask, I would be grateful . . . 'Cause that was the last time I heard was through Stewart.

ag: And I heard he was in good shape, had gotten a little plump.

wsb: Yes, that's what I heard too.

ag: And was no longer out of his skull and was kind of sweet.

wsb: I wonder if he's on anything now.

ag: I don't think so, I think he's quit drinking or something.

wsb: Well, he was on heroin for a time . . . .

sl: Allen . . . . I don't know what time you're leaving today.

ag: Round about, let's see, an hour or so . . . .

[Talking on the phone:] A lot has come together in the last two, three weeks . . . . You know, for many years I've been archiving my tape recordings. So now a company is going to put out a boxed set of four CD records, about 270 minutes of poetry and music. Several hours, three hours or so of the best of all the work that I've done over the years and Steven Taylor, my assistant musician, is putting them all together on a DAT special machine where they can be rearranged easily, sequenced. And Hal Willner is producing . . . supervise the whole project so it's all being taken care of with material that they've accumulated. And I don't have to do too much work on it . . . .

And I'm here . . . requested to come here, paid to come here to interview Bill, and write something . . . so I made ten ninety-minute cassettes of conversation . . . Steven Taylor will reduce that to . . . it's been less work for me, somebody else to put it together and edit it. So I feel a . . . it's getting a lot of work done . . . .

I had my angiogram. My veins are clear, there's no blockage, no collapse, no nothing. Apparently some . . . maybe a virus that affected my heart slightly . . . so the heart is slightly weaker. Means if I take it easy, I'm alright. Get enough sleep, not overwork and not overdrive. I think the image was an old car, if you just drive it fifty miles an hour, it will go on forever. But if you blast it up to eighty or ninety, it might break down . . . .

SL: Allen, I have to go.

AG: One moment.

SL: We'll be in touch.

JG: I just missed Steve. Where did he go?

WSB: Back to his house . . . . Oh, Spooner. Spooner cat. Come 'ere, Spooner. Come up, my Spooner cat, come up. Spooner cat. Come here, my Spooner.

AG: I need twenty minutes or ten minutes to pack . . . .

JG: Go ahead. Do your thing. Not such a hurry . . . .

AG: I read it to Bill this morning, the notes from Dr. Wolberg.

JG: What do you think?

WSB: Interesting.

JG: The Wolberg . . . do you think that must be you . . . you're the patient he's talking about?

WSB: Oh, there's no question of that.

JG: I thought so [laughs].

WSB: No question about that.

JG: His correspondence may have been preserved but his client files were destroyed.

WSB: His what?

JG: Client files.

wsb: Were destroyed.

jg: So you don't feel like, you know, disturbed or alarmed to read these old third-party assessments like Dr. Wolberg's assessment or something?

wsb: No no, not at all. Not at all. Now . . . I . . . I think that the trauma that was uncovered under hypnosis was . . .

ag: [Entering the room] I missed the conversation, was that . . . was it in doubt whether or not it was Bill?

jg: No.

wsb: There's no doubt at all. It is me. It was more with the . . . The trauma was with the nurse apparently and her girlfriend, who was another governess, and the vet, the veterinarian. The veterinarian was sort of her boyfriend and she visited the veterinarian on Thursdays. It was her day off.

jg: Yeah. Every Thursday?

wsb: Well, not every Thursday, but . . .

jg: Did you always go along?

wsb: Well, I went along sometimes and then finally I didn't. And I made a great fuss. Or at least they didn't want me along.

jg: A ha. Did the veterinarian have cows and things in his place?

wsb: Yes, must have had all kinds. . . . I think . . . shall we say, a pet of a horse and cow and yes, he must have but I don't remember.

jg: What was his name?

wsb: Well . . . I forget what his real name was. But somebody found him and talked to him. And he said, well, I . . .

jg: Said what?

wsb: No, I was just speaking . . . it's . . .

JG: You mean somebody found him at the time and talked to him about . . . ?

WSB: No, no, no, years later.

JG: Oh really? Who found him?

WSB: Who was it? I seem to remember . . . it was my mother that found him and talked to him and asked him if he knew of anything that might have been traumatic . . . .

JG: But . . . you told the story in the "Interzone," what about . . . ?

WSB: That's just . . . pure supposition.

JG: It's all so long ago. Hopefully it wouldn't be very painful to contemplate it.

WSB: But there's no reason to . . . to make me recall what transpired.

AG: Bill and I were talking before, so he tells it, oh let's see . . . whereas Wolberg didn't get to the root trauma, that there was some incident very explicit . . . the entrance of the spirit. The Ugly Spirit, and that Brion was the one that named the Ugly Spirit.

WSB: Yes.

AG: And did the shaman catch it?

WSB: He says that he caught it and got it out of the body, but it's still hanging around.

AG: He put it in the fire.

WSB: Now he's going to be back here on Tuesday, back in town, so, he wants to bless the house.

END OF TRANSCRIPT

———— ⦿ ————

William S. Burroughs looking at one of half dozen or more cut-
out plywood silhouettes made for him to paint, shotgun, &
collage by assistant friend Steven Lowe, Lowe's house, Lawrence Kansas March 19, 1992.
                                    Allen Ginsberg

BIBLIOGRAPHY

Albright, Daniel. "Yeats, A Vision, and Art History." *The Yeats Journal of Korea* (2011): 5-29.

Dawkins, Richard. *The Selfish Gene.* New York: Oxford University Press, 1976.

Ginsberg, Allen. "Exorcising Burroughs." *Observer* (26 April 1992): 26–30.

Grauerholz, James. "The Death of Joan Vollmer Burroughs: What Really Happened?" American Studies Department, University of Kansas, 2002.

Green, Michelle. *The Dream at the End of the World: Paul Bowles and the Literary Renegades in Tangier.* New York: Harper Perennial, 1991.

Kashner, Sam. *When I Was Cool: My Life at the Jack Kerouac School.* New York: Harper Collins, 2004.

Lotringer, Sylvère, ed. *Burroughs Live: The Collected Interviews of William S. Burroughs, 1960–1997.* Los Angeles: Semiotext(e), 2001.

Martin, Malachi. *Hostage to the Devil: the Possession and Exorcism of Five Living Americans.* Harper One, 1992.

Miles, Barry. *Call Me Burroughs: A Life.* New York: Twelve/Hachette Book Group, 2014.

Morgan, Ted. *Literary Outlaw: The Life and Times of William S. Burroughs.* New York: W. W. Norton and Company, 2012.

ACKNOWLEDGMENTS

A kind of peculiar family builds up around writers with five-decade careers; they are elders, peers, partners, apprentices, protégés, companions, secretaries, agents, scholars, collaborators, and publishers. In the spirit of word as virus, we are all in the same pool. For present purposes, I'll note a few persons directly related to the book, in chronological order of our acquaintance. I always thought of Bob Rosenthal as my slightly older and much wiser brother. In the course of taking care of Allen Ginsberg for more than twenty years, Bob supported everything I ever did with Allen with kindness, patience, and humor. Next came Anne Waldman, poet advocate and courage teacher these forty years. Then Barry Miles, our friend and occasional host in London and biographer of Ginsberg and Burroughs, for whose notes and encouragement I am very grateful. Thanks to James Grauerholz, without whose early support I might not have begun the book, for his 2002 paper on the death of Joan Burroughs, and for his expert advice. Thanks to Judy Hussie-Taylor for unerring support in all things and for identifying the title of the work. I am particularly indebted to Peter Hale for encouragement and help at every stage of the process over the course of three years. Heartfelt thanks go to Peter Carlaftes and Kat Georges for so expertly and swiftly doing the work of design and production, and for keeping me on deadline.

ABOUT THE EDITOR

Steven Taylor is a poet, musician, songwriter, and ethnomusicologist. He has published two books of poems and the musical ethnography, *False Prophet: Field Notes from the Punk Underground*. He has composed music for the theater, film, radio drama, and dance and has made more than a dozen records with various artists. His articles, reviews, essays, and poems have appeared in anthologies and zines. From 1976–1996 he collaborated on music and poetry works with Allen Ginsberg. Since 1984, he has been a member of the seminal underground rock band The Fugs. He has toured and recorded with Anne Waldman, Kenward Elmslie, and the New York hardcore band False Prophets. From 1995–2008 he was on the faculty at the Jack Kerouac School of Disembodied Poetics at Naropa University. He lives in Brooklyn.

RECENT AND FORTHCOMING BOOKS FROM THREE ROOMS PRESS

FICTION

Meagan Brothers
Weird Girl and What's His Name

Ron Dakron
Hello Devilfish!

Michael T. Fournier
Hidden Wheel
Swing State

William Least Heat-Moon
Celestial Mechanics

Aimee Herman
Everything Grows

Eamon Loingsigh
Light of the Diddicoy
Exile on Bridge Street

John Marshall
The Greenfather

Aram Saroyan
Still Night in L.A.

Richard Vetere
The Writers Afterlife
Champagne and Cocaine

Julia Watts
Quiver

MEMOIR & BIOGRAPHY

Nassrine Azimi and
Michel Wasserman
Last Boat to Yokohama:
The Life and Legacy of
Beate Sirota Gordon

William S. Burroughs & Allen Ginsberg
Don't Hide the Madness:
William S. Burroughs in Conversation
with Allen Ginsberg
edited by Steven Taylor

James Carr
BAD: The Autobiography of
James Carr

Richard Katrovas
Raising Girls in Bohemia:
Meditations of an American Father; A
Memoir in Essays

Judith Malina
Full Moon Stages:
Personal Notes from
50 Years of The Living Theatre

Phil Marcade
Punk Avenue:
Inside the New York City
Underground, 1972-1982

Stephen Spotte
My Watery Self:
Memoirs of a Marine Scientist

PHOTOGRAPHY-MEMOIR

Mike Watt
On & Off Bass

SHORT STORY ANTHOLOGIES

SINGLE AUTHOR
First-Person Singularities: Stories
by Robert Silverberg
with an introduction by John Scalzi

Tales from the Eternal Café: Stories
by Janet Hamill, with an introduction
by Patti Smith

Time and Time Again:
Sixteen Trips in Time
by Robert Silverberg

MULTI-AUTHOR
Crime + Music: Twenty Stories
of Music-Themed Noir
edited by Jim Fusilli

Dark City Lights: New York Stories
edited by Lawrence Block

Florida Happens:
Bouchercon 2018 Anthology
edited by Greg Herren

Have a NYC I, II & III:
New York Short Stories;
edited by Peter Carlaftes
& Kat Georges

Songs of My Selfie:
An Anthology of Millennial Stories
edited by Constance Renfrow

The Obama Inheritance:
15 Stories of Conspiracy Noir
edited by Gary Phillips

This Way to the End Times:
Classic and New Stories of
the Apocalypse
edited by Robert Silverberg

MIXED MEDIA

John S. Paul
Sign Language: A Painter's Notebook
(photography, poetry and prose)

FILM & PLAYS

Israel Horovitz
My Old Lady: Complete Stage Play
and Screenplay with an Essay on
Adaptation

Peter Carlaftes
Triumph For Rent (3 Plays)
Teatrophy (3 More Plays)

Kat Georges
Three Somebodies: Plays about
Notorious Dissidents

DADA

Maintenant: A Journal of
Contemporary Dada Writing & Art
(Annual, since 2008)

HUMOR

Peter Carlaftes
A Year on Facebook

TRANSLATIONS

Thomas Bernhard
On Earth and in Hell
(poems of Thomas Bernhard
with English translations by
Peter Waugh)

Patrizia Gattaceca
Isula d'Anima / Soul Island
(poems by the author
in Corsican with English
translations)

César Vallejo | Gerard Malanga
Malanga Chasing Vallejo
(selected poems of César Vallejo
with English translations
and additional notes by
Gerard Malanga)

George Wallace
EOS: Abductor of Men
(selected poems in Greek & English)

POETRY COLLECTIONS

Hala Alyan
Atrium

Peter Carlaftes
DrunkYard Dog
I Fold with the Hand I Was Dealt

Thomas Fucaloro
It Starts from the Belly and Blooms

Inheriting Craziness is Like
a Soft Halo of Light

Kat Georges
Our Lady of the Hunger

Robert Gibbons
Close to the Tree

Israel Horovitz
Heaven and Other Poems

David Lawton
Sharp Blue Stream

Jane LeCroy
Signature Play

Philip Meersman
This is Belgian Chocolate

Jane Ormerod
Recreational Vehicles on Fire
Welcome to the Museum of Cattle

Lisa Panepinto
On This Borrowed Bike

George Wallace
Poppin' Johnny

Three Rooms Press | New York, NY | Current Catalog: www.threeroomspress.com
Three Rooms Press books are distributed by PGW/Ingram: www.pgw.com